# GREAT FAMILY TRIPS IN NEW ENGLAND

A YANKEE BOOKS TRAVEL GUIDE

# GREAT FAMILY TRIPS IN NEW ENGLAND

## by Harriet Webster

YANKEE BOOKS

*For Kim, my good friend.*

*YANKEE* is a registered trademark of Yankee Publishing, Inc. Used by permission.

Printed in the United States of America on acid-free ∞, recycled paper ♻

Cover design by Dale Swensson
Interior design by Jill Shaffer

**Library of Congress Cataloging-in-Publication Data**

Webster, Harriet.
        Great family trips in New England.

        "A Yankee magazine publication."
        Includes index.
        1. New England—Description and travel—
1981—Guide-books. 2. Family recreation—New
England Guide-books. I.Title
F2.3.W392    1988    917.4'0443        88-250
ISBN 0–89909–159–8

**Distributed in the book trade by St. Martin's Press**

2   4   6   8   10   9   7   5   3   1     paperback

# Contents

New England Aquarium

*"Hands-on" aptly describes the experiences available to children at New England's many and varied family trips destinations.*

# Introduction

**F**amily trips are like a treasure chest waiting to be pried open. You expect jewels, but you don't know whether you'll find emeralds, rubies, or gold.

Perhaps you decide to spend a day introducing your kids to some spectacular New England scenery. You want to take them on their first canoe trip. You head for Vermont, with a picnic of course, and you paddle up the Battenkill so they can experience the beauty of the river. That much you can plan. The part that just happens is the blue heron that suddenly appears on the riverbank, the trout your eight year old catches . . . that's the stuff that makes memories.

There are several key components to taking successful family trips. First, there's the matter of advance planning. A good way to do this is to look through *Great Family Trips in New England* and pick out a couple of trip possibilities. Then sit down and share the information with your children. Which of the destinations you suggest do they find most attractive? Which of the specific suggestions within the chapter appeal to them most and which leave them cold?

Once you've agreed on where you want to go and what you hope to do, make a few telephone calls. We purposely exclude exact hours and admission fee information because it quickly becomes outdated. We do include telephone numbers because we want to encourage you to call ahead before leaving home, to be sure the museum will be open or that there's enough snow on the ground for cross-country skiing. (We also include the names and addresses of tourism information offices for all of the areas mentioned in the book.) For trips that you plan well in advance (as opposed to those you plan on the spur of the moment), you might ask an older child to write to the contact, requesting leaflets and asking any pertinent questions. The more kids are involved in the planning process, the greater their investment in making the trip a success.

In addition to good advance planning, try to set reasonable expectations. What do we mean by reasonable expectations? Well, to start with, don't make any promises. The book may mention that there's a zebra at a zoo in Rhode Island, but if your child's heart is set on seeing that zebra and little else matters, the whole trip is going to be ruined if, for some reason, that animal is no longer there. Kids are stubborn, and many an excursion has been spoiled by

*The more kids are involved in the planning process, the greater their investment in making the trip a success.*

the youngster who won't forgive his or her parents for not delivering on their promise. So instead of making promises about what you'll see and do, discuss possibilities. Try to infuse your kids with the attitude that taking trips means making discoveries and giving new experiences a chance.

Setting reasonable expectations goes hand-in-hand with flexibility. Have some backup plans if the weather turns sour. Don't worry if you can't do all that you planned to do; you can always come back another time. If you plan to stay overnight, loosen up on bedtimes. Kids are often both excited and a little frightened at the idea of sleeping in a new place, and you'll have an easier time if you acknowledge their feelings and roll with them than if you try to impose home routines. And admit to yourself that a day without three square meals isn't going to harm most kids. Just as they know that a family trip is a special occasion, they'll realize that making dinner out of a hot dog at 4 P.M. and an ice cream sundae at 7 P.M. is also a special event. Taken together, careful planning, setting reasonable expectations, and being flexible can go a long way toward tipping the scales in favor of some wonderful family outings.

This book is divided into twenty-six trips. Each trip describes the activities and attractions within a specific geographic area. We don't for a moment, however, expect that any two families will use the

*American heritage comes alive for children and their parents at attractions such as Old Sturbridge Village in Massachusetts.*

information in exactly the same way. Families take many different forms and so too must trips if they are to be successful. Budgets vary, amounts of time available vary, the ages of children vary, tastes and life-styles vary. That's why our trips include more than enough to do in a day. You'll want to mold the suggestions to meet the needs of your own group.

In many places throughout the book we've indicated the age range we think most appropriate for a particular attraction. Keep in mind that this is simply a guideline. No one knows your children better than you do, and ultimately it's the interests, skills, personality, and maturity level of the child that matter, not his or her exact age.

*Great Family Trips in New England* is filled with ideas for trips that appeal to children great and small, toddlers to teens. There are active, outdoor suggestions, educational opportunities, and places to go simply to have fun. There are city trips and country trips, summer trips and winter trips. Use the book as a menu, choosing the dishes that sound most tempting. Use it as a source of inspiration, sampling both the tried and true and options you've never before considered. We hope that through the trips you and your children will learn about the world and each other, and have a wonderful time in the process. You couldn't have picked a better part of the country to travel in.

# CONNECTICUT

T. Charles Erickson/Wadsworth Atheneum

*Connecticut's multifaceted amusements, such as this wall of mirrors at Hartford's Wadsworth Atheneum, will entertain your whole family.*

## Tobacco Valley

**N**orth-central Connecticut is a particularly good daytrip destination for families with children who vary in age. Among the farms where you can pick your own produce, the eighteenth-century prison, and a museum tracing the history of flight, there's plenty to occupy preteens as well as preschoolers. All of the places mentioned are within ten miles of each other, from Windsor to East Granby, and can be comfortably visited in a single day.

Fittingly housed in a cavernous hangar on the grounds of busy Bradley International Airport, the

**New England Air Museum** features a collection of fighters, bombers, helicopters, commercial aircraft, and other flying machines. The museum continuously monitors the messages sent from the Bradley Airport Tower, and as you check out the exhibits, you'll hear the voices of air traffic controllers delivering departure and approach directions to aircraft taking off and landing.

The museum chronicles the history of flight, focusing on the men who designed and flew the aircraft as well as on the amazing machines themselves. Here you'll discover that although inspired by birds, man first flew by buoyancy, not wings. The first aerial voyage took place on November 21, 1783, when François Laurent and Pilâtre de Rozier departed from the outskirts of Paris in a hot air balloon and sailed along the edge of the city for nearly half an hour before landing.

*Sound effects and flashing lights on the dial-studded control panel add to the excitement as the young flier tries to figure out how to make a jet soar.*

Important Connecticut aviation pioneer Edson Gallaudet is represented by a delicate model of the seaplane he designed before 1910, which was a precursor of the steam-powered airplane. No full-size version of the plane was ever built. The pre-1910 period is also represented by a Bleriot XI Monoplane, the first widely produced plane, symbolizing the start of the aircraft manufacturing industry. With delicate white wings stretched over a wooden frame, shiny wooden propeller, and metal and rubber "bicycle wheels" up front, the Monoplane looks like a huge moth. Its popularity soared following Louis Bleriot's flight across the English Channel in 1909.

You'll also see the world's first mass-produced helicopter, the R-4, which went into production in 1943. Ordered by the United States Army, it saw war service in Burma. Nearby the R-4 an exhibit focuses on rotor and fuselage development and explains how a helicopter flies.

Climb the steep wooden steps to the viewing platform and peer into the cockpit of the Republic F-105B Thunderchief (1957), the first U.S. aircraft designed specifically as a fighter bomber. It became famous during the Vietnam War. Makeshift theaters are set up throughout the hangar, where you can take a seat and watch films of planes in action. A video near the Thunderchief shows how in-flight fighter plane refuelings are handled.

Kids like to climb aboard the MB22 Flight Simulator to get a sense of what it's like to be a pilot. A museum staffer introduces the control panel, and the novice pilot discovers the complexity and challenge involved in flying a supersonic jet. Sound ef-

New England Air Museum

fects and flashing lights on the dial-studded control panel add to the excitement as the young flier tries to figure out how to make a jet soar. "Don't pull up the wheels now!" cautions the adviser. "You're still sitting on the ground. You'll go splat!" At the end of his or her turn, each child is given a certificate to take home, testifying to his or her flight training.

In addition to serious working planes, the collection includes recreational aircraft like the tiny experimental *Nick's Special*, a Formula I class racing plane produced by Goodyear in the 1950s. Planes in this class had to be powered by a four-cylinder engine to keep the cost of racing within the range of individuals and small groups. Then there's the ultralight Mosquito 166, built in 1980 for experienced hang glider pilots. Suspended from the hangar ceiling, it resembles a mammoth orange, black, and yellow bat. This particular glider logged twenty-five hours in the air, including a flight from New Hampshire's Mount Washington.

The field outside the museum also is filled with planes, some undergoing restoration. Feel free to wander right up to them or climb the makeshift stairs for a look inside. You'll also want to take a look in the museum shop, where airplane fans can stock up on flight patches, models, gliders, posters, books, and puzzles relating to flight.

Cider making has been a tradition on the site now occupied by **Allen's Cider Mill** for more than two hundred years. In 1783 Silas Cossitt, a former militia captain, and his bride built their homestead and began to manufacture cider and cider brandy, probably selling it at the nearby tavern owned by his father. The mill property was purchased by Arthur

Allen in 1919, and his granddaughter, Lois Allen Longley, and great-grandson continue to operate the business today.

Cider making begins in mid-September and usually continues well into May. The best time to observe the process is on a weekend morning, although cider also is made during the week. Call ahead if you plan to visit midweek. You'll see all the steps involved: the apples are grated, washed, and ground; the pulp is pressed; and the juice is then filtered three times. The bottling process can be viewed also. When cider making is not taking place, you can watch a video made right on the premises which follows all the steps, from picking to jugging. Free cider samples are always available, and the taste is something special. Lois Allen Longley takes pride in the product and notes that no preservatives are added and very few "drops" are used in the cider. "I always say that if you can't cook with it, you can't make cider with it," she remarks.

In addition to the mill itself, there's a full-size garden center and retail showroom where you can purchase fresh produce grown on the premises, along with jams and jellies. In the fall and winter the air in the showroom is rich with the spicy scent of hot mulled cider, and again samples are on the house.

Bring the kids in October, and they can head right out to the fields to select their own pumpkins in anticipation of Halloween. In summer and fall you can pick your own flowers — ten cents a stem — and herbs. And you can dig up your own chrysanthemums; they cost the same as the potted versions sold here but are much bigger.

There are also a gift shop featuring antiques and items with a country flair, a florist shop, and a crafts room. Throughout the rooms you'll see lovely wreaths and herbal arrangements and other items made from natural materials. You can purchase these ready-made or buy the materials right here and produce creations of your own.

Allen's Cider Mill sets the second full weekend of December aside for a special event designed to thank their customers. Everyone is welcome at the free buffet, which is replenished all day long. Feast on crackers and cheese; homemade cookies, brownies, and fruit bars; and cakes and tortes; and wash it all down with coffee, cocoa, and hot cider. Browse in the Christmas shop or choose a fresh-cut Christmas tree to take home. Wreaths and roping are available too, along with poinsettias and just about anything else you and your brood might need for holiday decorating. Santa holds forth in an antique sleigh, for the pleasure of the true believers in your family.

In the late spring and summer it's fun to stroll the grounds, enjoying the perennial, rose, and lily gardens. Mother's Day weekend is another special event, with a free carnation given to each mom who stops by. Your kids will enjoy pulling around one of the red wagons that serve as shopping carts as you stock up on garden plants. And with a little luck, you may find kittens basking in the sunshine.

If your children would like to harvest their own produce, take them to **Bushy Hill Orchard,** with its red barns and shiny green tractors, just a few minutes' drive from the cider mill. Peaches are usually ready midsummer, and apples come into their own in September. Back near the air museum you can pick strawberries, peas, beans, or pumpkins — depending upon the month — at **Brown's Harvest**. Combine your farm experience with a stop at the **Poquonot Playport,** just a quarter mile from Brown's. This intricate complex of wooden climbing structures incorporates swings, slides, towers, tunnels, and bridges, just the sort of stuff to set young imaginations flying.

Back in East Granby is the **Old New-Gate Prison and Copper Mine**. Copper was first discovered here in 1705, and the much celebrated Simsbury Mine was first worked two years later, financed by capitalists from Boston and New York, as well as far-flung London and Holland. Mining continued until 1773. That same year the colony of Connecticut decided to use the mine as a prison, naming it after the notorious New-Gate Prison in London. Burglars,

*Your tour of Old New-Gate Prison includes a stop at the "Confinement Area," where "difficult" prisoners were once shackled to the wall.*

Old New-Gate Prison

counterfeiters, and horse thieves were sent to New-Gate, where they were later joined by Tories and British prisoners of war. In 1776 New-Gate became the first state prison in what was to become the United States. More than eight hundred prisoners were incarcerated here during the next forty-two years.

When you approach the towering sandstone walls that surround the prison, you can't help admiring the beauty of the Litchfield Hills. It's difficult to imagine that the dark underground passageways where men lived and worked are part of such a scene. Your visit begins with a tape-recorded speech introducing the prison and its early history. Then you enter the mine itself for a tour of this subterranean world. Even in the heat of summer, temperatures hover in the mid forties in the mine, so bring along sweaters. Keep a firm grip on small children as you navigate the steep, sometimes slippery dirt floor that descends into the eighteenth-century prison. It's hard to believe that forty prisoners were packed into the "Lodging Area," where they slept in wooden cabinets designed to offer some protection from the dampness and continual dripping of water. When you reach the well where they got their drinking water, you're forty-five feet underground. Continue on to the "Confinement Area," ducking your head to avoid banging into the low ceiling. This is where difficult prisoners were shackled to the wall.

*Burglars, counterfeiters, and horse thieves were sent to New-Gate, where they were later joined by Tories and British prisoners of war.*

Elsewhere you'll see the ore shaft used to hoist copper ore to the surface when the prison functioned as a mine. The first prisoner confined at New-Gate climbed the sixty-five-foot shaft and escaped — never to be seen again — after only eighteen days of imprisonment. Most successful of the escape attempts was a mass exit of twenty-one prisoners in 1781. They departed through an old entrance with the help of an above-ground accomplice. A doomed but imaginative escape attempt occurred in 1806 when thirty prisoners used the blacksmith shop to forge keys from the pewter buttons on their uniforms. They unlocked their chains and started to flee but were soon caught. Your children will probably devise some inventive escape strategies of their own.

On leaving the dank, dark passageways, you'll want to explore the above-ground ruins, including the remains of the treadmill building, which housed offices, a hospital, cells for women, and an actual grain treadmill toward the end of the prison's operation. Although your tour of the prison is self-guided, the very knowledgeable guides posted here and there on the grounds will tell you stories about both the mine and the prison. (It may take a little prodding to start them talking.) You might learn, for example, that as bad as conditions at New-Gate were, practices here in some ways marked a new era in prison reform. It was common for prisoners to have their ears cropped, to forever mark them as outcasts, but this practice was never instituted at New-Gate. Whipping, however, was permitted.

## ACCESS

**WINDSOR.** Take I-91 to exit 40. Follow Route 20 west to Route 75. Follow Route 75 south to Windsor.

**EAST GRANBY.** Take I-91 to exit 40. Follow Route 20 west about 7 miles.

**NEW ENGLAND AIR MUSEUM. Directions:** Take I-91 to exit 40. Take Route 20 west to Route 75 north, following signs to the museum, which is on the grounds of Bradley International Airport. **Season:** Year-round. **Admission:** Charged. **Telephone:** (203) 623-3305.

**ALLEN'S CIDER MILL. Directions:** From Route 20 west, follow Route 10/202 north to Route 189. Turn right on Route 189/North Granby Road and continue 1 mile to mill, on the left at the corner of Mountain Road. **Season:** Year-round. **Admission:** Free. **Telephone:** (203) 653-6438.

**BUSHY HILL ORCHARD. Directions:** From intersection of Route 10/202 and Route 20, follow Route 20 west 1 mile to Bushy Hill Road. Turn right and continue to orchard, at 33 Bushy Hill Road. **Season:** July through December, depending upon crop. Call first. **Admission:** Free. **Telephone:** (203) 653-4022.

**BROWN'S HARVEST. Directions:** Located on Route 75 in Windsor about 1 mile from I-91. **Season:** June through October, depending upon crop. Call first. **Admission:** Free. **Telephone:** (203) 683-0266.

**POQUONOT PLAYPORT. Directions:** Located on Route 75 in Windsor, on the Poquonot School playground, about 1 mile from I-91. **Season:** Year-round; after 3:15 P.M. during school year. **Admission:** Free. **Telephone:** None.

**OLD NEW-GATE PRISON AND COPPER MINE. Directions:** Take I-91 to exit 40. Take Route 20 west through East Granby and follow signs to prison. **Season:** Mid-May through October. **Admission:** Charged. **Telephone:** (203) 653-3563.

**For further information** or lodgings and restaurant suggestions, contact the Tobacco Valley Convention and Visitors District, 111 Hazard Avenue, Enfield, CT 06082. Telephone: (203) 623-2578.

# Central Connecticut

Just outside of Hartford you'll find a group of towns with parks and museums that are both educational and fun to visit. All of them provide kids an opportunity to participate, not just to watch. Learn about the future of space exploration or travel back in time a couple of hundred million years (give or take a few) to a time when dinosaurs made Connecticut their turf. Make the acquaintance of parrots and opossums or learn about history and culture from a child's perspective. It wouldn't make sense to try to fit all the activities mentioned into a single day. They are grouped together because they're all within a half hour of Hartford and each other. Choose two or three (you can always hit the others another day), taking into account the ages and personalities of your children. And don't let rain or sleet slow you down; there are plenty of indoor options as well as outdoor ones.

New Britain is not the sort of city one visits simply to wander around. A busy commercial center with traffic to match, it is best approached with the goal of visiting a few specific attractions, one of which is actually located in neighboring Kensington. There is something to appeal to all age groups, but six to ten year olds will probably be most consistently satisfied.

At the **Copernican Space Science Center** in New Britain you can watch the heavens unfold above and around you in the small planetarium, a teaching

*From the trackway at Rocky Hill's Dinosaur State Park, you can get a good look at both dinosaur models (such as this Dilophosaurus) and actual dinosaur footprints.*

Dinosaur State Park

facility belonging to Central Connecticut State University. A member of the university staff introduces and narrates the weekly shows, which focus on subjects such as space travel, the chemistry of space, and the utilization of space in the future. Programs are usually held on Friday and Saturday evenings, and some Saturday afternoons; call ahead for exact times. Programs geared to the interests of children last thirty-five minutes. Slightly longer programs intended for adults are also good for older kids or those with a serious interest. If the sky is clear, the observatory on top of the center is open for public viewing following the show. Here you'll have a chance to look through the second largest public telescope in the United States, as a staff member helps you locate celestial phenomena.

*At the Copernican Space Science Center in New Britain you can watch the heavens unfold above and around you in the small planetarium.*

The emphasis is on the "culture of childhood" at the **New Britain Youth Museum,** which features two to four special exhibits each year. The staff members here believe that children should be treated with respect. That translates into well-designed, clearly labeled displays that incorporate authentic artifacts.

A recent exhibit called "Circus Days," for example, boasted midget Tom Thumb's boots and lion tamer Clyde Beatty's chair, along with circus posters and programs and lots of model circuses, one of which had real sawdust in the ring and hundreds of tiny spectators in the stands. A permanent display includes replicas of carved wagons used by the Barnum & Bailey, Ringling Brothers, and Forepaugh circuses during the late 1800s and early 1900s. One wagon has a pair of golden sphinxes on top and exotic desert scenes painted on the sides. In the small outdoor play area kids can scramble up into a wooden circus wagon and transform themselves into roaring lions or whatever else strikes their fancy. Or they can climb aboard a large, chunky wooden elephant with a wonderful fraying rope tail that looks as if it actually belongs on a horse.

The museum stocks a table with toys — like Lincoln Logs and counting rods and even a magic mirror optical toy — that kids are welcome to use. Children can also sign out board games at the gift shop counter to use in the museum. On Wednesday and Saturday afternoons they can join in a one-hour participatory program. Activities sometimes relate to the special exhibit on view and sometimes reflect a seasonal or historical theme. The sessions appeal to five to ten year olds (children under five may attend if a parent stays with them). During the circus show, participants learned to apply clown makeup. Other programs have revolved around ice cream making, tie dying, and making homemade school supplies (quill pens and notebooks like those used in early New England schools). It's wise to call ahead to reserve a space in these programs.

Before you leave, let your youngsters shop at the gift counter where about half the merchandise costs less than a dollar, including enameled animal pins, compasses, wooden flutes, Chinese yo-yos, beaded earrings, and indoor boomerangs.

Most children's museums have a section devoted to live animals, and while the youth museum is indeed the home of several caged birds, it doesn't really have space for much else. It solves that problem via its sister facility, the **Hungerford Outdoor Education Center,** located in nearby Kensington. Housed in an elegant, restored 1920s horse stable, Hungerford has plenty of room for hands-on exhibits and resident animals. Outdoors kids can pet the pigs, sheep, and goats and introduce themselves to geese, ducks, and chickens. Inside the barn animals vary from the endearing capuchin monkey to the not-so-cute tarantula, from ring-necked doves to rabbits. There are parrots too and a boa constrictor, and less exotic residents like mice and hamsters.

The emphasis at Hungerford is on wildlife rehabilitation and teaching visitors to respect and properly care for animals. Other goals include teaching about ecology, nutrition, and outdoor exploration. To this end, the staff has designed and installed a series of exhibits that challenge visitors to test their own knowledge and to fill in the gaps. The exhibits are housed in the refurbished stalls, which are immaculate and handsome, incorporating the original wood (you can find hoof marks if you look really hard) and brickwork. In one stall you learn that a cow is a ruminant, which means it has four compartments to its stomach and chews its cud. A single cow can produce as much as eighty pounds, or forty quarts, of milk in a day. Press the nine buttons on the fancy control board; each one illuminates various parts of the cow's internal workings important in digestion and the production of milk.

In another stall a giant mural challenges kids to find what's wrong in the picture. To check themselves, they can lift panels that reveal answers like "pet playing with electrical cord" or "dog left locked up in car." Another question board asks them to decide which animals should be kept as pets, which

*The emphasis at Hungerford is on wildlife rehabilitation and teaching visitors to respect and properly care for animals.*

*Kensington's Hungerford Outdoor Education Center gives kids a chance to get close to the animals.*

shouldn't, and why. Still another stall contains an exhibit about the process of clearing land, plowing, planting, and harvesting. The Center also includes a play area for small fry, complete with playhouse, animal books, puzzles, puppets, and toys.

Allow time to wander the grounds at Hungerford to enjoy the wonderful gazebo complete with rose garden, an extensive herb garden, and a raised bed vegetable garden. The former bridle paths have been recycled as nature trails, and they loop in and out of a landscape that includes a pond and a swamp as well as woods. Hungerford also runs Saturday Exploring, a series of indoor and outdoor programs. Depending upon the week you attend, your child might get to handle snakes and other reptiles, walk through the swamp (wear boots!), or attend (with a favorite stuffed animal) a tea party that includes live animal guests. Call ahead for schedule.

For a low-key, relaxed outing, spend an afternoon in Glastonbury. Begin at the **Old Cider Mill,** where cider is made sporadically throughout the summer and daily from Labor Day through Thanksgiving. Because the apples are pressed according to need, it's important to call ahead if you want to be sure to see cider being made when you visit. Out back of the mill you can watch the apples traveling from the wooden hopper up the conveyor belts on their way to the press. Here you might also see the plastic jugs being filled with the finished product. It all depends on how far along the process is when you stop by. But there's plenty else to catch your attention.

Here you can pick your own blueberries in July, and your own vegetables throughout the summer and early fall. Bring your own containers; you'll be charged by the pound. Kids enjoy petting and feeding the farm animals — sheep, goats, and rabbits, and sometimes pigs and ducks — and that's perfectly fine so long as they give them only animal food purchased in the mill. You are welcome to bring along a lunch to eat at the picnic tables on the patio overlooking the field where the animals live. If you've neglected to bring your own provisions, step into Grandma's Pantry, a section of the mill, and treat yourself to cold drinks (hot mulled cider when the weather turns cold), giant muffins, and oversized cookies. Take-home items include homemade pies, jams and jellies, cheeses, syrups and honeys, and other regional food products. The Old Cider Mill also includes the Old Mill Country Store, which is stocked with Christmas decorations and do-it-yourself supplies for those who want to make their own wreaths and other holiday ornaments.

Just a few doors down from the mill at the **Connecticut Audubon Society Holland Brook Center,** the hands-on exhibits focus on the native flora and fauna and the Connecticut River ecosystem. A touch table is filled with intriguing artifacts like antlers, seed pods, wooden burls, feathers, starfish, and shells, as well as magnifying glasses for viewing these items. In the weather corner you can push the bar on the weather radio for an up-to-the-minute weather report. Challenge yourself with weather riddles (You cannot see me with your eyes, but I make trees move when I go by. Answer: wind) or work on a weather puzzle.

The center has a few resident live animals, like the yellow rat snake, who prefers to pass the time sequestered in a hollow tree trunk, and the giant hissing cockroach (honest). You can peer into the eyeshine box and learn about the mirrorlike structure in the back of some animals' eyes that accounts for the fact that their eyes seem to shine at night when light is directed at them.

Individual tables are set up for activities like shell printing, which creates a good take-home souvenir. The lovely puppet theater is richly stocked with animal puppets ranging from turtles, ducks, and chipmunks to a large blue whale. Parents can take a break in the comfortable reading area while kids make themselves at home in this cozy, unpretentious place, with its own nature shop filled with records, books, toys, and fanciful animal- and plant-related novelties.

The center adjoins thirty-eight-acre Earle Park, which has a network of nature trails that you're free to explore. If you bring along a picnic, you can eat it

*A worker pours apples into the press at Glastonbury's Old Cider Mill, where cider making goes on regularly from Labor Day until Thanksgiving.*

Diane Levy

at one of the tables beside the Center or take a walk through the woods and enjoy it sitting on a bluff overlooking the Connecticut River.

Next stop Manchester, the perfect destination for children with lots of energy who thrive on learning through doing. No need to be quiet or to sit still as they indulge their spirit of discovery, indoors and out. Kids will seldom experience a warmer welcome than they'll receive at the **Lutz Children's Museum**. The museum has two areas that are always devoted to participatory exhibits designed to encourage children to learn through their own experiences. Depending upon what's current when you visit, your kids may get to build a shoulder-high dinosaur model, experiment with sign language, or decipher codes. The exhibits change regularly, but all relate to art, history, science, nature, or ethnology.

The Lutz also features a live animal exhibit devoted to small native, domestic, and exotic creatures. Your children are likely to make the acquaintance of an opossum, a skunk, or perhaps a corn snake. Many of these animals have been injured or orphaned and will eventually be released. One section of the Lutz Museum shop — stocked with intriguing artifacts, projects, equipment, and supplies that encourage kids to discover through doing — is set aside for kid-sized budgets, with all items priced at one dollar or less. Out back of the museum, your kids can work off some steam crawling and climbing as they stretch their muscles on some imaginative play equipment.

Complement your museum visit with a stop at nearby **Wickham Park,** a 215-acre expanse of gardens, woodlands, open fields, and ponds. This park is packed with special places to discover. Rabbits and squirrels frequent the walking trails, where even deer and fox have been known to appear. The pleasant picnic areas have tables, benches, and grills, and there's a cabin where refreshments are sold on weekends and holidays. Most children are enchanted by the aviary, which accommodates more than fifty native and exotic birds. A nearby playground is geared to the needs of the toddler set, and older kids can use the tennis, volleyball, and shuffleboard courts free of charge. There's also a gracious oriental garden complete with arched bridge and tea house. In the winter, when weather conditions allow, the park reopens for sledding on weekends and holidays.

Last on the list is Rocky Hill, where the subject is dinosaurs, and the emphasis is on authenticity, a statement you should interpret as a warning. Preschoolers who are enchanted with dinosaurs are

*You can be sure you'll get your money's worth at Manchester's Lutz Children's Museum.*

*These 185-million-year-old Eubrontes tracks are about as close as you want to get to that ancient flesh-eating reptile.*

Dinosaur State Park

likely to be disappointed. There are no Disneyesque models to see, just genuine footprints. As you gaze over the serene landscape that envelops **Dinosaur State Park,** it's difficult to imagine that 185 million years ago, just a few miles south of what is today Hartford, huge, flesh-eating reptiles skulked here along the shores of a lake now long gone. They left their tracks in a large area of bedrock discovered in the 1960s. Today many of those tracks are enclosed beneath a 122-foot geodesic dome.

Inside the dome you'll first encounter several displays of dinosaur fossils and models. Then step onto the trackway, a long platform that passes just a few feet from footprints left behind by Eubrontes, who is believed to have reached a length of eight to twenty feet. The tracks are a series of three-toed impressions that vary from ten to sixteen inches in length.

Planning ahead is an absolute must when your destination is Dinosaur State Park, unless you're in the habit of driving around with a bag of plaster of Paris and a bottle of cooking oil in your car. That's because while you're here you can make your own casts of real dinosaur tracks to take home. The casting area is stocked with fossils, metal rings (sometimes needed as a frame to prevent the plaster from oozing away), rags, and a water supply. You need ten pounds of plaster of Paris and one-quarter cup of cooking oil for each casting you plan to make. And since it's easy and there's no fee, you might as well make a few!

**NEW BRITAIN.** Follow I-84 to exit 40. Take Route 71 south, following signs into New Britain.

**GLASTONBURY.** Follow I-84 to Route 2. Take Route 2 south to exit 7.

**MANCHESTER.** Follow I-84 to exit 60. Take I-384 east to the Route 83 exit.

**COPERNICAN SPACE SCIENCE CENTER. Directions:** From I-84, take exit 40. Take Route 71 south in the direction of New Britain (following signs to Central Connecticut State University). Route 71 becomes Stanley Street. At Central Connecticut State, turn left on Wells Street. Science Center will be on your right, past the second stop sign. Free public parking garage is on the right just beyond the center. **Season:** Year-round; selected evenings. **Admission:** Charged. **Telephone:** (203) 827-7419.

**NEW BRITAIN YOUTH MUSEUM. Directions:** From I-84, take exit 35. Follow Route 72 east to Columbus Boulevard exit; go straight through the light. At the next light turn right onto High Street. Museum is on the right at 30 High Street, behind the public library. **Season:** Year-round. **Admission:** Free. **Telephone:** (203) 225-3020.

**HUNGERFORD OUTDOOR EDUCATION CENTER. Directions:** From I-84, take exit 35. Follow Route 72 east to Corbin Avenue exit. Turn right on Corbin Avenue and continue to Farmington Avenue. Center is located at 191 Farmington Avenue, about a 15-minute drive from the Youth Museum. **Season:** Year-round. **Admission:** Charged. **Telephone:** (203) 827-9064.

**OLD CIDER MILL. Directions:** Follow I-84 to Route 2 exit. Follow Route 2 south to exit 7. Turn right on Route 17 and continue through Glastonbury. Located at 1287 Main Street (Route 17) in Glastonbury. **Season:** Easter through December 31. **Admission:** Free. **Telephone:** (203) 633-4880.

**CONNECTICUT AUDUBON SOCIETY HOLLAND BROOK CENTER. Directions:** Follow Route 2 south to exit 7. Turn right on Route 17 (Main Street) in Glastonbury. Center is located at 1361 Main Street. **Season:** Year-round. **Admission:** Charged. **Telephone:** (203) 633-8402.

**LUTZ CHILDREN'S MUSEUM. Directions:** Follow I-84 to exit 60. Take I-384 east to the Route 83 exit. Go south on Route 83 to museum, located at 247 South Main Street (Route 83). **Season:** Year-round. **Admission:** Charged. **Telephone:** (203) 643-0949.

**WICKHAM PARK. Directions:** The park is located about 500 feet west of exit 60, I-84, at 1329 West Middle Turnpike. **Season:** Early April through late October. **Admission:** Free. **Telephone:** (203) 528-0856.

**DINOSAUR STATE PARK. Directions:** Follow I-91 to exit 23 and follow signs to park. **Season:** Year-round. **Admission:** Charged. **Telephone:** (203) 529-8423.

**For further information** or lodgings and restaurant suggestions for Glastonbury and Rocky Hill, contact the Olde Towne Tourism District, 2400 Main Street, Glastonbury, CT 06033. Telephone: (203) 659-1219. For information on New Britain, contact the Central Connecticut Tourism District, 227 Main Street, Suite 104, New Britain, CT 06051. Telephone: (203) 225-3901. For information on Manchester, contact the East-of-the-River Convention and Visitors' Bureau, 20 Hartford Road, Manchester, CT 06040. Telephone: (203) 646-2223.

# Hartford

With a population of more than 136,000, Connecticut's capital is definitely an urban experience. Navigating an unfamiliar city of this size can be difficult, so it makes sense to ditch your car and depend instead on your feet and on bus service. As soon as you exit the interstate, you'll see signs directing you to pay parking facilities. Follow them! Once you've disposed of your car, you're ready to begin exploring the downtown area.

The best way to get your bearings in Hartford is to head directly for the **Old State House,** which serves as a combination museum, visitor center, and gift shop. This is the starting place for walking tours and also where you can find city maps and tons of brochures describing Hartford attractions and activities. If you visit on a Monday, Wednesday, or Friday morning during the summer or early fall, you'll discover a delightful farmer's market spread out on the brick plaza in front of the State House. Local farmers sell their produce and flowers out of the backs of their trucks while pushcart vendors sell fast food that varies from barbecued chicken to steak subs. Nearby benches provide places to sit and map out your sightseeing strategy while your kids feed the pigeons. From here it's an easy walk to several museums and other points of interest.

As you walk through the downtown area, your children are likely to clamor for a ride aboard one of the bright red English double-decker buses that travel the streets. **Red Rover Limited Buses** offer both transportation and sightseeing. Trips are fully narrated, so while you're avoiding the traffic and the difficulties involved in negotiating an unfamiliar city, you also get some background on major points of historic interest. The complete route is six and a half miles. Your ticket entitles you to ride all day, getting on and off as you choose at any of the thirteen designated stops, which include museums and other attractions. The trip takes about one hour if you go straight through without stopping.

You'll certainly want to get off at **Bushnell Park,** a generous splash of green in the center of the city. Complete with pond and plenty of lawn space for tossing a Frisbee, this downtown oasis is a good place to stretch your legs and take a break from the rigors of sightseeing. Pushcarts bordering the park sell everything from hot dogs to Greek salads, which makes it a good place to eat lunch too. And it is the home of an unexpected treat — an elaborate old-time carousel. Created in 1914 by "Stein and Goldstein, the Artistic Carousel Company," the **Bushnell Park Carousel** has forty-eight hand-carved, brightly painted horses, along with two ornate chariots. Light from more than eight hundred bulbs reflects in the oval, square, and rectangular beveled mirrors, making the carousel a shimmering, magical place. Add to that music produced by the Wurlitzer band organ — waltzes, polkas, and marches — and you've got a hefty dose of romantic atmosphere right in the middle of the city. Pick out your favorite mount and go for a whirl, mane flying and golden hooves kicking high.

From the park, it's just a short walk to the gold-domed **State Capitol,** home of the state legislature and the governor's office. The imposing marble and granite neo-Gothic edifice looks more like a castle than an office building. Equally ornate inside as out, it has skylit stairwells, balconies, hand-painted col-

Diane Levy

*Hartford's gold-domed, marble and granite, neo-Gothic State Capitol looks more like a castle than an office building.*

umns, stenciled beams, and patterned marble floors. During your free tour, you'll learn how a bill becomes a law, and you'll see lots of artifacts relating to early New England history. If you're lucky, you might even catch a glimpse of the governor. Most of the legislative sessions and hearings are open to the public, and older children are often fascinated by a close-up of government at work.

The bus tour also stops at America's first public art museum, the **Wadsworth Atheneum,** which contains more than forty thousand works of art covering every major period. The collection of nineteenth-century American landscapes seems to register well with young visitors, as do the mummies and the fountain sculpture. Children are also impressed by the Great Hall, where gold-framed paintings are stacked three and four high on red walls beneath an ornate vaulted ceiling.

What's particularly nice about visiting the atheneum is that the staff here is keyed in to kids. They seem to understand that looking at art doesn't come easily, and to help kids appreciate what they're seeing, they've come up with a unique concept: taped tours geared especially to the interests of children. The tapes, prepared by the staff to accompany visiting exhibits, include sound effects (the dog in the Mary Cassatt painting barks), treasure hunts (look for the portrait of the one-eyed man), and lots of clues (Can you find a portrait of an artist? Artists use palettes, easels . . . ). In between the fun, the listener learns about concepts such as composition and impressionism, and it's all painless! Each tape recorder

Wadsworth Atheneum

*Leonardo would be proud of this young visitor, making a discovery (or two) at the Wadsworth Atheneum, America's first public art museum.*

is equipped with a second earphone, so mom or dad can listen along, if the child chooses.

If your kids are sports fans, they've probably heard of the **Hartford Civic Center,** home of professional ice hockey's Hartford Whalers. Located a few blocks from Bushnell Park and accessible by foot or bus tour, this huge complex includes the 16,500-seat Veterans' Memorial Coliseum and hosts a large variety of entertainment and events, including professional wrestling matches, exhibition basketball games, concerts, and special family shows. Call the box office for current ticket information.

Now it's time to reunite with your car to visit several places located outside of the downtown area. If your brood is hungry when you get back to the Old State House, step across the street to **The Pavilion,** an art deco–style, multilevel indoor shopping plaza with towering blue pillars, an atriumlike ceiling that lets the sunlight pour in, lots of brass trim, and a glass elevator. There are lots of elegant stores, but the real draw for a visiting family is the second-story Garden Court, an assortment of self-service fast food restaurants. Here you'll find pizza and pasta, burritos and tacos, croissants, deli sandwiches, and — from a stand called Boonoonoonoos — southern treats like sweet potato pudding, plantain tart, and oxtail with beans. Each member of your troupe can choose a different kind of fare, to be enjoyed at a table in the common dining area.

For dessert, travel less than a block from The Pavilion to **Ashley's Ice Cream.** Connecticut boasts five Ashley outlets in all, and each makes its own ice cream right on the premises. At Ashley's, the ice cream is made by hand in four-gallon batches. Ashley's skips the artificial additives and concentrates instead on fresh fruits and other high-quality ingredients. They make seventy-five flavors total, serving twenty-three at any given time. They also make their own waffle cones. You can have your ice cream straight, or you can order it with a selection of mix-ins, up to three of which can be worked into a single large scoop.

Children familiar with the exploits of Tom Sawyer will enjoy a visit to **Nook Farm** (also on the Red Rover route), settled in the last half of the nineteenth century by interrelated families and friends who formed a famous literary colony in the process. Here you'll tour both the Mark Twain House and the Harriet Beecher Stowe House. A combined tour of the two houses takes one and a quarter hours; tickets to the individual houses are not sold.

*Children familiar with the exploits of Tom Sawyer will enjoy a visit to Nook Farm.*

*Mark Twain wrote seven major works — including* Huckleberry Finn — *while a resident of this exotic Victorian home.*

Diane Levy

Your visit to the fancy Victorian-era house where Samuel Clemens wrote seven major works, including *The Adventures of Tom Sawyer* and *The Adventures of Huckleberry Finn,* provides opportunity to step back into the Gilded Age. Born in 1835 and raised in Hannibal, Missouri, Samuel Clemens left school at age twelve and set about trying his luck at a series of jobs that ranged from printer's devil (errand boy in a printer's office) to reporter, from riverboat captain to gold miner.

When he finally found his niche as a writer, he settled on a pen name that evoked memories of his time on the Mississippi River. In order to measure the depth of the river, the boatman lowered from the deck a rope with marks six feet apart (six feet equals one fathom). When the first mark on the rope disappeared beneath the water's surface, he called out, "Mark one!" indicating one fathom in depth. When the second one disappeared, he shouted, "Mark twain!" or two fathoms.

A Victorian marvel complete with fancy carved woodwork, painted bricks, turrets, and bay windows, this is the house where Clemens and his wife Livy raised their three daughters and entertained dozens of distinguished guests. Children may not be interested in the guide's description of the architecture and furnishings, but they'll enjoy hearing about the exploits of the family and its famous father. Clemens was so infatuated with state-of-the-art gadgetry that he had one of the earliest telephones installed, a "butterstamp" model that called for the user to speak and listen through the same device, whipping it back and forth from ear to mouth. When the guide presses a button, you'll hear actor Hal Holbrook imitating Mark Twain complaining about the confounded thing. In the master bedroom kids will be intrigued to discover that Clemens and his wife slept with their heads at the foot of the bed so that they had a good view of the elaborately carved headboard and the bedposts with removable angels that they'd purchased at great cost.

The Stowe house is less spectacular than the Twain house, but very much worth a visit. This is where Harriet Beecher Stowe, author of *Uncle Tom's Cabin*, lived with her husband and her grown twin daughters. The house is filled with cheery objects and furnishings, many pieces hand decorated by Ms. Stowe, who with her sister coauthored *The American Woman's Home*, a popular late-nineteenth-century handbook expounding the most modern ideas concerning home decoration and domestic economies.

For children, you can't do better than a leisurely visit to **The Science Museum of Connecticut**. Exhibits here cater to a broad age range, making the museum popular with twelve year olds as well as preschoolers. The museum even has its own planetarium, second largest in New England, and its own aquarium, which incorporates a Caribbean reef backdrop in an eleven thousand-gallon tank containing hundreds of colorful tropical fish. You can find out how sea animals sound by listening to an underwater recording of the voices of the sea robin, puffer, dolphin, sperm whale, and some of their friends. There's a hands-on tank too, where kids can roll up their sleeves and shake hands (gently) with a crab or a starfish. Little kids are thrilled to try on a real sea turtle's shell or a diver's flippers.

In the Discovery Room you can step inside the infinity tunnel, where two parallel mirrors make reflections and reflections of reflections of — you! Try to figure out whether the floating rings are actually floating or learn about physics as you experiment with the bicycle wheel gyroscope. You can also turn yourself into a human battery, observing the electrical current that flows through a meter as you create different chemical reactions by placing your hands on copper and aluminum plates. The echo tunnel is great for kids who thrive on the sound of their own voice, and a reflections table outfitted with a two-way mirror enables you to transpose your head onto someone else's shoulders.

In the "Key to Your Heart" exhibit, each child gets a "passkey" that unlocks parts of the exhibit when slipped into a slot. Here you'll learn how physical activity affects blood pressure and how habits like smoking and eating a high cholesterol diet affect your arteries. The museum features daily live animal

*Kids can roll up their sleeves and shake hands (gently) with a crab or a starfish.*

demonstrations and a full-size outdoor sperm whale model that you can walk right into.

For a different perspective of the city, take a cruise along the Hartford waterfront and down the Connecticut River. The **Deep River Navigation Company** offers several trips, two of which particularly interest families. For younger children, the hour-long midday cruise to Wethersfield Cove is just right. Lunch is sold aboard the *Lady Fenwick*, but you are welcome to bring your own picnic. Older, more patient kids (particularly those who wish they could wander the river like the legendary Tom Sawyer) will enjoy the two-and-a-half-hour journey south to Glastonbury. As you glide out into the countryside, the captain will comment on points of interest, including highlights of the Hartford skyline, the bridges, the Trinity Boathouse, and the Rocky Hill ferry.

## ACCESS

**HARTFORD.** Take I-84 to exit 52 or I-91 to exit 31.

**OLD STATE HOUSE. Directions:** Follow signs from I-84, exit 52, or I-91, exit 31. Located within walking distance of all the downtown Hartford attractions mentioned below. **Season:** Visitor Information Center open year-round. **Admission:** Free. **Telephone:** (203) 522-6766.

**THE PAVILION. Directions:** Located at the corner of Main Street and State House Square, just across from the Old State House. **Season:** Year-round. **Admission:** Free. **Telephone:** (203) 241-0100; (203) 527-0100.

**ASHLEY'S ICE CREAM. Directions:** Located at 19 Asylum Street, ½ block from Main Street, just beyond the Old State House. **Season:** Year-round. **Admission:** Free. **Telephone:** (203) 241-0161.

**RED ROVER LIMITED BUSES. Directions:** Tickets and route maps are available at the Old State House or from any of the double-decker buses. All bus stops are clearly marked. **Season:** Year-round; Tuesday through Saturday. **Admission:** Charged. **Telephone:** (203) 525-5155.

**BUSHNELL PARK CAROUSEL. Directions:** Located on the Jewell Street side of Bushnell Park in downtown Hartford. **Season:** Mid-April through September. **Admission:** Charged. **Telephone:** (203) 728-3089.

**STATE CAPITOL. Directions:** Located at 210 Capitol Avenue, at the corner of Capitol Avenue and Trinity Street, overlooking Bushnell Park. Tours depart from main lobby. **Season:** Guided tours on weekdays, February through June and September through November. **Admission:** Free. **Telephone:** (203) 240-0222.

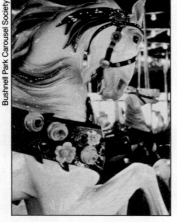

Bushnell Park Carousel Society

*Hooves high, mane flying, this mighty mount is just the right size for the junior bronco busters in your family.*

**WADSWORTH ATHENEUM. Directions:** Located at 600 Main Street in downtown Hartford. **Season:** Year-round; closed Mondays and major holidays. **Admission:** Charged. **Telephone:** Information tape (203) 247-9111; other calls (203) 278-2670.

**HARTFORD CIVIC CENTER. Directions:** Located at One Civic Center Plaza in downtown Hartford. **Season:** Year-round. **Admission:** Charged. **Telephone:** (203) 727-8080.

**NOOK FARM. Directions:** Follow I-84 to exit 46. Take Sisson Avenue to Farmington Avenue, less than a mile. Turn right on Farmington Avenue. Entrance to Nook Farm on your right. **Season:** Year-round; closed Monday from September through May. **Admission:** Charged. **Telephone:** (203) 525-9317.

**THE SCIENCE MUSEUM OF CONNECTICUT. Directions:** Take I-84 to exit 43. Take a right on Park Road and an immediate left on Trout Brook Drive. Museum is 2 blocks ahead on the right at 950 Trout Brook Drive. **Season:** Year-round. **Admission:** Charged. **Telephone:** (203) 236-2961.

**DEEP RIVER NAVIGATION COMPANY. Directions:** Take I-91 to exit 27, Brainard Road–Airport Road. Follow signs to Brainard Road. Go left at the end of the ramp, north on Brainard Road. Turn left at the fork marked Regional Market. The Charter Oak Landing dock entrance is on the right, ¼ mile beyond the Regional Market. **Season:** June through October. **Admission:** Charged. **Telephone:** (203) 526-4954.

**For further information** or restaurant and lodgings suggestions, contact the Greater Hartford Convention and Visitors Bureau, One Civic Center Plaza, Hartford, CT 06103. Telephone: (203) 728-6789. Or stop in at the Visitor Information Center in the Old State House.

# New Haven

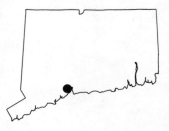

**P**ut New Haven on your "any time" list. Best known as the home of Yale University, this southern New England city can entertain your family in bad weather as well as fair, any season of the year. Museums are the big news here — museums with particular appeal for young visitors.

Your children may not be ready to apply to Yale, but they are probably ripe for a visit to the university's **Peabody Museum of Natural History,** one of the oldest and largest natural history museums in the world. The big draw is the world-famous collection of dinosaurs, housed in the Great Hall. A full-scale fossil of Brontosaurus dominates the hall,

*Dinosaurs galore await visitors to the Peabody Museum of Natural History, one of the world's oldest and largest natural history museums.*

where you'll also make the acquaintance of Stegosaurus, Camptosaurus, and Anatosaurus. The horned dinosaurs Torosaurus and Triceratops are represented by skulls, and there is the cast of a skull from famed Tyrannosaurus rex. A "new" dinosaur, Deinonychus (or "terrible claw"), is slated for installation in 1988. Distinguished by the large sickle-shaped claw on each of its hind legs, this previously unknown species of dinosaur (its skeleton was discovered near Billings, Montana, in 1964) resembled a large bird more than a reptile.

Young dinosaur enthusiasts will also be attracted by the 110-foot-long Pulitzer Prize–winning mural *The Age of Reptiles,* by Rudolph Zallinger, as well as by Zallinger's 60-foot-long mural *The Age of Mammals.* To remember their visit, they can pick up a poster of the reptiles mural or another souvenir in the DinoStore, which features bracelets, wallets, lunch boxes, notebooks, rubber stamps, and bath sponges, all decorated with dinosaurs. Other choices include activity books, puzzles, and charts, as well as real fossils and shells, many priced under a dollar.

Elsewhere in the rambling museum, you'll see meteorites, dioramas of North American flora and fauna, and artifacts depicting the past culture of Meso-Americans and South Americans, Egyptians, and Plains Indians. Rock collectors will find much to examine in the Hall of Minerals. In the Hall of Invertebrates, insect collectors can get a close-up of mounted specimens of unusual and common centipedes, scorpions, butterflies, beetles, wasps, and grasshoppers. Here, too, shell collectors can see how many specimens they recognize in the display of 160 mollusks from the Florida and Caribbean regions (can you find a tulip shell? an angel wing?).

Although the Peabody is predominantly an old-fashioned museum, it certainly does not ignore a child's need to interact with exhibits. The first of five sections in the evolving Hall of Human Origins, a major new permanent exhibit, focuses on the great diversity found among primates, the characteristics that make primates unique in the animal world, and the differences between modern and fossil primates. Using a computer game, kids identify primates by matching stuffed specimens, skulls, and photographs with clues describing physical characteristics. A tape recording introduces children to the voices of sifakas, howlers, baboons, and chimpanzees; and a film shows the varying styles of locomotion and hand grasping practiced by primates, from baboons to chimpanzees to human beings. Four additional sections of the exhibit are slated for completion by 1990.

On weekends the museum has special programs of interest to children, including natural history films (for those eight and older) and guided tours of the Great Hall of Dinosaurs. Visitors age six and up are welcome to participate in hands-on activities in the museum's Discovery Room most weekend afternoons, with additional hours scheduled in the summer (call ahead to be sure). Kids can learn about taxidermy by handling skins, make a rubbing from a replica of the Rosetta stone, examine plant and animal specimens under a microscope, and try out activities designed to nourish their interest in natural history.

Children up to seven years of age will have a wonderful time at the **Connecticut Children's Museum,** where the signs say "Please Touch!" The ringing of a cash register and the clacking of typewriter keys attest to the industriousness of young visitors in the miniature village that serves as the core of the museum. Here little kids can get a job in the post office, the local restaurant, the school, the grocery store, or the television station. There's lots of real equipment to handle and dress-up clothing to put on. The museum staff encourages parents to play with their children, and the setup provides plenty of imaginative role-playing opportunities designed to stimulate thoughtful conversation and the free expression of feelings and ideas. A daughter pumps gas for her father's car in one part of town while a

*Children up to seven years of age will have a wonderful time at the Connecticut Children's Museum, where the signs say, "Please Touch!"*

son checks his mom's heartbeat with a stethoscope over at the hospital. Kids are encouraged to handle things, to find out how they work.

In addition to providing lots of opportunity for fantasy play, the museum runs weekend drop-in workshops (free with museum admission) that are keyed to a different theme each month. Parents join their four to seven year olds in making projects that vary from sculpture to music, architecture to collage. All in all, this is a museum where children learn by imagining and manipulating, touching, seeing, hearing, comparing, creating, and inventing. Come prepared to have fun, and allow plenty of time.

If there are older, mechanically inclined kids in your family, stop by the **Eli Whitney Museum,** located at the scene of the oldest continuously used industrial site in New England. The focus is on Whitney's contribution to the history of manufacturing and technology and the effects of his innovations on American life. Based on his reputation after he invented the cotton gin, Whitney was awarded a large government contract in 1798 — an order for ten thousand muskets. He built an armory on this spot to fulfill the contract, but the project was not an easy one. Writing to a friend in November of 1798, Whitney lamented, ". . . had it not been for the late snow storm my building . . . would have been raised today. I have 40 or 50 hands in my employ and am almost worn out with fatigue and anxiety. I have not a moment's leisure, day or night."

*Travel back in time as you board a working trolley for a three-mile trip through the Connecticut woods, hills, and meadows.*

Yet Whitney succeeded in his endeavor. Not only did he produce the required guns, but in the process he developed the concepts of interchangeable parts and division of labor which were to become the basis of the American system of manufacturing. The permanent exhibit is limited to a series of panels about Whitney's work and life. But the museum also regularly hosts traveling exhibits, such as the recent "Wheels at Work," which included three interactive stations where children could experiment with waterwheels, pulleys, and gears. Call ahead to find out about the current exhibit.

Had your fill of museums? For a change of pace, take a cruise through New Haven Harbor aboard the two-hundred-passenger **M/V** *Liberty Belle*. Seats are located around the edge of the canopy-covered upper deck, which is outfitted with roll-away side panels for weather protection. The enclosed main cabin occupies most of the lower deck. A half-hour midday jaunt is short enough to keep even toddlers interested. Hot dogs, sandwiches, and sodas are

*This museum moves! The Shore Line Trolley Museum includes carbarns, restoration shops, and a working trolley.*

served aboard, or you can bring along a picnic. An hour-long late afternoon harbor cruise is a relaxing way to bring a busy day to a close. Two-and-a-half-hour afternoon trips provide a chance to see more of the Connecticut coastline as you cruise to Branford Harbor or Morris Cove, while the captain provides a lively commentary on points of interest. Live music is also part of the fun.

To experience still another mode of transportation, head out to the **Shore Line Trolley Museum** in East Haven, where a motorman will take you on a tour of the carbarns and restoration shops where old electric trolleys are brought up to snuff. You'll learn about the history of the cars and then have an opportunity to travel back in time as you board a working trolley for a three-mile trip through the Connecticut woods, hills, and meadows. Feel free to take an additional ride if you like. A summer/fall attraction, the museum reopens on weekends each December to give Santa Claus a chance to welcome young visitors aboard. Hot chocolate and cookies are served, adding to the air of festivity.

Now that we've mentioned food, there are a couple of options you ought to know about. Let's face it — where there are students, there are bound to be plenty of places to eat. Yale weaves through downtown New Haven, and right on the edge of the campus are two student haunts that you should consider. The whole family will enjoy the sinfully delectable, absolutely fattening confections dished out at

**Thomas Sweet Ice Cream & Chocolate.** It is essential that you shelve all notions of good nutrition before entering these doors.

At Thomas Sweet, ice cream, chocolate, and other sweet things are made fresh daily on the premises — right in front of your eyes, in fact. You may arrive just in time to see large sheets of chunky homemade cookies being pulled from the oven. In addition to traditional favorites, the ice cream flavors include innovations such as butter brickle and chocolate cinnamon. The specialty here is the Thomas Sweet Blend-In. Using a special machine, the server will mix your choice of ice cream with as many as three blend-ins, chosen from a huge selection that includes everything from Heath Bars to fresh fruits to Oreos. You'll end up with a luxuriously smooth confection, served up in a homemade waffle cone if you desire. Thomas Sweet also offers sundaes, milk shakes, malts, and even egg creams. Take your ice cream out to the adjoining atrium, with its glass roof and three glass walls (the fourth is brick and complements the quarry tile floor). There are plenty of small round tables and bentwood chairs with padded seats, and decorative blue banners hang from above. If you prefer, you can eat at a picnic table in the sunny outdoor courtyard.

Prefer chocolate to ice cream? You'll have a field day choosing from chocolate-covered candy apples, chocolate-dipped pretzels, truffles, clusters, and barks. Then there are the novelty items — from Porsche to tennis racket, guitar to calculator — which come in milk, dark, and white chocolate.

Is there a bookworm in your family? Treat your favorite young reader to a visit to the **Atticus Bookstore Café.** Let your child choose a new book in the children's corner and then take a seat at the counter or one of the tables right in the middle of the store. A fresh croissant, muffin, or scone makes a delightful snack, or opt instead for pastilles (described in the menu as "gourmet Ring Dings") or a generous slice of chocolate marble mousse pie. Atticus also offers soups, sandwiches, a fruit and cheese plate, and exotic sodas like apple strawberry, Orangina, and black cherry. Best of all, it's considered good manners to read while you eat.

*Novelty items — from Porsche to tennis racket, guitar to calculator — come in milk, dark, and white chocolate.*

## ACCESS

**NEW HAVEN.** Follow I-91 to exit 3.

**PEABODY MUSEUM OF NATURAL HISTORY. Directions:** Take I-91 to exit 3, Trumbull Street. At second light, turn right on Whitney Avenue. Museum is located at 170 Whitney Avenue; street parking usually available. **Season:** Year-round. **Admission:** Charged. **Telephone:** (203) 432-5050.

**CONNECTICUT CHILDREN'S MUSEUM. Directions:** Take I-91 to exit 3. Traveling on Trumbull Street, turn left on Orange Street (a very short distance from exit 3; keep alert for it). Museum is at 291 Orange Street. **Season:** Year-round. **Admission:** Charged. **Telephone:** (203) 777-8002. **Note:** The museum is moving to this location in late spring of 1988; call before visiting to make sure it has reopened.

**ELI WHITNEY MUSEUM. Directions:** Located on Whitney Avenue about 5 blocks beyond the Peabody Museum of Natural History, at the intersection with Armory Street. **Season:** Year-round; limited hours. **Admission:** Free. **Telephone:** (203) 777-1833.

**M/V *LIBERTY BELLE*. Directions:** Take I-95 (Connecticut Turnpike) to exit 46 and follow signs to the *Liberty Belle* on Long Wharf Pier, 1 minute from the turnpike. **Season:** Late May through September. **Admission:** Charged. **Telephone:** (203) 562-4163.

**SHORE LINE TROLLEY MUSEUM. Directions:** From I-95 west, take exit 52. Take High Street toward East Haven. Cross Route 1 and then turn left on Main Street, then right on Hemingway Avenue. Turn left on River Street and continue to museum. From I-95 east, take exit 51. Turn right at second traffic light onto Hemingway Avenue and proceed as above. **Season:** Memorial Day through Labor Day; some December weekends. **Admission:** Charged. **Telephone:** (207) 467-6927.

**THOMAS SWEET ICE CREAM & CHOCOLATE. Directions:** Follow Trumbull Street to second light. Turn left and continue into downtown area. Pass the Historic Green and turn right on Chapel Street. Located at 1140 Chapel Street. **Season:** Year-round. **Admission:** Free. **Telephone:** (203) 562-8179.

Liberty Belle Ltd.

*A thirty- or sixty-minute cruise of the Connecticut coast aboard the* Liberty Belle *is brief enough to hold the interest even of very young travelers.*

**ATTICUS BOOKSTORE CAFÉ. Directions:** Located at 1082 Chapel Street, next to the British Art Center. **Season:** Year-round. **Admission:** Free. **Telephone:** (203) 776-4040.

**For further information** or restaurant and lodgings suggestions, contact the Convention and Visitors Bureau, 900 Chapel Street, New Haven, CT 06510. Telephone: (203) 787-8367.

# Mystic

**W**inter, spring, summer, or fall — who cares? Toddlers, ten year olds, or teens — no problem. Mystic is almost always right for a family getaway. This popular coastal Connecticut town, once an important shipbuilding center, boasts two major attractions and a host of small shops and activities. If you have only a day, you'll probably want to divide it between the Mystic Seaport Museum and the Mystic Marinelife Aquarium. If you have two days, we suggest you do the seaport on one and the aquarium on the other, which will allow plenty of time to discover other aspects of Mystic.

At **Mystic Seaport Museum,** a self-contained living history village, the calendar flips back to the nineteenth century. Experience the sounds, sights, and smells of a bustling seaport as you explore the dozens of boats and buildings spread out along the banks of the Mystic River. Pick up a curling iron or a razor strop at the Grocery & Hardware Store or purchase some live leeches at the Drug Store to relieve the misery of an ailing acquaintance in need of a bloodletting. Have your harpoon mended at the Shipsmith Shop or head over to the Spouter Tavern (named for the tavern in Melville's *Moby Dick*) to catch up on the gossip or have a game of dominoes. Mystic Seaport is the sort of museum that fuels young imaginations. Here a child can assume the role of sailor, sea captain, or plain old-fashioned child.

As soon as you arrive at the seaport, check the calendar of today's events posted at the entrance. You'll find out when you can play games on the village green, observe nautical craft demonstrations, learn about fish smoking or oystering, or attend a program on whaling and whalemen. You'll also learn about planetarium shows and boat rides scheduled for the day. Once inside the seaport, head straight for the children's museum to get information about spe-

*Chanteymen like these provide authentic entertainment at Mystic Seaport.*

cial activities scheduled for young visitors. You'll soon have a sense of how to plan your time.

At the children's museum your youngster can get a real feel for what it was like to be a child in an early seaport by exploring an exhibit titled "Children Who Went to Sea." The exhibit tells the story of kids who lived aboard sailing vessels during the late 1800s, when captains often took their families along on their travels. After all, a whaling trip could last several years. The exhibit contains a reproduction "captain's family cabin," which children eight years and under are invited to enter and explore. Here they can join in activities such as scrimshaw and ropework, popular among seafaring children. There are reproduction games, books, and dolls to play with too. Nineteenth-century dress-up clothes help children enter into the spirit of the period. Your kids can ride the rocking horse, play with Noah's Ark, or make a tower of the wooden alphabet blocks. And when they're tired, they can climb into the bunk bed, peer out the porthole, and try to imagine what it would be like to awaken each morning to a view of the endless sea.

Older kids needn't feel excluded. A table of Victorian amusements offers them several challenges. It's not as easy as it looks to make the jointed wooden lumberjack do a jig on the flat board placed on your knee, nor is it simple to catch the wooden ball in the cup-on-a-handle. It's fun to take a look through the

*Have your harpoon mended at the Shipsmith Shop or head over to the Spouter Tavern to catch up on the gossip or have a game of dominoes.*

*A costumed staff member will take kids on a tour of the seaport, including a couple of behind-the-scenes spots adults aren't permitted to visit.*

stereopticon or experiment with one of video's early ancestors, the phenakistoscope.

It seems only natural that boats are important at the seaport. In fact, the museum has more than three hundred of them, several of which really stand out. Be sure to allow time to visit the *Charles W. Morgan*, the last surviving wooden whale ship (1841). Step aboard for a look at the cavernous try-pots used for converting blubber to whale oil. Peek into the cramped quarters where the ship's officers and crew lived for years at a time. When you're up on deck, keep in mind that, fully rigged, the ship can carry approximately thirteen thousand square feet of sail (that's nearly one-third of an acre). You can also board the *L.A. Dunton*, an early twentieth-century fishing schooner.

For a ride down the river, take a trip on the **Sabino**. Built in 1908, it is one of the few coal-fired steamboats still in operation. From May to October, you can hear her steam whistle resonate throughout the valley as she treats passengers to a half-hour narrated cruise of the waterfront.

You can ride the *Sabino* even if you don't plan to visit the seaport. During the day she serves museum guests, but in the evening she offers daily ninety-minute excursions down the Mystic River to Fishers Island Sound. Several evenings are set aside for music cruises featuring either a barbershop quartet or a Dixieland jazz ensemble. Children are welcome on all cruises. Bring along a sweater or jacket since it gets cool on the water. Also feel free to bring any refreshments you wish. Food and drink are not sold aboard.

While you're in the museum, you're likely to make the acquaintance of some of the first-person interpreters who frequent the seaport. Dressed in period clothing, these people assume the role of typical nineteenth-century seaport inhabitants. One will entertain with tales of life on the high seas while another may lead an impromptu sing-along, complete with banjo and concertina: "Those New York Mas don't bake no pies, they feed their kids on moldy flies!"

For a special treat, sign up your child for an "Ice Cream Tour," offered daily from late June through Labor Day (a small fee is charged). A costumed staff member will take kids on a tour of the seaport, including a couple of behind-the-scenes spots adults aren't permitted to visit. They'll also have an opportunity to try some old-fashioned pastimes, like walking on stilts and rolling wooden hoops (not as easy as it looks!). The tours conclude with an ice cream break. While your kids are off with the guide, you'll have a child-free hour to spend visiting parts of the seaport that might not appeal to your offspring.

The other major family attraction in Mystic is the **Mystic Marinelife Aquarium,** complete with a two-and-a-half-acre outdoor complex called Seal Island, where five species of seals and sea lions live in recreated natural habitats. The aquarium, home to more than six thousand specimens of sea life, seeks to educate visitors about the way sea creatures look, live, and behave. In addition to dozens of fish tanks, great and small, there are many interactive exhibits. Look through a series of lenses to find out what a fish sees. Ever wonder what a fish feels like? You'll know before your visit is over. Peer into a tank filled with weed-covered rocks and try to pick out a fish that looks like a weed-covered rock! And learn how to estimate a fish's age. (Hint: it's a bit like determining the age of a tree.)

You'll want to attend one of the daily animal-training sessions held in the Marine Theater. If you sit in the first couple of rows, you're just asking for a bath. When a trio of Atlantic bottlenose dolphins splash down after demonstrating their jumping abilities by leaping twenty feet into the air, they displace a lot of water. The dolphins also strut across the water's surface on their tails, jump through hoops, and generally prove themselves charming and entertaining. On the rare occasion when they're displeased, they tend to show their chagrin by cackling, whistling, and slapping the water with those powerful tails. The training sessions often include appear-

*The performers are all wet at the Mystic Marinelife Aquarium, where seals, sea lions, and dolphins are part of the act.*

ances by whales and sea lions, in addition to the dolphins.

If you're hungry when you leave the aquarium, treat yourself to a great, gloppy ice cream treat at nearby **Sonny's Ice Cream Parlor.** There are a few red-and-white, ice cream parlor–style chairs and tables, but mostly you come for the goodies to go, not the ambiance. Enjoy the scrumptious sundaes, banana splits, floats, shakes, or egg creams. Other choices include chocolate-covered bananas, strawberries, and pineapple chunks; cones of frozen yogurt and soft ice cream; and chocolate chip ice cream sandwiches. You can also order your ice cream served up in a waffle cone or bowl — "so delish you'll eat the dish."

Another way to take a sightseeing break is to spend an hour or two exploring Mystic's endearing downtown. Lined with historic homes and store buildings, many of which date back to the nineteenth century, Mystic's Main Street lies on both sides of the Mystic River, crossing via a fifty-year-old drawbridge. The bridge provides an excellent vantage point for walkers to view the sailboats and lobster boats, rowboats and even the occasional canoe that tie up along the riverbanks.

*There are bears in stocking caps, bears in sea captain hats, even a bear in a Scotch plaid tam and matching scarf.*

You're bound to find your own favorites among the many attractive specialty shops, but here are a few you shouldn't miss. **Good Hearted Bears** has tiny bears, great big bears, bear puppets, bear soap, bear stickers, bear paper party goods, and just about anything else you can think of that lends itself to the bear motif. The shop also carries a whimsical line of little felt bears in kit form, along with kits for making costumes and accessories like a straw hat or a pinafore, a bed with linens, or a braided rug.

The bears that hunker down cozily on the shelves of this cheerful shop are no ordinary bears. These natty critters come in many sizes and shapes, and they tend to be stylishly dressed. There are bears in stocking caps, bears in sea captain hats, even a bear in a Scotch plaid tam and matching scarf. You might choose a soldier bear or a surgeon bear, or perhaps your heart will be captured by a baseball player or a ballerina. We even made the acquaintance of a green-skinned fellow who calls himself the Hunch Bear of Notre Dame.

At **Mystical Toys** the emphasis is on unusual, imported, and educational toys, many of which are not surprisingly pricey. What makes this a pleasant place to take children are the baskets of inexpensive toys — the kinds of small gifts that take the sting out of a long car trip. Starting at about fifteen cents, these items include tiny circus and farm animals, whistles and kazoos, rubber sharks and snakes, magnifying glasses, necklaces, and miniature dolls. The shop also stocks a line of "Take Along Games," puzzles, memory, cards, and collecting games that are perfect for amusing young travelers. There's a good supply of Caedmon tapes, for kids who pass long hours in the car listening to their personal cassette players. Louis Jordan reads *Babar*, Michael Pond reads *Paddington Bear*, and so on.

Right next door, you're in for a delectable, cavity-conscious experience at **Kane's Fudge Dock**. Tom and Doreen Kane are friendly, cheerful folks who turn out fudge, caramel corn, peanut brittle, and waffle cones on the premises, right before your eyes. Tom is the resident candy maker, and you're likely to find him cooking the fudge in a big copper kettle or pouring it onto one of the two large marble slab tables where it is "creamed" and formed into a loaf. Doreen often works in the Main Street window, making waffles using two small round irons and then forming the waffles into cones on molds. She'll be happy to serve you up a finished product filled with delicious ice cream (high quality, high butterfat, super rich, and delicious) made by a small New England producer who specializes in flavors like Mississippi mud and strawberry cheesecake.

When it's time for more nourishing fare, you can't beat **Abbott's** for New England seaside charm and absolutely fresh seafood. A coastal Connecticut landmark, Abbott's specializes in lobster in the rough. You can eat at a picnic table right at the edge of Fishers Island Sound (out in the sun or under a striped canopy) or in the enclosed dining room if the weather threatens. Abbott's is located in Noank, just a ten-minute drive from downtown Mystic. Once a shipbuilding center, Noank today remains a working fishing village, and it is not unusual to see boats pulling up to the restaurant dock to unload the day's crustacean catch. You can visit the holding pound, if you'd like, to see how Abbott's takes care of up to twenty-two thousand pounds of live lobsters.

You can see why lobster is the main item on the menu at Abbott's in Noank, a short drive from Mystic.

In addition to lobster, the menu lists several types of seafood rolls, clams on the half shell, mussels, shrimp, crab, and a mixed seafood plate. For kids who don't trust food that swims, the hot dog plate is a safe standby. Soft drinks are available, and you are welcome to bring along your own beer or wine (you'll pass a package store about a quarter of a mile before you arrive at Abbott's). Cheesecake and carrot cake are the most popular desserts. Altogether a pleasant, cheerful, informal eating spot, Abbott's is perfect for families. Just take care to avoid the crowds at peak weekend hours.

If you visit Mystic in the fall, make a stop at **Clyde's Cider Mill,** the last steam-powered cider mill in New England. Jack Buckyn's red and green Boomer & Boschert Press has been in action on this site since 1898. It can press seventy bushels of apples at a time, producing some of the best cider around. For two months each fall, the press, located in a cream-colored barn with a cupola, operates almost daily. A family business, Clyde's is a friendly, unpretentious place. The press dominates the showroom, the air smells like apples, and the 15 hp steam engine that powers the press croons and whistles away in the engine room, which is fully visible. If you want to be absolutely sure of seeing the process, plan your visit for one o'clock or three o'clock on a Saturday or Sunday afternoon.

In addition to cider, Clyde's sells chunky chrysanthemums, straw flowers, Indian corn, mulling spices, fudge, caramel and candy apples, homemade pumpkin bread, and, of course, fresh crisp apples. For parents, Clyde's produces a limited amount of hard cider, seasoned a full year in wooden kegs in the barn cellar. The supply usually lasts only a couple of weeks, so you'll have to visit right at the start of the season in late September or early October if you want to grab some of this nippy rarity.

*If you visit Mystic in the fall, stop at Clyde's Cider Mill, the last steam-powered cider mill in New England.*

## ACCESS

**MYSTIC.** Follow I-95 to exit 90. Follow Route 27 south about 1½ miles. Turn right on Route 1, following signs to Mystic.

**MYSTIC SEAPORT MUSEUM. Directions:** Follow I-95 to exit 90. Follow Route 27 south 1 mile to Seaport Museum. **Season:** Year-round. **Admission:** Charged. **Telephone:** (203) 572-0711.

*SABINO.* **Directions:** Enter through the South Gate of Mystic Seaport, near the Seaport Store. *Sabino* ticket booth will be to your right, at the head of the first dock. **Season:** Mid-May through mid-October. **Admission:** Charged. **Telephone:** (203) 572-0711.

**MYSTIC MARINELIFE AQUARIUM. Directions:** Follow I-95 to exit 90. Follow signs to aquarium, located on Coogan Boulevard, within minutes of the interstate. **Season:** Year-round. **Admission:** Charged. **Telephone:** (203) 536-3323.

**SONNY'S ICE CREAM PARLOR. Directions:** Located on Route 27, between Days Inn and the Ramada Inn, ¼ mile from aquarium. **Season:** Year-round. **Admission:** Free. **Telephone:** (203) 536-2223.

**GOOD HEARTED BEARS. Directions:** Located at the corner of Pearl and West Main streets in Mystic. **Season:** Year-round. **Admission:** Free. **Telephone:** (203) 536-2468.

**MYSTICAL TOYS. Directions:** Located at 36 West Main Street in Mystic. **Season:** Year-round. **Admission:** Free. **Telephone:** (203) 536-7131.

**KANE'S FUDGE DOCK. Directions:** Located at 40 West Main Street in Mystic. **Season:** Year-round. **Admission:** Free. **Telephone:** (203) 536-4516.

**ABBOTT'S. Directions:** Located about 10 minutes from downtown Mystic, in Noank. From Route 1 in Mystic, take Route 215 south in the direction of Noank. Turn left on Mosher Avenue and continue to T-intersection with stop sign. Turn left on Main Street. Go 1 block and turn right on Pearl Street. Abbott's is on the left. **Season:** May through Columbus Day. **Admission:** Free. **Telephone:** (203) 536-7719.

**CLYDE'S CIDER MILL. Directions:** Located in Stonington, less than 10 minutes from I-95. From exit 90, follow Route 27 north toward Stonington. Bear right at Old Mystic General Store, continuing on Route 27. Bear right at firehouse and continue on Stonington Road. Mill will be on the left. **Season:** Last weekend in September until Thanksgiving. **Admission:** Free. **Telephone:** (203) 536-3354.

**For further information** or restaurant and lodgings suggestions, contact the Mystic Chamber of Commerce, 2 Roosevelt Avenue, Mystic, CT 06355. Telephone: (203) 536-1641.

# MAINE

*Visitors pause to enjoy a moment of calm at Acadia National Park's Thunder Hole, where the waves often arrive with a roar, much to the delight of children.*

## The Portland Area

The emphasis is on learning and having fun at the same time when you spend a day in the Portland area. Here you can encourage your children to investigate subjects as diverse as computers and crafts, medicine and model railroads in the morning, and introduce them to coastal ecology and marine life in the afternoon. Many of the activities are available year-round, so keep this trip in mind for mud season as well as midsummer.

The exhibits at **The Children's Museum of**

**Maine** get a good work out, and staff members wouldn't have it any other way. This is a place for learning by getting involved. Even babies can join in the fun as they crawl up the carpeted ramps and steps in the Infants & Toddlers Park, a space set aside just for them. There are tunnels, elevated platforms, and a slide to navigate; a big wooden rocking horse with flowing rope mane and tail to ride; and a goofy circus mirror to make faces at. Also popular with preschoolers is the Fire Room, where they fantasize about being a fire fighter as they put on a heavy slicker, slide down the pole, drive the truck, hook up the hose, and put out the imaginary fire. In Snug Harbor they can similarly put themselves in the role of the lobsterman as they row out to the miniature lighthouse in a real skiff. Or, if they've a mind to, they can instead crawl into a wooden trap and see how it feels to be a lobster.

Grade-school kids will enjoy the computer lab where they can experiment with different software designed to teach and reinforce sequencing, plotting, and graphing skills. A program called Mask Parade allows them to design and print out a mask, which they can then color, cut out, and wear. Another piece of software simulates an assembly line. Here the child gets to set up a factory and produce a product, all on the computer. The six- to ten-year-old crowd also likes the Science Lab, where they can experiment with magnets by leading a ball through a maze or using a compass to find the north and south poles on a globe. At Station KITE they can appear on camera in the role of anchorperson, weather forecaster, sports reporter, or the celebrity of their choice.

And that's not all. There are an art room and a water-play room, as well as Dr. P. D. Atricks, a make-believe medical and dental clinic. Children can play checkers at Tom & Bill's Country Store or work out on the balance beam and chinning bars in the physical awareness area. Kids of all ages like to watch the Kite Express. A push of the button and the trains chug forward, twisting through tunnels and over bridges, around the mountain and through the tiny towns. A whistle blows; streetlights glow.

The museum has a small basement room with a snack vending machine where you are welcome to eat a lunch you've brought from home, or settle in at one of the picnic tables outside. Plan to spend one to two hours here, playing and learning alongside your kids.

After visiting the museum, cross the street and stop in at the **Children's Resource Center,** where

*Even babies can join in the fun as they crawl up the carpeted ramps and steps in the Infants & Toddlers Park.*

*A discriminating shopper examines the goods at Portland's Children's Resource Center.*

Michael Quan

the term recycling takes on new dimensions. This is nirvana for do-it-yourselfers, young or old. Each year the nonprofit center gathers, sorts, and sells thirty-five tons of materials that have been discarded by Maine industries. The place is absolutely stuffed with low-cost art materials — buttons, ribbons, wood items, plastic pieces, metal things, and much more — all neatly displayed on shelves and in rows of barrels, Plexiglas bins, and boxes. In the bathroom the bathtub is stuffed to overflowing with chunks of foam rubber awaiting transformation into stuffed animals, pillows, or anything else you might imagine. The Paper Room is filled with cardboard, poster board, envelopes, cards, plain paper, glazed paper, colored paper, pads, and textured paper. In the Fabric Room, you can choose from dozens of remnants, wallpaper sample books, vinyl, fleece, fake fur, canvas, and on and on.

You don't need to worry about what you'll do with all this tempting stuff once you get it home. Your kids are sure to have their own thoughts, and inspiration is everywhere. Sample projects made from the materials hang from the walls and ceilings wherever you turn. In addition, you can purchase Idea Sheets for ten cents apiece. Each one shows you how to make a specific project, be it mobile, hat, puppet, necklace, paper flowers, or even your own homemade paper.

Some materials are sold by the piece while others are sold by the pound or the foot. Place your items in a shopping bag and keep a running tally on the outside, making note of each item and its price. Shopping turns into a lively math lesson as kids count, measure, weigh, and cut, en route to the cash register.

The museum and the recycle center are on the outskirts of Portland, but you'll also want to get a look at the thriving downtown area. A good way to get oriented to Maine's largest city is to make for the waterfront, specifically Long Wharf. Here you can take a boat trip with the **Longfellow Cruise Line,** which operates five excursions each day. The M/V *Longfellow* is fifty feet long and can carry ninety passengers on its open upper deck and enclosed lower deck. Depending upon the interests of your brood, choose from the Lobster Fisheries and Island History Cruise, the Light House and Shipwreck Cruise (where you'll hear the sad and gruesome tale of Ram Island Light), or the Naturalist Cruise. On the latter, the emphasis is on watching seals and feeding seagulls as you pass their nesting grounds. Each of these narrated cruises lasts ninety minutes. If your kids are less patient, pack up a picnic lunch and climb aboard for a fifty-minute midday tour of the harbor.

From Long Wharf it's just a few steps to the Old Port Exchange, a restored area of nineteenth-century buildings that have been recycled as fashionable restaurants and shops. There are loads of places to eat, from pizzerias and bakeries to handsome pubs and bistros. While you're in this part of town, stock up on good reading matter at **The Enchanted Forest,** a bookstore devoted to children's fare. The comfortable, carpeted shop has high ceilings and lots of light and is an altogether cheerful, relaxed place. Best of all, the staff really knows and loves children's literature. They'll help a child find just the right book.

*From Long Wharf it's just a few steps to the Old Port Exchange, a restored area of nineteenth-century buildings that have been recycled as fashionable restaurants and shops.*

The store stocks both contemporary titles and old favorites, reprints of the classics you read as a child. In the section marked "chewables," you'll find a good collection of board books for the very young. There are sections for children in transition from picture books to chapter books, sections for preteens and teens, and a section of foreign language titles where you can pick up favorites like *Bonsoir Lune* (*Goodnight Moon*), *Jorge El Curioso* (*Curious George*), and *Petit Stuart* (*Stuart Little*). In addition, you can choose from high-quality cassettes and some unusual "literary" video cassettes. Tasteful writing and art toys and activity books are available too. Story hour is held on Sunday afternoons; call ahead for the exact time.

Just across the street from the bookstore is **ABC: Apple Bee Company,** stocked to the ceiling with educational toys and supplies, including lots of equipment used in schools. From easels to puppet theaters, magnets to beanbag globes, counting games to science equipment, the stock covers the gamut of children's interests. Nothing tacky or tasteless here, just good solid products that make learning fun.

Just a couple of doors away, **Mariner's Church Bakery** sells sandwiches, croissants, crusty breads, and desserts, along with bottles of fruit juice and good coffee. Bentwood chairs and tiny tables allow you to have an intimate chat with your offspring. If you have small children or if your crew tends to be rambunctious, get your goodies to go.

Less than twenty minutes south of Portland are two places that deserve a visit, both geared to teaching families about a different aspect of nature. Made up of more than three thousand acres of tidal marsh, salt creeks, fresh marsh, and uplands, Scarborough Marsh serves as a resting, feeding, and breeding habitat for numerous species of wildlife. At the **Scarborough Marsh Nature Center** you can look at the aquariums and mounted wildlife on exhibit, watch a slide show, and consult a self-guiding brochure as you stroll along the marsh nature trail, keeping alert for birds, plants, and other marsh life. Another great way to become familiar with the marsh is to rent a canoe, available by the hour or the half day. Paddles, life preservers, and maps are provided, so all you need to bring is yourselves. If you would rather go canoeing with an experienced naturalist guide, sign on for one of the ninety-minute canoe tours provided at different times of the day throughout the week. Bring your own canoe or use one belonging to the center.

The naturalist-guided family marsh adventure helps kids and adults learn together about salt marsh ecology. Other programs center on wildflowers and wild edibles, birding, and astronomy. A program especially for preschoolers encourages them to use all five senses as they discover the plant and animal life that thrive in the marsh. Advance reservations are

*A program especially for preschoolers encourages them to use all five senses as they discover the plant and animal life that thrives in the marsh.*

*If trailside bird watching at Scarborough Marsh Nature Center doesn't satisfy you, you can bring along (or rent) a canoe for a closer look at things.*

not necessary, but you should call or write ahead for a schedule with current information.

A growing concern located by the side of Route 1, the **Maine Aquarium** is a good place to learn about marine life, both local and exotic. The first folks you'll meet are the Magellanic penguins, who swim and strut about in a spacious glassed-in enclosure complete with slide. You'll come next to the touch pools, where a staff member shows kids how to handle sea urchins, horse mussels, crabs, limpets, and other creatures frequently found in coastal Maine tide pools. "You have to hold your breath when you go under the water," she explains. "These animals have to hold their breath when they come out of the water, so let's not keep them out too long." Picking up a starfish, she'll show that it's best to hold it flat in your hand, observing that it's fragile and "you'd feel real bad if all of a sudden all you had in your hand was a leg."

Move on next to the dozens of aquariums, filled with fish from different environments. Sturdy wooden boxes are placed in front of the raised viewing windows, making it easy for small kids to step up and get a good look. You'll see largemouth bass in the Maine lake habitat and rare blue lobsters in the Saco Bay tank, while the river tank lets you see the shimmering rainbow trout close-up. Be sure not to miss the giant Pacific octopus, an undulating orange-brown mass of tentacles and head clinging to the back of its tank, staring through slitty eyes. Its vision, we learned, is nearly as good as ours. We also learned that this shy and retiring creature seldom leaves its den except to look for food.

Among the tropical sea life is the venomous lionfish, which belongs to the scorpion fish family and looks like a tropical flower as it flares its striped, featherlike fins defensively, earning it the nickname "turkeyfish." As you venture on to the Amazon, Ca-

*You can't blame an adult for wanting to get into the act when kids go "on the air" at the Children's Museum of Maine.*

Michael Quan

ribbean, and Pacific tanks, you'll see an electric eel and a moray, as well as dozens of tiny, luminescent jewel-like fish. There are also a special room for Sparky, Fuzzy, and Red, the aquarium's three harbor seals, and a spacious shark tank where you can go eyeball to eyeball with a nurse shark, lemon shark, or giant grouper. In warm weather explore additional exhibits outside.

## ACCESS

**PORTLAND.** Follow I-95 to exit 6A. Take I-295 north to Route 1A (which becomes Commercial Street) to the Old Port Exchange district.

**THE CHILDREN'S MUSEUM OF MAINE. Directions:** Follow I-95 to exit 8 and turn right on Riverside Street. At next light, turn right on Warren Avenue. Continue to end and then turn right on Forest Avenue. Stay in right-hand lane, which will become Stevens Avenue. Museum is located ¼ mile down on the right, at 746 Stevens Avenue. **Season:** Year-round. **Admission:** Charged. **Telephone:** (207) 797-5483.

**CHILDREN'S RESOURCE CENTER. Directions:** Located at 741 Stevens Avenue, across the street from The Children's Museum of Maine. **Season:** Year-round. **Admission:** Free. **Telephone:** (207) 797-0525.

**LONGFELLOW CRUISE LINE. Directions:** Travel east on Commercial Street (Route 1A) to Moulton Street. Ticket office is located at Long Wharf, across from the intersection of Commercial and Moulton streets. **Season:** May through December. **Admission:** Charged. **Telephone:** (207) 774-3578.

**THE ENCHANTED FOREST. Directions:** Located at 377 Fore Street in the Old Port Exchange district. **Season:** Year-round. **Admission:** Free. **Telephone:** (207) 773-8651.

**ABC: APPLE BEE COMPANY. Directions:** Located on 374 Fore Street in the Old Port Exchange district. **Season:** Year-round. **Admission:** Free. **Telephone:** (207) 772-8940.

**MARINER'S CHURCH BAKERY. Directions:** Located at 366 Fore Street in the Old Port Exchange district. **Season:** Year-round. **Admission:** Free. **Telephone:** (207) 773-2253.

**SCARBOROUGH MARSH NATURE CENTER. Directions:** Follow I-95 to exit 5. Take Route 1 north to Scarborough and turn east on Pine Point Road (also marked as Route 9 west). Continue ½ mile to nature center, on the left. **Season:** Mid-June through Labor Day. **Admission:** Free; program and rental fees. **Telephone:** (207) 883-5100. **Note:** There are no rest-room facilities available at the center.

**MAINE AQUARIUM. Directions:** Follow I-95 to exit 5. Go north on Route 1 about 1 mile to aquarium, on the right. **Season:** Year-round. **Admission:** Charged. **Telephone:** (207) 284-4511.

**For further information** or restaurant and lodgings suggestions, contact the Maine Publicity Bureau Visitor Center, 142 Free Street, Portland, ME 04101. Telephone: (207) 772-2811.

# Ogunquit

Ogunquit is blessed with three miles of sandy coastline, from lively surf to protected inlet. Backed in some places by graceful dunes, in others by dramatic rock formations, the series of beaches offers a rare diversity. In the language of the Abnaki Indians, who camped along the Ogunquit River hundreds of years ago, the name Ogunquit means "beautiful place by the sea," a definition that still rings true today. Thanks to six clean, well-maintained beaches, you can spend nearly a week in Ogunquit without ever swimming at the same place twice.

Before settling down on the sand you may want to rent some equipment to make your day more comfortable or entertaining. The **Norseman Motel,** located right across from the main beach parking area, runs a concession overlooking Ogunquit Beach. Here you can rent beach chairs, beach umbrellas, and inflatable and solid floats. If you've come just for the day you might also want to make use of the locker facilities, showers, changing rooms, and the snack bar.

Although sun and swimming and digging in the sand are the big attractions here, there's plenty else to do. Ogunquit's beauty, for example, isn't limited to its beaches. **Perkins Cove,** a small protected inlet, is picturesque and intriguing. Kids will enjoy crossing the wooden footbridge that spans the mouth of the cove. It's a drawbridge with directions for operation posted on either side. Who knows? You might just have to become bridge tender, allowing a tall masted craft passage to the open sea.

Right at the entrance to the cove, you'll spot **Barnacle Billy's.** In addition to the ample indoor dining space, there are a brick patio with umbrella-covered tables, a wooden deck perched on the edge of the cove, and a second-story sun deck reached by a spiral staircase. The fare includes barbecued chicken, garlic bread, and hamburgers along with seafood specialties like lobster stew and shrimp rolls. Barnacle Billy's is also an ice cream stand.

*The name Ogunquit means "beautiful place by the sea," a definition that still rings true today.*

Barnacle Billy's dock serves as headquarters for **Finestkind Scenic Cruises.** Here's an opportunity to get an intimate look at one of Maine's most colorful industries — lobstering. Climb aboard an authentic lobster boat and head out to sea. While the lobsterman steers the craft, his helper talks about the history and geology of the area and about lobster legend and lore. In colonial days lobsters were so plentiful that they could be scooped off the rocks in places. They were known as "poor man's food" because only those who could afford nothing else would bother with them. You'll also learn about lobstering terminology and regulations (a "berried" lobster is a female breeder carrying eggs, and the law says you've got to throw her back).

Once you arrive at a trap, the lobsterman slides into his rubber coveralls and uses a hydraulic lift to pull the trap to the water's surface. If he's lucky, it will contain a couple of "keepers" (lobsters meeting the legal length requirement). If he's not, it might contain a "short" (the opposite of a keeper), a dead pollack, and maybe a couple of starfish and sea urchins. He's likely to chop the fish up for bait, and he'll probably distribute the urchins and starfish to young passengers before moving on to another trap. Kids will also have the opportunity to handle a lobster, after they've seen its claws safely banded. By the time the fifty-minute trip is over, your young ones will know how to determine the sex of a lobster, and they'll be able to point out the "kitchen," "parlor," and "shark's mouth" on a lobster trap.

Bring sweaters along as it tends to get chilly on

the water. This is particularly true on the early morning departure, which includes a donut, orange juice, and coffee. Finestkind also offers a fifty-minute starlight cruise and an hour-and-a-quarter lighthouse sightseeing cruise.

Older kids might enjoy a half-day (4 P.M. to 8 P.M.) deep sea fishing trip aboard the 1983 forty-foot fiberglass fishing boat, the *Bunny Clark,* captained by Ogunquit native Tim Tower. All you need to bring is a brown bag supper and a warm sweater; all fishing equipment and bait are provided. You'll go bottom fishing for cod, pollack, halibut, haddock, hake, cusk, and wolf fish. Equipped with enough rod holders and seating to accommodate everyone, most of the deck is covered with a canopy that offers protection from rain and spray. If you like to fish but aren't interested in taking the fillets home, the crew will tag and release your catch, using them in fish migration studies. Reservations are recommended (you can make them by calling Barnacle Billy's), and you should plan to arrive at the dock half an hour before departure time. Full-day trips are also available.

Crowded with lobster boats, rowboats, sailboats, and even inflatable boats, the Perkins Cove area is a hive of activity. Long known as a favorite

*Older kids might enjoy a half-day deep sea fishing trip aboard the 1983 forty-foot fiberglass fishing boat, the* Bunny Clark.

The Bunny Clark

*You should see the one that got away!*

*The beauty of Ogunquit inspires many people.*

Don Richeson

haunt for artists, its streets are lined with galleries, small specialty shops, and restaurants, every one just yards from the ocean. You're sure to discover your own favorites among the stores, but do make a point of stopping in at **Perkins Cove Candies,** a cheerful shop lined with wooden shelves containing dozens of baskets, jars, and trays overflowing with special sweets. It's not unusual for thirty-two pounds of peanut brittle to change hands in a single weekend. The taffy, fudge, and chocolates are made expressly for the shop and come in all sorts of flavors and shapes. With large white Japanese lanterns hanging from the high ceiling, a stenciled flower and bird wall motif, and an unbeatable view of the Atlantic shoreline, the shop is a delightful place to agonize over whether to go for the dark chocolate-covered cashew patties, the Dutch mints, the peanut butter fudge, or a bag full of cinnamon imperials, gummy bears, or Boston baked beans. There's lots of penny candy (though it costs two cents apiece and up) and gourmet popcorn as well.

For lunch try the **Lobster Shack,** a bustling, unpretentious, self-service eating place where you can feast on lobster rolls and clam rolls, steamers and chowder, hot dogs and hamburgers, and of course, boiled lobster. For dessert try a hefty portion of apple pie, blueberry pie, or chocolate fudge cake, served with a scoop of ice cream if you like. The ambiance is relaxed and informal, strictly paper plates and red-and-white-checked plastic table-cloths. For families with small children, there's even a high chair.

For an afternoon snack — maybe a fruit-filled croissant, a homemade muffin, an oversized chocolate chip cookie, a chunk of carrot cake, or a cinnamon swirl — try **Ma Perkins' Kitchen,** near the entrance to the cove. Make your choice at the glass and wood counter; then carry your purchases out to a chair on the screened porch.

Along with Perkins Cove and the beaches, Ogunquit has yet a third natural attraction that should not be missed. A mile-long footpath linking Perkins Cove to the downtown area, **Marginal Way** stretches along the cliffs overlooking the sea (signs posted at the cove and on Shore Road in the center of town direct you to the path). Juniper, bayberry, beach roses, and other wildflowers grow along the path, and there are lots of stone benches where you can pause to savor the views. Waves splash against the rocks as you follow the twists and turns, stopping perhaps to clamber down to examine a tide pool on the ocean's rocky edge, or to wade in the sea, or to have a picnic on the rocks. Swimming is permitted at two small beaches.

Whichever direction you walk Marginal Way, from Perkins Cove to downtown or the reverse, you'll probably be ready for a ride back to the start and your car. Hop aboard one of the four turn-of-the-century trolleys operated by **Ogunquit Trolley.** The bright yellow and red cars have wooden bench seats, brass trim, and etched glass. They make frequent stops throughout Ogunquit, and the charge is nominal.

Looking for a place to eat in the downtown area? **Einstein's Deli Restaurant** fits the ticket for breakfast, lunch, or dinner. The fare runs the gamut from bagels and omelets to burgers and sandwiches, spaghetti with meatballs to a turkey dinner. For a hearty breakfast at a thrifty price, try the **Egg and I, Pancake House,** just outside of town. The menu lists twelve kinds of pancakes (including chocolate chip, strawberry, and blueberry), six kinds of waffles, and fourteen kinds of omelets. Kids seem particularly pleased with pigs in a blanket, sausage links neatly wrapped in buttermilk pancakes. The Egg and I stays open for lunch too.

If your children enjoy live theater, you'll want to cap off their time in Ogunquit with a visit to the **Ogunquit Playhouse,** which has presented lively summer stock productions for well over fifty years. The program features revivals of favorite musicals and comedies and includes both matinees and evening performances. The theater is housed in a sprawling, white wooden building with green awnings and green trim surrounded by meticulously

*Hop aboard one of the four turn-of-the-century trolleys operated by Ogunquit Trolley. The bright yellow and red cars have wooden bench seats, brass trim, and etched glass.*

manicured grounds. A visit to the Playhouse can be a delightful treat for children in the twelve and up age range — even younger for some shows.

## ACCESS

**OGUNQUIT.** Follow I-95 to York exit. Take Route 1 north and continue to the center of Ogunquit.

**NORSEMAN MOTEL. Directions:** Follow Route 1 north to the intersection with Shore Road in center of Ogunquit. Go directly across intersection to Beach Street. Located on Beach Street, overlooking Ogunquit Beach. **Season:** Rentals from Memorial Day through Labor Day; inn open April through October. **Admission:** Fees charged. **Telephone:** (207) 646-7024.

**PERKINS COVE. Directions:** Following Route 1 north into Ogunquit, turn right on Bourne's Lane (at sign to Perkins Cove), just beyond the Josias River. Bear right on Shore Road and continue to cove parking areas. **Note:** There is free municipal parking at Perkins Cove, but it is almost impossible to get a space on weekends. Pay lots are within easy walking distance.

**BARNACLE BILLY'S. Directions:** Located at the entrance to Perkins Cove. **Season:** May through mid-October. **Admission:** Free. **Telephone:** (207) 646-5575.

**FINESTKIND SCENIC CRUISES. Directions:** Dock is adjacent to Barnacle Billy's at Perkins Cove. **Season:** July through Labor Day; limited schedule for May, June, September, and October. **Admission:** Charged. **Telephone:** (207) 646-5227.

*BUNNY CLARK.* **Directions:** Trips depart from the town dock in Perkins Cove. **Season:** April 1 through October 31. **Admission:** Charged. **Telephone:** Reservations accepted at Barnacle Billy's: (207) 646-5575.

**PERKINS COVE CANDIES. Directions:** Located at Perkins Cove. **Season:** May through Columbus Day; weekends through early December. **Admission:** Free. **Telephone:** (207) 646-5368.

**LOBSTER SHACK. Directions:** Located at Perkins Cove. **Season:** May through mid-October. **Admission:** Free. **Telephone:** (207) 646-2941.

**MA PERKINS' KITCHEN. Directions:** Located at the entrance to Perkins Cove. **Season:** May through mid-October. **Admission:** Free. **Telephone:** (207) 646-4416.

**OGUNQUIT TROLLEY. Directions:** Frequent marked stops along Route 1 (Main Street) and Shore Road. Stops put you within easy walking distance of all major points of interest, from Perkins Cove to Ogunquit Beach and Footbridge Beach. **Season:** Memorial Day through Columbus Day. **Admission:** Small charge. **Telephone:** Call the

Don Richeson

*A sample from Barnacle Billy's ice cream stand leaves this taste tester all smiles.*

Chamber of Commerce at (207) 646-2939 or (207) 646-5533.

**EINSTEIN'S DELI RESTAURANT. Directions:** Located at the corner of Route 1 and Shore Road in the center of town. **Season:** Year-round. **Admission:** Free. **Telephone:** (207) 646-5262.

**EGG AND I, PANCAKE HOUSE. Directions:** Located on Route 1 north in Ogunquit. **Season:** Memorial Day through Columbus Day. **Admission:** Free. **Telephone:** (207) 646-8777.

**OGUNQUIT PLAYHOUSE. Directions:** Located on Route 1 in Ogunquit, south of the center of town. **Season:** Late June through Saturday before Labor Day. **Admission:** Charged. **Telephone:** (207) 646-5511.

**For further information** or restaurant and lodgings suggestions, contact the Ogunquit Chamber of Commerce, Box 2289, Ogunquit, ME 03907. Telephone: (207) 646-2939.

# Mount Desert Island

The third-largest island on the eastern seaboard, Mount Desert is blessed with pink granite mountains, craggy cliffs, deep valleys, dramatic stands of hardwood and firs, crystalline lakes, and shallow icy mountain streams that feed into the sea. Raccoon, mink, skunk, red fox, beaver, chipmunk, snowshoe hare, and white-tailed deer make their homes in the forest or by the shore, along with 327 species of birds. The island was first inhabited by the Abnaki Indians, who called it "Pemetic," or "the sloping land." French explorer Samuel de Champlain in the early 1600s first coined the name "L'Isle des Mont Deserts," which translates as "island of the deserted, lonely, or barren mountains." Mount Desert is today in many ways unchanged from the 1600s.

Your visit to the island will center on Acadia National Park, which offers a tremendous variety of recreational opportunities. Even a short visit will be memorable, but if at all possible, plan to spend at least a few days.

Begin your stay at the park with a stop at the **Hulls Cove Visitor Center,** where you can watch a short film introducing the park, its history, geological attributes, flora, and fauna. Here you can pick up information on campgrounds, naturalist programs, hiking trails, and other features and services. The

*To the summit! A young hiker races for the top of Acadia National Park's Cadillac Mountain.*

knowledgeable park rangers who staff the center will gladly help you plan your stay.

For an overview of the park, drive along the Park Loop Road, a twenty-mile route that connects lakes, mountains, and seashore. It leads to Cadillac Mountain Summit Road, which climbs up the mountain to the highest point on our Atlantic coast, offering splendid views of Blue Hill, Penobscot, and Frenchman bays.

A good way for bikers to become familiar with the park is to take to the network of carriage paths. Financed by John D. Rockefeller (who also donated eleven thousand acres of wilderness) and designed by landscape architect Frederick Law Olmsted, the paths were built between World War I and the early 1930s. Graced by sixteen hand-cut stone bridges, each one especially designed to complement its setting, the paths make it easy to explore some of the park's more secluded areas. Sixteen of the fifty-seven miles of paths have been especially surfaced for bicycles, making this an excellent opportunity for a family bike excursion free from the noise and hazard of cars. The remaining paths are perfect for hiking.

If you would like to experience the park from the water, go canoeing. You can rent equipment from **National Park Canoe Rentals** at the northern end of Long Pond, where swimming is also permitted. Canoes are available by the half or full day. The water is tranquil, and the necessary instruction is provided on the spot, so don't worry if you have never lifted a paddle before. Reservations are strongly advised, particularly on weekends.

The most popular swimming spot in the park is the lovely sandy beach at **Echo Lake,** where children can play in the sand and splash in the clear water under the watchful eyes of park lifeguards.

There are a number of private camping facilities outside the park, but Acadia also has two campgrounds of its own, each situated in a forest setting within easy walking distance of the ocean. Both have designated sites that can accommodate trailers up to thirty-five feet, but neither has utility hookups. Each has an outdoor amphitheater where evening slide programs are held. (You don't have to stay at the campground to attend.) Do be forewarned that sites are in heavy demand. In-season reservations are accepted for **Blackwoods Campground.** Write or call the park for an advance reservation form. **Seawall Campground** operates on a first-come–first-served basis. Cars line up very early in the morning during the height of the season, waiting for spaces as departures occur. If you are arriving at Mount Desert in the afternoon, particularly on a Friday or Saturday, be prepared to spend the night in a motel. Then one person can head out at 7 A.M. to get in line for a site while the rest of the family sleeps in.

Be sure to bring along plenty of warm clothes and rain gear. The temperature ranges from forty-five to eighty-five degrees Fahrenheit in the summer, with spring and fall readings in the thirty to seventy degree Fahrenheit range. Bringing along insect repellent is always a good idea, but it's absolutely essential in June, when mosquitoes and black flies are most common.

The park Naturalist Program provides many activities designed to introduce visitors to the natural history and ecology of Acadia. Kids particularly enjoy the Naugahyde Whale Program, during which they "dissect" (and then reassemble) a ten-foot model of a pilot whale. They learn about mammal physiology by comparing whale and human musculature, skeletal structures, and internal organs. Children from eight to eleven can sign up for the Nature's Way Walk, where they'll have the chance to explore the park in small groups with the help of naturalists. Other specialty programs include photo walks and workshops for aspiring nature photographers and Stars Over Acadia (identifying celestial phenomena from the summit of Cadillac Mountain).

In cooperation with the Naturalist Program, **Frenchman's Bay Boating Company** sponsors a daily, early morning, two-hour cruise. A park naturalist travels aboard, describing the geological history of the area and the wildlife as you glide past ocean cliffs and summer mansions, keeping an eye out for sea birds and marine animals. You may well see a bald eagle or osprey, especially if you've brought

*Kids particularly enjoy the Naugahyde Whale Program, during which they "dissect" (and then reassemble) a ten-foot model of a pilot whale.*

*The Naturalist Program incorporates a full spectrum of guided walks, ranging from the early morning Birders Walk to Night Prowl, which focuses on nocturnal animals.*

along binoculars. Kids get particularly excited when they spot seals and porpoises. There's something about seeing them in the ocean that's different from seeing them in an aquarium or zoo. In addition to the naturalist cruise, the company also operates ten other sightseeing trips each day. There are several one-hour-long options, perfect for young children, who are still likely to see porpoises.

The Naturalist Program also incorporates a full spectrum of guided walks, ranging from the early morning Birders Walk to Night Prowl, which focuses on nocturnal animals. The walks are rated easy to strenuous, with opportunities for every member of the family. Choose a leisurely shoreline walk, where the focus is on the delicate ecological balance in the area extending from the edge of the forest to the low-tide line. Or take a challenging three-hour climb up Acadia Mountain, where you'll be rewarded by spectacular views of Somes Sound, the only natural fjord on the eastern coast of the United States. For a complete schedule of the Naturalist Program, and to reserve space, check at the Visitor Center. With the exception of the cruises, all the activities are free of charge.

The staff at the Visitor Center will direct you to the starting points for two independent hikes that are both easy and gratifying (there are many others to choose from). Wonderland follows an abandoned roadway that leads to the coast, where you're greeted by a pebble beach and accessible tide pools perfect for exploration. The Ship's Harbor Trail is a circular nature walk with thirteen points of interest. Purchase an inexpensive trail guide at the center, and you're in business. The guide focuses on the interrelation of man, nature, and disaster. You'll discover, for example, that certain animals are dependent on certain types of vegetation. At the ocean's edge you'll see the scene of an eighteenth-century shipwreck. What would you have done if you were one of the survivors, cast ashore with no weapons and few tools?

For a different taste of social history, spend half an hour at Sieur de Monts Spring, where you can visit the tiny **Robert Abbe Museum of Stone Age Antiquities** and walk in the Wild Gardens of Acadia. Very small children may be more interested in the pond and stream nearby than in the museum itself, which contains many fine Indian artifacts like imaginative jewelry fashioned from animal bones and baskets decorated with porcupine quills. Boys who are enamored of pocket knives should be sure to take a look at the display tracing the evolution of the crooked knife (or "biketagenigan," to the Penobscots), beginning with an animal's curved incisor tooth and progressing to a lead blade set into a wooden handle. The knife was used for making everything from basket splints to birchbark canoes.

In the adjoining gardens you'll see plants that you've encountered throughout the park, but this time they're labeled so you'll know what you're looking at. The plants are organized by habitat, and a map is provided to help you locate areas of particular interest. In the Mixed Woods habitat, for example, you'll find lady's slippers, wild oats, Canadian lily, wood anemone, and the bright (and poisonous) red and white baneberries. The Beach habitat is filled with beach pea, sea milkwort, and skullcap, and other areas replicate the Bog, Dry Heath, Meadow, Mountain, Island, Coniferous, Ponds and Marshes, and Roadside habitats.

Before leaving Mount Desert, be sure to visit two places outside of the park. Exhibits at the **Natural History Museum at College of the Atlantic** focus on Mount Desert's sea birds, plant life, and marine animals. There are a twenty-two-foot-long Whale on Wheels skeleton to assemble and a skeleton of the moose, Maine's official state animal. Special interpretive programs, which center on subjects like nature drawing and plant and animal identification, are held nearly every morning (call ahead to check the time).

At Southwest Harbor you can spend an hour or more in the delightful **Mount Desert Oceanarium,** a low-key, cozy facility designed to teach families about the sea life and fishing industry so important

*Exhibits at the Natural History Museum of the College of the Atlantic focus on Mount Desert's sea birds, plant life, and marine animals.*

to coastal Maine. Kids get to activate all their senses as they learn about tides and weather, seaweed, seagulls, and all sorts of sea creatures. The very young like to climb up in the wheelhouse and pretend they're steering a ship at sea. Older kids will enjoy learning about the ocean through interactive exhibits that let them do such things as find out how much they weigh under water. Or taste two types of salt and see if you can tell which is sea salt and which is table salt.

Everyone enjoys the Living Room, which houses more than twenty tanks of live sea life from the coast of Maine. Over at the touch tank, you'll get to handle a starfish, sea urchin, or a slimy sea cucumber as a staff member explains their habits. In the Lobster Room, you'll find out all about this famous Maine product and industry, as a licensed lobsterman explains how a lobster eats, reproduces, and gets caught. You'll also learn how traps are constructed, baited, set, and hauled. Still other exhibits provide the opportunity to don headphones to listen to the sounds of the sea, including the songs that whales sing.

Just a short walk away from the oceanarium, you can introduce your kids to the joys of a fresh broiled lobster at **Beal's Lobster Pier.** Enjoy your meal at a picnic table overlooking the busy Southwest Harbor waterfront, where lobster boats, pleasure boats, and fishing boats unload the day's catch. Clams, crabmeat, and shrimp are available too, along with sandwiches and ice cream.

*Echo Lake is Acadia's most popular family swimming spot.*

Carolyn J. Casey

## ACCESS

**MOUNT DESERT ISLAND.** Follow I-95 to Bangor. Then take Route 1A south 26 miles to Ellsworth. From Ellsworth, take Route 3 to Mount Desert Island. Continue east on Route 3, following signs to Bar Harbor.

**HULLS COVE VISITOR CENTER. Directions:** Follow Route 3 east to Hulls Cove. Park entrance and Visitor Center will be on your right. **Season:** Acadia National Park is open year-round; Visitor Center open May 1 through November 1. Park headquarters on Route 233, 3 miles west of Bar Harbor, open for information November 1 through May 1. **Admission:** Free. **Telephone:** (207) 288-3338.

**NATIONAL PARK CANOE RENTALS. Directions:** From the Hulls Cove Visitor Center, follow Route 3 south to Route 233. Turn right on Route 233 and then right on Route 198. Follow signs to Somesville. Take Route 102 (Pretty Marsh Road) south 2 miles to rental facility. **Season:** June through October. **Admission:** Charged. **Telephone:** (207) 244-5854.

**ECHO LAKE. Directions:** Located on Route 102, south of Somesville. **Season:** Mid-June through Labor Day. **Admission:** Free. **Telephone:** (207) 288-3338.

**BLACKWOODS CAMPGROUND. Directions:** Located off Route 3, five miles south of Bar Harbor. **Season:** Year-round; reservations accepted from June 15–September 15. **Admission:** Charged. **Telephone:** (207) 288-3338.

**SEAWALL CAMPGROUND. Directions:** Follow Route 3 to Mount Desert Island. Then take Route 102 south to Southwest Harbor. Bear left on Route 102A and continue 2 miles south to entrance. **Season:** Late May through late September. **Admission:** Charged. **Telephone:** (207) 244-3600.

**FRENCHMAN'S BAY BOATING COMPANY. Directions:** Follow Route 3 east to Bar Harbor. Located at the municipal pier in Bar Harbor. **Season:** Memorial Day through early October. **Admission:** Charged. **Telephone:** (207) 288-5741.

**ROBERT ABBE MUSEUM OF STONE AGE ANTIQUITIES. Directions:** From the Visitor Center, take the Park Loop Road to Sieur de Monts Spring entrance and the museum. **Season:** Mid-May through mid-September. **Admission:** Charged. **Telephone:** (207) 288-3519.

**NATURAL HISTORY MUSEUM AT COLLEGE OF THE ATLANTIC. Directions:** Located on Route 3, about ½ mile west of Bar Harbor. **Season:** Mid-June through Labor Day. **Admission:** Charged. **Telephone:** (207) 288-5015.

**MOUNT DESERT OCEANARIUM. Directions:** From Ellsworth, follow Route 3 south to Mount Desert Island and junction with Route 102. Follow Route 102 south to Southwest Harbor. Turn left at the flashing light at the intersection. Oceanarium is on your right. **Season:** Mid-May through mid-October. **Admission:** Charged. **Telephone:** (207) 244-7330.

**BEAL'S LOBSTER PIER. Directions:** Located on Clark Point Road in Southwest Harbor, between the Coast Guard base and the Mount Desert Island Oceanarium. **Season:** May through September. **Admission:** Free. **Telephone:** (207) 244-3202.

**For further information** about Acadia National Park, contact the Superintendent, P.O. Box 177, Bar Harbor, ME 04609. Telephone: (207) 288-3338. For lodgings and restaurant suggestions, contact the Chamber of Commerce, 93 Cottage Street, P.O. Box 158, Bar Harbor, ME 04609. Telephone: (207) 288-5103.

# MASSACHUSETTS

*Costumed interpreters aboard Plymouth's* Mayflower II *will make you feel as though you've been transported back in time to February 1621.*

## Plymouth

Plymouth and Pilgrims go together like peanut butter and jelly. A visit to this famous Bay State seaside town is a history lesson, the perfect way to reinforce the early American history your children learn in school. There is a great deal to see and do, easily enough to fill two days, and the best place to get started is at historic **Plymouth Rock.** Now the rock might not look all that imposing, but it's the symbolic quality that counts. Over the years souvenir hunters have chipped away at this national monument, removing three thousand pounds of it.

Add to that the fact that much of the rock is underground, and you'll begin to forgive its rather unassuming size.

Today the famous rock is protected by a columned portico. A park ranger is on hand to speak of its history. He points to the water and explains that the Pilgrims first landed in Provincetown, some fourteen miles distant across Cape Cod Bay. Dismayed by the sandy soil, they set out in search of more fertile land, following the coast. Delayed by a storm, they finally came ashore here at the rock, eager to find a place to settle before winter arrived. To their pleasant surprise, they found land that had been cleared by Indians who had already left the area. They found fresh water springs and a high hill overlooking the bay, a good vantage point to keep an eye alert for French, Indians, and other enemies.

When you finish admiring the rock, walk to adjacent Pilgrim Memorial Park, which stands at the edge of the harbor and overlooks a bevy of boats including the *Mayflower II*. With plenty of shade trees, this is a pleasant spot for a picnic.

Continue your discovery of the past by stepping aboard the ***Mayflower II,*** and stepping back into the year 1621. On the dock leading to the gangway you'll see an exhibit describing the people who traveled to the New World in the 1600s, a migration that included the Pilgrims. These adventurous men, women, and children sought a new life, free from the economic, social, and religious barriers that characterized the Old World. Here you'll discover that of the 102 passengers aboard the original *Mayflower*, half were called "saints" (the Separatists who came in search of religious freedom) and the other half "strangers" (those who pursued economic advantage). Eventually, saints and strangers became known collectively as Pilgrims.

Once aboard the *Mayflower II*, you'll find yourself transported to February 1621, just a couple of months after the Pilgrims' arrival in Plymouth Harbor. They live on the ship and travel ashore daily to work on the simple structures that will soon become their permanent homes. The costumed staff members practice a technique known as first-person interpretation, which means that each member plays the role of a specific person who actually sailed aboard the *Mayflower*. While they will gladly converse with you, they know nothing of the events of the world after 1621, which is for them the present. Ask them what they thought of George Washington,

*While staff will gladly converse with you, they know nothing of the events of the world after 1621, which is for them the present.*

and they'll only look perplexed, never having heard of the fellow (why, he wasn't even born yet).

Elbow your way through the hammocks and heaps of rope as you explore the ship. You'll pass small pockets of domesticity — beds on the floor, a cradle, clothing, pottery — and you'll wonder how they managed to survive two unhealthy months at sea, crowded together in this dark, dank place. An elderly bedridden woman explained to us that she was "having a touch of the great sickness, like everyone is dying of. I might be dead before morning." When a visitor asked a crewman working on the deck whether this ship is the same size as the original *Mayflower*, the crewman knitted his eyebrows quizzically and responded, "I never seen a ship could grow or shrink." (Remember, for him this *is* the original ship.)

The *Mayflower II* is actually part of the living history museum, **Plimoth Plantation,** located a few miles out of town. Just a short walk from the ship you can stop in at the **Plimoth Plantation Information Center and Museum Shop** and pick up a copy of the Mayflower Compact (the document that established the government of Plymouth Colony), a copy of the original passenger list, Pilgrim hats, books, and toys. Plymouth is full of tacky souvenir shops, but the goods here are much more appealing. If you plan to visit Plimoth Plantation, hold off on your souvenir hunting further. That shop is the best of all.

To continue your Pilgrim experience, cross the street and climb the thirty-seven steps up Coles Hill, where you can peer out across the bay through a coin-operated viewer. Here you'll also see the sarcophagus containing the bones of the Pilgrims who died during their first winter in the New World. At the crest of the hill you'll find the **Plymouth National Wax Museum,** with more than two dozen tableaux illustrating the Pilgrim story. Some of the scenes are grim, like that depicting the terrible winter of 1621, when nearly half the *Mayflower* passengers perished from disease and exposure. Others, like one portraying the 1628 May Day festivities, are distinctly cheerful. Historically significant moments, such as the signing of the Mayflower Compact and the Massasoit Treaty (in which Massasoit, the Wampanoag chief, promised he would not permit his people to harm the colonists as long as he lived), are included too. Special effects add to the drama as you wander through the dark halls, where light, sound, and animation provide unexpected surprises, in-

*You might want to check into a half-day deep sea fishing trip. Bait is supplied, and you can rent rods and reels so you don't have to bring any equipment along.*

cluding a violent storm. Most children find the wax figures fascinating, but do take care with very young ones. The noise and the ghostly pallor of the lifelike faces may well strike them as downright scary.

If you find you've overindulged in Pilgrims and need a brief respite, take a walk along the waterfront. You'll soon arrive at the **Town Wharf,** where the fishing fleet ties up. This is a working wharf with lots of truck traffic. It's also a great place to feast on fresh seafood. Several fish markets on the wharf serve ready-to-eat meals in a very informal setting. One has a self-service cafeteria while another has picnic tables tucked between the harbor and the asphalt parking area. Head to the left at the back of the parking lot, and you'll find a couple of more spots, even one with waitress service.

While the decor and amenities vary, all of these places feature seafood. The fare includes stuffed quahogs, fried popcorn shrimp, crab cakes, fish cakes, steamers, fried squid, lobster, and crab rolls, along with extras like corn on the cob and fresh apple pie. Most places also serve hot dogs and hamburgers, for kids who are confirmed meat eaters.

While you're on the wharf, you might want to inquire about whale watching expeditions at the ticket and information booth for **Capt. John Boats.** These trips last four to five hours (shorter than many other whale watches), which makes them a good bet for families with children ten years old and up. Each trip includes a slide presentation about whale behavior and ecology, and a naturalist is always on board to answer questions.

Or you might want to check into a half-day deep sea fishing trip. Offered morning and afternoon, these last four hours. Bait is supplied, and you can rent rods and reels so you don't have to bring any equipment along. Depending upon the season, you might catch cod, haddock, mackerel, rock eel, flounder, or dogfish. The comfortable Capt. John excursion boats vary in length from sixty-five to eighty-five feet, and each is equipped with snack bar (for breakfast or sandwiches), rest rooms, and an enclosed cabin.

When you finish eating and exploring the wharf, walk a bit farther along the waterfront (still moving away from the *Mayflower II*), and you'll come to a long stone breakwater that stretches out into the harbor. There's only a rope railing on the ocean side and the harbor side is wide open, so it's not a safe place for small children unless you really keep a hand on them. Older kids — whom you still

*Massasoit's pledge that his Wampanoag Indians would not harm the Pilgrims as long as he lived eased the plight of Plymouth's founders.*

*Feeding the ducks at the Jenny Grist Mill rates high on children's lists of favorite activities in Plymouth.*

need to watch — find walking the breakwater a wonderful adventure. It feels as though you've marched into the middle of the sea. The day we visited lots of folks were fishing from the wall, so you might want to bring along some gear.

At **Cranberry World,** just a five-minute walk from the breakwater, kids get to do some sampling of their own. Ocean Spray Cranberries, Inc., has created a first-rate visitor center in a reconstructed clam factory. The exhibits here focus on the cranberry, one of only three native American fruits, the other two being the blueberry and the Concord grape. There are several brief color videos, including an interview with a Cape Verdean cranberry bog owner, who explains how his family became involved in the cranberry business. Pick up a telephone attached to the diorama of a cranberry bog and listen to a taped narration. You'll learn that the two tiny figures who look as if they're mowing a lawn are actually raking cranberries, that berries are harvested in a circle, and that wildlife flourishes in and around the bogs.

Lots of modern and antique harvesting equipment is on display. Kids are most intrigued by the separators, which divide superior cranberries from average ones, average ones from unacceptables. The berries are graded according to bounce. Those that fly effortlessly over a four-inch barrier are sold as fresh fruit, while those with less leap are relegated to sauces and drinks. Ask the hostess to demonstrate.

At the end of your visit you can sample several types of cranberry beverages, including cranraspberry, cranapple, and cranicot (a tasty cranberry-apricot combination). You may also be lucky enough to see a brief cooking demonstration and end up with free samples of cranberry-strawberry shortcake. If you visit Plymouth in the summer, you might want to save your visit for the evening, after most other attractions have closed, since Cranberry World remains open until 9 P.M. in July and August.

More free evening entertainment is available across the street from Cranberry World and a couple of blocks back toward the *Mayflower II*. The **Village Landing Marketplace** shopping center has a colonial theme. Specialty shops and boutiques line the cobblestone and brick paths, which are limited to pedestrian traffic. Concerts are held four days a week at the outdoor bandstand in the center of the marketplace. The fare varies from folk music and folk dancing to big band and barbershop, from country and western to jazz. Munch on something delicious from the **Candy Apple** while you enjoy the show. This small shop is chock-full of wonderful confections like licorice laces, giant nonpareils, chocolate mint lentils, milk chocolate soccer balls, and fudge.

Leaving the waterfront area, pay a visit to the **Jenney Grist Mill** at Town Brook Park. There's lots of parking near the mill, or you can take the pleasant, ten-minute walk from Plymouth Rock, which passes through pretty Brewster Gardens and continues along the banks of Town Brook. Jenney Grist Mill is a working reproduction of Plymouth Colony's first grist mill. The water turns a huge cypress wheel, producing power to grind corn, wheat, and rye. Inside the mill, which is a gift shop, you can purchase a loaf of fresh bread or a bag of corn to feed the ducks who frequent the pond.

Take a break at one of the white tables on the fenced wooden deck overlooking the mill pond and enjoy a treat from **TC's Scoop,** an ice cream emporium housed in one end of the mill complex. We strongly recommend a "Big Olaf," a homemade ice cream cone that resembles a large waffle rolled into a cornucopia. Have it filled with a generous mound of negative chocolate chip (white chocolate in chocolate ice cream) or cranberry sherbert, or do it up royal by having it prepared as a walk-away sundae.

If you visit Town Brook Park early in May you're likely to catch the annual herring run. Adult fish jump as high as two feet as they make their way up the fish ladder, leaving behind the saltwater in favor of their freshwater spawning ground. When the herring are "running," the stream is absolutely thick with them.

Allow several hours for your visit to **Plimoth Plantation,** the unique living history museum where

*We strongly recommend a "Big Olaf," a homemade ice cream cone that resembles a waffle rolled into a cornucopia.*

Mark Johnston Associates/Village Landing Marketplace

*The traffic is strictly pedestrian at Village Landing Marketplace.*

*Inside the walls of Plimoth Plantation, children's fantasies about Pilgrim life can become reality.*

the calendar came to a halt in 1627. Your visit begins in the Orientation Center. A slide presentation introduces the village and its inhabitants, and describes the reasons the Pilgrims came to the New World and the hardships they endured. Just as at the *Mayflower II*, each person you meet in the village plays the part of a specific Pilgrim. The dress, speech, attitudes, and manner differ with the individual, depending upon social status, region of origin, and personality.

The village itself is a humble, dusty place, set out on a gentle slope leading down toward the bay. Here the villagers go about their business, their chores determined by the season. You might find them planting or harvesting, working in their herb gardens, building fences or even houses.

The first person we came upon was Humility Cooper, hard at work splitting wood on a ninety-degree day, dressed in a long sleeved jacket and a long wool skirt. We then chanced upon a half-completed house that looked like a large thatched roof sitting over a hole in the ground. "It's an easy way to keep warm, making it underground," remarks a passing Pilgrim, who explains that it will be occupied by John Billington, whose house burned down last winter.

The footing is rough, and you can smell the fresh hay and farm animals as you wander past a clutch of chickens and into one of the homes, where a Pilgrim woman strews southernwood on the floor to help freshen the air. In answer to a visitor's question about local medical practice, she leans on her broom and gives her no-nonsense seventeenth-century opinion. "A physician is a very learned man. He's been to university, got a lot of degrees, and all that knowledge. He might look you up and down and see there's something wrong, but he doesn't do much. Now a surgeon, he learns his skills from another surgeon like a daughter learns from a mother. Now he'll *do* something, maybe cut off a limb or pull a tooth or bleed you with leeches."

The more you enter into the spirit of the village, the more rewarding your visit will be. Encourage your children to start conversations with the Pilgrims and to offer to help with the chores, be it carrying feed to the pigs or hanging out the bedding to air on the fences. And don't forget to allow time to visit the Wampanoag Summer Campsite, reached by traveling a short path through the woods. Here the Indians, interpreted by Native Americans, go about their tasks, from setting the corn to fishing for herring, from tending crops to making cordage and baskets of basswood bark. As the summer becomes fall, they prepare food storage pits; harvest the corn, nuts, and cranberries; and prepare for deer hunting.

Throughout the season many special events are held in the village. These include weddings, fur trading sessions, court sessions, the arrival of Dutch messengers, a funeral, and more. Write to the museum for a calendar of events if you want to plan your visit to coincide with one of these happenings.

Before leaving, take some time to browse in the handsome museum shop, which includes a good selection of children's books, along with Pilgrim hats and accessories. Kids who like to make things can choose a berry basket kit or other kits designed for crafting seventeenth-century cordage, making a cornhusk doll, or teaching kids to spin their own yarn. In 1988 the museum moves into its ambitious new visitor center, which includes the museum shop, formal exhibits, a restaurant, and two theaters.

*Encourage your children to start conversations with the Pilgrims and to offer to help with the chores.*

## ACCESS

**PLYMOUTH.** From Boston, follow I-93 south to Route 3. Follow Route 3 south for 37 miles to Plymouth. Take Route 44 (Samoset Street) east to Route 3A (Court Street). Turn right on Court Street, which becomes Main Street (Route 3A). Turn left on North Street, which will bring you to Water Street. The State Pier will be directly in front of you, and Plymouth Rock will be a short walk to the right of it.

*MAYFLOWER II.* **Directions:** Berthed at the State Pier in Plymouth Harbor. **Season:** April through November. **Admission:** Charged. **Telephone:** (617) 746-1622.

**PLIMOTH PLANTATION INFORMATION CENTER AND MUSEUM SHOP. Directions:** Located between the State Pier and Plymouth Rock. **Season:** April through November. **Admission:** Free. **Telephone:** (617) 746-6544.

**PLYMOUTH NATIONAL WAX MUSEUM. Directions:** Located at 16 Carver Street, at the top of Coles Hill (across the street from Plymouth Rock). **Season:** March through November. **Admission:** Charged. **Telephone:** (617) 746-6468.

**CAPT. JOHN BOATS. Directions:** Ticket office located on the Town Wharf, at the end of Route 44. **Season:** April through October. **Admission:** Charged. **Telephone:** (617) 746-2643.

**CRANBERRY WORLD. Directions:** Located on Water Street on the Plymouth waterfront. **Season:** April through November. **Admission:** Free. **Telephone:** (617) 747-1000.

**VILLAGE LANDING MARKETPLACE. Directions:** Located at 170 Water Street on the Plymouth waterfront. **Season:** Year-round; entertainment from Memorial Day through Labor Day. **Admission:** Free. **Telephone:** (617) 746-4600.

**JENNEY GRIST MILL. Directions:** Follow Route 3A (Main Street) south to Summer Street. Turn right on Summer Street and then left at sign for Town Brook Park. Located in Town Brook Park. **Season:** Year-round. **Admission:** Free. **Telephone:** (617) 747-0811.

**PLIMOTH PLANTATION. Directions:** Located 3 miles south of Plymouth Rock on Route 3A (Main Street/Court Street). **Season:** April through November. **Admission:** Charged. **Telephone:** (617) 746-1622.

**For further information** or restaurant and lodgings suggestions, contact the Plymouth County Development Council, Box 1620, Pembroke, MA 02359. Telephone: (617) 826-3136.

# Boston

No matter what the weather, the ages or interests of your children, Boston is a terrific destination. There are splendid museums to visit and time-proven traditions to experience. You can wander in a marketplace that feels like a street circus or step aboard a boat steeped in history. Explore the city on foot or examine it from a vantage point sixty stories high. Plan to visit Boston more than once. If you followed all the suggestions in this chapter, you'd need several days, and these suggestions are only a

beginning. The more time you spend in "the Hub," the more you'll want to return.

A nonprofit educational organization, **Boston by Foot** has introduced thousands of visitors to Boston's rich architectural heritage. On Sunday afternoons, children eight to twelve years old and their adult friends can join an hour-long guided tour called "Boston by Little Feet," which encourages them to speculate (how many bricks do you think there are in City Hall Plaza?), question, and appreciate the city's look and feel. Each child receives an illustrated map of the route, which makes a good souvenir.

For an aerial view of the city, or at least as close as you can get without taking an airplane, travel 740 feet off the ground by elevator to the **John Hancock Observatory.** From this glassed-in deck, you'll see the gold-domed State House, the harbor, the Charles River, Fenway Park, and lots of other notable city spots. High-powered Funscopes provide a closer look at the famous landmarks. For a pleasant history lesson, take a seat on one of the carpeted tiers and look down at the city while a tape narrated by late architectural historian Walter Muir Whitehill describes changes that have occurred since Boston's early days. Here you can also watch a fast-paced film that presents a collage of city faces, places, and experiences. Then step into the "time machine" and peer down at a relief map depicting the pre-Revolutionary period. Tiny homes, shops, churches, public buildings, pathways, and streets light up, and disembodied voices describe the drama of the Boston Tea Party, Paul Revere's ride, and the battles of Bunker Hill and Charlestown. Period folk music adds to the ambiance.

The city's foremost collection of family-centered attractions is found in the Museum Wharf

*The John Hancock Observatory, 740 feet above Boston, offers families a bird's-eye view of the city called "the Hub."*

*The more time you spend in "the Hub," the more you'll want to return.*

area. The area's main attraction, the **Children's Museum,** is housed in a huge renovated warehouse overlooking a small nook of Boston Harbor. There is so much to do here, for toddlers to teens, that a description can only scratch the surface. Suffice it to say you'll be able to blow giant bubbles, dress in Victorian-era clothing, appear on closed-circuit television, match wits with a computer, and animate your own drawings on a zoetrope carousel. Young imaginations get wrapped up in role-playing in the supermarket area and the dental office, not to mention the factory assembly line.

The youngest members of your group can play in safety in Playspace, a protected area that's off-limits to big kids. Here little ones explore a castle complete with ramps, a slide, a hidden compartment, a lookout tower, and a carpeted moat filled with toys. In The Clubhouse, which is just for nine to fourteen year olds, kids can perform on stage to create dazzling patterns on a video screen. They can also enter a music booth to do some jamming on special guitars hooked to a synthesizer, try out education and entertainment software in the microcomputer corner, and mull over food choices and cooking in the simulated diner.

*The museum changes exhibits frequently, bringing back old favorites and installing new ones.*

The museum changes exhibits frequently, bringing back old favorites and installing new ones. One of the most recent and most ambitious exhibits, Mind Your Own Business, focuses on you and your body. A series of imaginative interactive exhibits encourages kids to ask questions and helps them to acquire timely, accurate information that will help them take responsibility for their own health and well-being. One display illuminates digestion by tracing a day in the life of a hamburger. Others explore taste, touch, smell, and skin color. There are telephones where kids can, in privacy, get the lowdown on sensitive subjects like sexually transmitted diseases or the development of their own bodies by listening to prerecorded tapes. Some displays encourage them to express their feelings, while others explain why certain intriguing but unmentionable phenomena — like body noises — occur.

Allow at least two hours for your visit, and do try to avoid rainy weekends. The less crowded the museum, the more your kids will relax and enjoy it.

Before you leave, you may want to let them fill a grocery bag with odds and ends from the barrels in the recycle center. These are stocked with industrial leftovers that vary from chunks of foam rubber to shoe decorations, rubber grids to fake fur remnants.

Or stop in at the museum shop, which is laden with attractive, tasteful toys from around the world. The back room is lined with big glass jars filled with inexpensive items that make it easy to shop on a youthful budget.

If you get hungry while at Museum Wharf, you can eat at the fast food restaurant adjoining the Children's Museum or, in warm months, you can purchase salads, yogurt, and ice cream at the outdoor take-out stand, shaped like a giant milk bottle. Settle down on one of the benches and watch the boats while you eat.

If there are computer enthusiasts in your family, you'll want to visit the **Computer Museum,** adjacent to the Children's Museum. The exhibits chronicle the history of the amazing machines, from their infancy in the early 1950s right up to the present. You can watch a short videotape of a 1952 "See It Now" show, hosted by Edward R. Murrow. He puts the famous Q-7 (also known as the "Sage") through its paces, asking the machine to calculate how much money the Indians would have amassed had they invested the twenty-four dollars they got for the sale of Manhattan Island in 1626 at 6 percent. Q-7 spits out a ten-figure number. Elsewhere in the museum you'll see chunks of the positively prehistoric Whirlwind computer (back in the 1950s it took five years to construct and filled a whole floor at MIT) and a piece of Univac, the first computer used to predict election results.

Children will be drawn to the hands-on stations throughout the museum where they can experiment with computer graphics and image processing. One station leads you through a program that explains how "memory" works, and another allows you to design a spiffy futuristic car. All of the programs are

*You'll see chunks of the positively prehistoric Whirlwind computer (back in the 1950s it took five years to construct and filled a whole floor at MIT).*

*Kids need no invitation to attend a party on board the Boston Tea Party Ship.*

self-explanatory. You just have to be willing to wait for a turn.

Moored at the Congress Street Bridge, a few steps from Museum Wharf, is the **Boston Tea Party Ship and Museum,** where you can relive the drama of the famous rebellion both aboard the floating brig *Beaver II* and in the adjacent museum building. Guides in colonial costume offer lively commentary as you view exhibits. These include a garden of tea plants and a model of eighteenth-century Boston that traces the route of the Tea Party participants, as well as two slide shows. In the "Where Do You Stand?" display you can determine whether you're a Patriot, Loyalist, middle-of-the-roader, or passive supporter. Once you've decided, step behind the corresponding, authentically costumed, life-size headless stand-up figure and have your picture snapped. Aboard the *Beaver II*, a full-size replica of one of the three Tea Party ships raided by angry patriots on December 16, 1773, you can hurl a bale of tea into the harbor below (and then pull it back up again by the attached rope).

Outside Museum Wharf you'll find two other major facilities in the city that cater to families. Although it's a pleasure to visit the **New England Aquarium** any time of year, there's an added bonus on warm, fair weather days, when you can relax at Water Park, the plaza in front of the aquarium building. Buy your lunch from the pushcarts that hang out here, peddling hot dogs, pretzels, ice cream, and the like, and then settle down by the edge of the park's cascading pools. Kids will be attracted to the seven enthusiastic harbor seals who cavort in the nearby outdoor seal pool.

The aquarium building itself is designed so that the only light comes from within the exhibits. As you wind your way up the ramp that spirals around the largest circular glass–enclosed tank in the world, you'll feel as though you've slipped beneath the surface of the sea. Press your face up to one of the viewing windows and only an inch or two separates you from barracuda, sharks, sea turtles, and other creatures of the deep. At certain times of day you can watch a scuba diver tending to the needs of tank residents, who seem undisturbed by his presence.

In addition to the tank, which simulates a Caribbean coral reef habitat, you'll see dozens of other aquariums. The walkways in the building are quite dark, so keep a hand on your small kids, particularly if you visit on a crowded day. More than seven thousand saltwater and freshwater fish live here, includ-

*Press your face up to one of the viewing windows and only an inch or two separates you from barracuda, sharks, sea turtles, and other creatures of the deep.*

*Any bets on who wins this staring contest at Boston's Museum of Science?*

ing Siamese fighting fish, shovelnose sturgeon, and diminutive seahorses, not to mention an eel that can produce more than six hundred volts of electricity. The Tidal Pool is particularly popular with young children, who love the opportunity to handle (if they dare) horseshoe crabs, starfish, and other small saltwater animals.

Kids of all ages are thrilled by the antics of the aquatic acrobats who strut their stuff at the floating pavilion *Discovery*, located next to the aquarium building. Admission to a forty-five-minute performance is included in the cost of your aquarium ticket. Find a seat in the bleachers (you're almost guaranteed to get splashed if you sit in the front few rows) that surround the edges of the forty-five- by thirty-five-foot swimming pool where sea lions and dolphins show off their tricks. The former specialize in retrieving colored hoops, balancing beach balls on their noses, playing catch, and clapping appreciatively for themselves. The latter sparkle when it comes to synchronized jumping, testimony to both their strength and intelligence. The trainers discuss the animals' habits and personality quirks, making the show educational as well as entertaining.

There's so much to see at the **Museum of Science** that you should allow half a day. That way your children can take in a performance at the Charles Hayden Planetarium, as well as a showing in the Mugar Omni Theatre, where action-packed adventure films are projected on a tilted dome screen that's seven stories high. Teens who are into computers will want enough time to drop by Computerplace, where they can experiment with different hardware, software, games, and simulations. And young children will be able to drop in at the Discovery Room (check hours ahead of time), where they can assemble science puzzles, observe specimens under magnifiers, listen to their own heartbeat, and participate in lots of other activities designed to expand their understanding of the natural world.

Of course, those are just some of the special programs. Major exhibits also abound. Many are participatory, like the television synthesizer, where a youngster can turn her brother purple by "colorizing" his image. Learn about the sea at the giant wave tank, or watch baby chicks peck their way out of their shells at the Giant Egg incubator, or step inside a space capsule for a simulated countdown. Watch a live animal demonstration, listen to the Transparent Woman explain how her body works, and take in a lightning demonstration courtesy of the Van de Graaf generator. There are more than three hundred exhibits in all, some temporary and some permanent. When you get tired or hungry, take a break in one of the museum's two cafeterias or in the fast food restaurant. There's also a terrific gift shop to check out, filled with science toys and books in a broad price range.

For a change from museums, there are several Boston traditions your kids will enjoy. The legendary **Boston Red Sox** have created baseball magic at Fenway Park since 1912, and they're still at it today. For enthusiasm and loyalty, Boston fans are hard to beat, so keep your own allegiance under raps if you're from away. Watch star hitters like Wade Boggs contend with the vagaries of the Green Monster (the imposing left-field wall of the park) in the tradition of Ted Williams and Carl Yastrzemski. From box seats to bleachers, Fenway franks to peanuts in the shell, the atmosphere at this well-loved ballpark is one-of-a-kind.

*If your children have already made the acquaintance of Mr. and Mrs. Mallard and their children, heroes of Robert McCloskey's* Make Way for Ducklings, *their faces will light up when you suggest a visit to the Swan Boats in the Public Garden.*

If your children have already made the acquaintance of Mr. and Mrs. Mallard and their children Jack, Kack, Lack, Mack, Nack, Ouack, Pack, and Quack, heroes of Robert McCloskey's storybook, *Make Way for Ducklings*, their faces will light up when you suggest a visit to the **Swan Boats** in the Public Garden. If they don't already know the Mallard family, pick up a copy and introduce them to the heartwarming tale of a young duck couple in search of the perfect Boston neighborhood in which to raise their family. They eventually settle on the pond in the

*Historic Faneuil Hall and its accompanying marketplace and red brick plaza offer everything from baklava to sword swallowers.*

Public Garden where the Swan Boats have cruised for more than a century.

Painted bright green with a touch of red, each boat consists of a platform built on two pontoon-like structures with pointed tips that tilt up at either end. A great white metal swan commands the rear of each boat, overlooking the rows of varnished benches where the passengers sit. Sitting between her wings, the captain propels the boat by pedaling. Each boat can hold thirty-five passengers, and a ride lasts ten to fifteen minutes. Before boarding, purchase popcorn from a vendor. Your children will want to share it with the ducks who trail the boat, in the tradition of the young Mallard family.

For a newly revitalized Boston tradition, you can't beat a visit to **Faneuil Hall Marketplace,** a large indoor/outdoor complex of shops, restaurants, and pushcarts. The long central building used to serve as the heart of the city's wholesale food market. Today it shelters elegant stands that sell everything from baklava, goose liver pâté, and fresh oysters to chocolate chip cookies, pizza, and fried dough. Or select a fresh fruit cup, Chinese food, sourdough bread, or a yogurt sundae. Definitely something for every taste! And although eating and shopping are the major activities here, there's a third aspect that's really special — the parade of street entertainers that sets up shop on the plazas and walkways, particularly on warm weekend afternoons. You might see a sword swallower or an organ grinder complete with monkey, a juggler or a clown magician, as well as a variety of musicians. The atmosphere is festive albeit frenetic, upbeat, and distinctly cheerful. Just be sure to figure out a meeting place in advance, should your group become separated, because the crowds can get large here.

## ACCESS

**BOSTON.** From the north, follow I-93 south. From the south, follow Route 3 north, which becomes I-93. From the west, travel east on I-90 (Massachusetts Turnpike) to I-93, then north on I-93. It is a good idea to obtain a Boston street map for getting around in the city.

**BOSTON BY FOOT. Directions:** Office located at 77 North Washington Street. Boston by Little Feet tours meet at the Samuel Adams statue on Congress Street, near Faneuil Hall. **Season:** May through October. **Admission:** Charged. **Telephone:** (617) 367-2345.

**JOHN HANCOCK OBSERVATORY. Directions:** Located at Copley Square in the John Hancock Tower. **Season:** Year-round. **Admission:** Charged. **Telephone:** (617) 247-1976.

**CHILDREN'S MUSEUM. Directions:** From the north, follow I-93 south to High and Congress streets exit. Take third left onto Congress Street and continue across the bridge, following milk bottle signs. From the south, follow I-93 north to Atlantic and Northern avenues exit. Take immediate right over Northern Avenue Bridge, following milk bottle signs. Located at 300 Congress Street, Museum Wharf. **Season:** Year-round. **Admission:** Charged. **Telephone:** (617) 426-8855. **Note:** There is a large outdoor parking area at the base of the Northern Avenue Bridge, 1 block from Museum Wharf.

**COMPUTER MUSEUM. Directions:** Located at 300 Congress Street, Museum Wharf, in the same building as the Children's Museum. **Season:** Year-round. **Admission:** Free. **Telephone:** (617) 423-6758.

**BOSTON TEA PARTY SHIP AND MUSEUM. Directions:** Located at the Congress Street Bridge, adjacent to Museum Wharf. **Season:** Year-round. **Admission:** Charged. **Telephone:** (617) 338-1773.

**NEW ENGLAND AQUARIUM. Directions:** From I-93, take Atlantic and Northern avenues exit. Take Atlantic Avenue to Central Wharf, following signs to aquarium. **Season:** Year-round. **Admission:** Charged. **Telephone:** (617) 973-5200. **Note:** There is an indoor public parking facility in front of the aquarium.

**MUSEUM OF SCIENCE. Directions:** Located at Science Park, off Monsignor O'Brien Highway. **Season:** Year-round. **Admission:** Charged; additional charges for Charles Hayden Planetarium and Mugar Omni Theatre. **Telephone:** (617) 742-6088.

**BOSTON RED SOX. Directions:** Home games played at Fenway Park, 1 block from Kenmore Square. **Season:** April through October. **Admission:** Charged. **Telephone:** (617) 267-1700.

**SWAN BOATS. Directions:** Boats depart from the Lagoon

Carol Goodstein

*Here's a rare "backstage" glimpse of three performers from the New England Aquarium's great water show.*

in the Public Garden, bordered by Beacon, Charles, Boylston, and Arlington streets. **Season:** Mid-April through late September. **Admission:** Charged. **Telephone:** (617) 323-2700.

**FANEUIL HALL MARKETPLACE. Directions:** Follow directions to New England Aquarium. From the aquarium parking garage, walk along State Street away from the harbor, passing under the expressway. Turn right onto Commercial Street and walk a short distance to the marketplace. Or take I-93 Callahan Tunnel/Dock Square exit and park in any of the nearby garages. **Season:** Year-round. **Admission:** Free. **Telephone:** (617) 523-2980.

**For further information** or restaurant and lodging suggestions, contact the Greater Boston Convention and Visitors Bureau, Prudential Plaza, Boston, MA 02199. Telephone: 1-800-858-0200.

# Charlestown

It used to be that responsible parents visiting Boston with kids in tow trekked out to Charlestown to pay an obligatory visit to the USS *Constitution*, just as they'd make sure their kids got to visit the Statue of Liberty when in New York. And while "Old Ironsides" certainly was (and is) an intriguing vessel to explore, it always seemed a shame that there wasn't more to do in Charlestown. Oh, there was the famous monument, but together the two stops didn't even fill a morning. That was then. This is now, and now is very different.

Today a visit to Charlestown focuses on the **Charlestown Navy Yard,** which closed as a government facility in 1974. Since that time it has evolved into a delightful place to spend the day learning about American history, shipping, and commerce. As frosting on the cake, Charlestown is one of those rare destinations that can be happily visited any time of year. As a matter of fact, if you have the option, we'd advise skipping it in the summer simply because the line to see the USS *Constitution* gets so very long.

Begin your visit to the Charlestown Navy Yard with a stop at the **Visitor Information Center,** where National Park Rangers will answer questions and help you plan your day. Here you'll also find a schedule of special guided walking tours, which you may wish to join. A ten-minute slide show focusing on the yard's role in both naval and shipbuilding history is shown at frequent intervals throughout the day. You'll learn how an archaic shipyard has been recycled into a complex integrating light industry, commercial ventures, housing, and recreational space.

Here at the center you can also see models of some of the types of vessels built at the yard during its long tenure as a naval facility. From 1800 until 1974 the yard was responsible for building, repairing, and modernizing thousands of United States Navy ships. Among these vessels (and depicted in the models) were the USS *Merrimack*, the first steam-operated, screw propeller warship, and the CSS *Virginia*, an ironclad warship that took part in the first naval battle between ironclads, back in 1862.

The center also houses visiting exhibits on history and ships. Typical of these was the recent interactive, computer-assisted display designed to illustrate the impact of the United States Constitution during its two-hundred-year history. By touching the screen with your finger, you could call forth information on a significant constitutional issue, be it child labor laws, freedom of speech, or the rights of illegal aliens.

When you leave the center, your children will probably want to head straight for the famous ship. The oldest commissioned warship afloat anywhere on the globe, the **USS *Constitution***, fondly referred to as Old Ironsides, was first launched in 1797 at the then astronomical cost of $302,718. She measured 204 feet from stem to stern, and she flew a full acre of sail. Today she is manned by forty-six active-duty U.S. sailors, one of whom will take you aboard for a tour. On the main deck you'll pass cannons with names like Sweet Sue and Raging Eagle. Kids are particularly intrigued by the "head," a long board with three holes in it leading directly to the sea. So much for environmental protection.

Children also enjoy clambering down the ladderlike steps leading to the lower decks where they can peek into the purser's cramped quarters (his desk, with the addition of a mattress, doubled as a bed) and take a look at the surgeon's office, where the floor is painted red to camouflage any blood that might spill. "Back then," your guide might explain, "if a surgeon was good he could cut off an arm or a leg, burn the end, and put tar on it, all in about thirty seconds." No wonder the ship was built to hold eight thousand gallons of rum along with the other provisions. The sailors probably needed it for medicinal purposes.

Hard life or not, lots of young visitors find

*The USS* Constitution, *fondly referred to as Old Ironsides, was first launched in 1797 at the then astronomical cost of $302,718.*

Ben Barnhart

*"Old Ironsides" and the Bunker Hill Monument are two reasons why Boston's Charlestown neighborhood is a destination unto itself.*

themselves yearning to sign on for a tour of duty as a powder monkey, one of the nimble young boys who passed buckets of gunpowder from the powder magazine to the upper decks in times of battle.

Your children will continue to learn about life at sea at your next stop, the **USS** *Constitution* **Museum.** Here hands-on exhibits give them a chance to "sleep" in hammocks just as sailors did aboard Old Ironsides. They can also try their hand at nautical knot tying. And they can assume the role of ship captain by taking part in a computer simulation that challenges them to escort a squadron safely across the Atlantic for a rendezvous at Gibraltar. Young captains contend with storms, diminishing supplies, hostile crews, and damage the ship sustains at sea. At each crisis point the computer offers a series of choices, and the captain's decision determines the events that unfold. What lies ahead? Success or tragedy? One voyage will differ radically from another, depending upon the captain's judgment.

The museum also contains paintings, prints, model ships, historic naval documents, and many antique maritime artifacts. You'll see handguns, muskets, cutlasses, boarding pikes, and other pieces of equipment commonly used by the crew. During the summer months the museum sponsors a living history program that sends actors dressed in period costume out into the navy yard to play the roles of nineteenth-century Charlestown residents, demonstrating traditional maritime arts such as cooperage, scrimshaw, and model making.

The USS *Constitution* isn't the only ship you can board at the yard. Take a walk along the main deck of the **USS *Cassin Young,*** a destroyer built right here at the Charlestown Navy Yard in 1943. The ship saw action in the battles of Leyte Gulf, Iwo Jima, and Saisan. Although decommissioned in 1967, she is kept in working order and is manned by former crew members and men who served on other destroyers. They'll be happy to answer your questions as you peer into the galley and the officers' mess. You'll also see the central communications room, where eleven men worked elbow to elbow in a space of about ten square feet, tending to radar, communications, and navigational equipment. The feeling is downright spooky as you find yourself in the company of gun turrets, torpedo tubes, and other serious weaponry. If you want to see more of the ship, take advantage of the forty-five-minute guided tour offered by the Parks Department. This is your chance to get a look at the bridge and to go below deck to see where the officers and crewmen lived. The tours are free of charge, and the schedule is posted in the Visitor Information Center. You can also telephone ahead to check times.

*You'll see the central communications room, where eleven men worked elbow to elbow in a space of about ten square feet, tending to radar, communications, and navigational equipment.*

You'll probably want to spend a while just wandering around the navy yard and the waterfront. There's a small refreshment stand where you can purchase hot dogs, ice cream, and pretzels to stave off hunger while you take a walk. Stroll by the 1805 commandant's house, the elegant mansion that served as the home of the commanding officers of the navy yard and the Commandants of the First Naval District until the navy yard closed in 1974. Take a look at Dry Dock #1, used to repair ships since 1833. Rigging squeaks, boats rock gently, seagulls perch on wooden pilings, flags fly overhead. Looking out across the water at downtown Boston, you'll see huge cranes, planes and helicopters taking off from Logan Airport, and maybe even a Coast Guard cutter.

Adjacent to the navy yard you'll find the **Bunker Hill Pavilion.** Here you can watch "The Whites of Their Eyes," a half-hour multimedia presentation on the Battle of Bunker Hill (which actually took place on nearby Breed's Hill), one of the first major battles of the American Revolution.

The program begins with a brief slide show in

the lobby. The narrator, who assumes the role of Paul Revere, describes the atmosphere of unrest in the colonies during the mid-1700s and the events that led to the battle itself. You'll hear about the Boston Tea Party and Revere's ride to warn the patriots of the approach of British troops. On the eve of the battle you'll enter the fifteen-screen theater. Music plays, and a voice sings out: "It's been just over seven weeks since cannon balls were heard at Lexington and Concord, the shot heard 'round the world."

Maps, paintings, old prints, and newspaper clippings flash on the screens in rapid succession as the story unfolds. Costumed mannequins light up, and their voices tell another side of the story. Describing the travail of preparing for battle, a patriot writes a letter to his wife explaining, "We bear it all, sensible that our cause is righteous." Another voice describes the anxiety the troops experience as they frantically build entrenchments and breastworks. Finally, the flash of gunshot . . . the boom of the cannon . . . tragedy. A young soldier tells his family, "He was so near me that my clothes were besmeared with blood and brains . . . cannonball took his head clear off." Even though the colonists lost the battle, they proved themselves a formidable opponent, withdrawing only after their ammunition was exhausted. By way of finale a folk song fills the theater and rings true: "They'd met the best and stood the test with stubborn Yankee pride."

After the show, make a pilgrimage to the battle scene itself. The **Bunker Hill Monument,** a 220-foot obelisk with 294 steps, poses on the summit of Breed's Hill, overlooking rows of houses built on the ten acres of battlefield sold off as house lots in 1838 to support construction of the monument. Something about a climbable monument draws children like a magnet. While an adult's first thought might be to find an elevator, children thrive on the endless stairs. Once you reach the top, you'll be rewarded with a panoramic view of Boston Harbor, downtown Boston, and Charlestown itself.

If you are combining a visit to Charlestown with a stay in Boston, you can travel to the navy yard by boat. **Boston Harbor Cruises** offers a "Constitutional Cruise," a narrated trip from Long Wharf to the Charlestown Navy Yard. The captain notes points of historic interest visible from the water, like the Old North Church, as well as contemporary landmarks. The round trip takes forty-five minutes, but you'll want to get off to explore the navy yard. Equipped with galley and both open and enclosed

*Even the passage between Boston and the Charlestown Navy Yard becomes an adventure thanks to Boston Harbor Cruises.*

decks, the comfortable cruise boat departs from Boston on the half hour throughout the day. It picks up returning passengers at the navy yard on the hour, so you can take as much time as you like.

## ACCESS

**CHARLESTOWN.** Traveling on I-93 north or south to Boston, follow signs to Charlestown Navy Yard and USS *Constitution*.

**CHARLESTOWN NAVY YARD VISITOR INFORMATION CENTER. Directions:** Located in the Charlestown Navy Yard. **Season:** Year-round. **Admission:** Free. **Telephone:** (617) 242-5601.

**USS *CONSTITUTION*. Directions:** Located in the Charlestown Navy Yard. **Season:** Year-round. **Admission:** Free. **Telephone:** (617) 426-1812.

**USS *CONSTITUTION* MUSEUM. Directions:** Located in the Charlestown Navy Yard. **Season:** Year-round. **Admission:** Charged. **Telephone:** (617) 426-1812.

**USS *CASSIN YOUNG*. Directions:** Located at the Charlestown Navy Yard. **Season:** Main deck open mid-April through October; closed when it rains. **Admission:** Free. **Telephone:** (617) 242-5601.

**BUNKER HILL PAVILION. Directions:** Located at the Charlestown Navy Yard. **Season:** Year-round. **Admission:** Charged. **Telephone:** (617) 241-7575.

**BUNKER HILL MONUMENT. Directions:** From I-93, take Charlestown exit. Turn right on Warren Street, then right on Monument Avenue. Continue to top of hill and the monument. **Season:** Year-round. **Admission:** Free. **Telephone:** (617) 242-5641.

**BOSTON HARBOR CRUISES. Directions:** Trips depart from Long Wharf, Atlantic Avenue, in Boston (adjacent to the New England Aquarium). **Season:** Mid-June through Labor Day; abbreviated spring and fall schedule. **Admission:** Charged. **Telephone:** (617) 227-4321.

**For further information** on guided tours and special events at the navy yard, contact the Visitor Information Center listed above.

# Cape Ann and the North Shore

Your visit to Cape Ann, a rocky promontory that juts out into the Atlantic Ocean thirty-odd miles north of Boston, will center on Gloucester, the oldest commercial fishing port on the East Coast. Plan to

Alexandra Meyns

THEY THAT GO
DOWN TO THE SEA
IN SHIPS
1623 – 1923

*You shouldn't be surprised to come across this landmark in Gloucester, the oldest commercial fishing port on the East Coast.*

spend lots of time outdoors, swimming, fishing, picnicking, and generally enjoying the rugged coastline and the informal atmosphere. Nearby you can take in a professional magic show, tour a castle, and pick your own apples. There's plenty to keep you busy, whether you plan a daytrip or a longer vacation.

Cape Ann, a popular tourist destination, has lots of motels and inns to choose from, but they're not inexpensive. As an alternative, consider camping. Pitch your tent at the **Cape Ann Camp Site,** an attractive wooded campground with more than three hundred sites located on one hundred acres of wooded hillside overlooking saltwater marshes. Instead of randomly assigning places, the owners encourage you to scout out your own site. As you drive through the maples and pines, navigating the winding road in search of the perfect spot, take your time. Because of the contours of the land, which includes granite boulders, dips, and rises, plenty of lovely surprises await those who ferret them out.

The fact that the topography is varied has another advantage in that this doesn't feel like a large campground. There's also plenty of space for children to play out of the way of cars. Just be sure that if you find a site you *must* have again next year, you make a note of the number. (When the owners get a

*Plan to spend lots of time outdoors, swimming, fishing, picnicking, and generally enjoying the rugged coastline and the informal atmosphere.*

request for "the site by the huge boulder," well, let's just say there are a lot of huge boulders.)

Each site is equipped with a rock fireplace and a picnic table. Hookups are available for those with trailers, but if you're a tent camper who likes to keep distance from the big rigs, you won't have any difficulty here since many of the sites are accessible only to tenters. There are flush toilets and coin-operated hot showers, washers, and dryers. Ice, wood, and basic supplies like milk, ice cream, and macaroni and cheese are sold at the camp store. Reservations are accepted and are a good idea on summer weekends, when there's a three-day minimum stay for Friday arrivals and a two-day requirement for Saturday arrivals. During the week reservations aren't really necessary.

One of the biggest assets of the campground is its location, just one mile from **Wingaersheek Beach,** a wonderful sweep of sand, sea, and sandbars backed by gentle dunes. Beach parking is at a premium in Gloucester, and the lots are often closed to nonresidents by 9 A.M. on summer weekends. That needn't worry you if you stay at the campground. You can just pack your gear in a backpack and take a pleasant twenty-minute hike down the country lane, past saltwater inlets, and on to the beach, where pedestrians are always welcome. The water is protected here, calm and accessible for kids. There are lots of nooks and crannies to explore, and at half tide pools form between massive rocks, providing warm, shallow places where small children occupy themselves blissfully by the hour.

*The water is protected here, calm and accessible for kids.*

In contrast, **Good Harbor Beach,** located on the other side of Gloucester, is best known for its surf and provides lots of excitement for body surfing enthusiasts on days when the waves beat against the shore with a vengeance. Both beaches have food concessions, as does **Stage Fort Park,** which has a small beach, a playground area, rocky trails to explore, and a wide open view of Gloucester Harbor. The park also has a bandstand, where free outdoor concerts are held throughout the summer.

Leaving the park, head for the Magnolia section of Gloucester for a guided tour of **Hammond Castle Museum,** a reproduction twelfth-century version, complete with moat and drawbridge, parapets, turrets, and lots of winding passageways. The focal point of the castle, built in the 1920s by prolific inventor John Hayes Hammond, Jr., is a massive pipe organ (also made by Hammond), housed in an eighty-five-foot tower.

Alexandra Meyns

As you tour the castle, your guide will offer serious comments concerning architecture and artwork, as well as intriguing anecdotes about Hammond. Children tend to be impressed by the interior courtyard, which frames a small swimming pool edged with statuary and greenery. Hammond thoughtfully equipped the courtyard with a glass ceiling that opens, so that on a warm, clear night he could splash beneath the stars. Yet despite his wealth, poor Hammond sometimes had to do without. He never quite managed to implement one of his pet ideas — guest rooms with walls and floors attached to turntables that would make it possible for an unsuspecting visitor to doze off in a modern room with an ocean view only to awaken in a windowless medieval torture chamber. Strange fellow, this Hammond.

The castle has a small café that serves light meals, and a gift shop where kids can stock up on toy soldiers and other medieval materials. Lots of special events are held at the castle, including workshops and performances especially for children and concerts and medieval celebrations that appeal to the entire family. Call ahead for a calendar of events.

It would be a shame to visit Cape Ann without getting out on the water, and there are several easy ways to do it, depending upon your tastes and the ages of your offspring. The tamest option — and to our mind the best for young children — is a one-hour narrated harbor tour aboard the *Dixie Belle*. The open-sided, canopy-covered boat glides through Gloucester Harbor, providing close-up views of the famous fishing fleet, lobstering vessels, Ten Pound Island, Rocky Neck (an artists' colony), and other waterfront landmarks.

*The only things at sea bigger than whales are the eyes of a youngster who has just spotted one off the port bow.*

For a more ambitious voyage, sign on for a two-and-a-half-hour narrated tour that takes you completely around Cape Ann. As a special highlight, crew members put on a lobstering demonstration. They'll pull a couple of traps (and raffle off the lobsters they find) and explain a little bit about the industry and the animal. For information on either of these trips, you should contact the **Daunty Fishing Fleet,** which also conducts four-hour fishing trips, departing at 9 A.M. Bring a sweater to fend off the cool breeze as you cast a line in search of the flounder, mackerel, pollack, and bluefish frequently caught in the protected Cape Ann waters. Rods and reels are provided.

Should you be ready to head farther out to sea, go on a whale watch. When the whales cooperate, these trips can be a fantastic experience. When the whales don't, the trips can be dreary and seem to last forever. So it's best to ask in advance how often whales have been sighted in recent days. A naturalist always sails aboard the **Cape Ann Whale Watch** boat to provide information on whale physiology and behavior. You'll spend about an hour chugging out to Stellwagen Bank, where the whales gather to feed on the rich supply of shrimp, sand eels, herring, and plankton that collects on the underwater ledges. You might see finbacks, which sometimes grow to eighty feet in length (weighing in at some sixty tons) and perhaps diminutive minkes (lightly tipping the scales at six to eight tons). And you'll probably see humpbacks. They're fun to watch because they breach (leap into the air) most often of any of the whales. Bring along a pair of binoculars so you can get a close-up view as the "gentle giants" make passes within yards of the boat and generally show off their stuff.

In downtown Gloucester, where you'll purchase your boat trip tickets, there are two small, family-operated bakeries worth going out of your way for. You'll find this pair of unpretentious eateries (where the conversation is as likely to be in Italian as English) at the lower end of Main Street, nearly next door to each other. **Virgilio's Italian Bakery** is famous for its homemade bread, light and crusty loaves that have become standard fare for hungry crews on the fishing boats. It is also widely known for its St. Joseph's sandwiches, a tasty mix of Italian cold cuts, oil, and spices, served up on a roll that's really a small version of the beloved bread. At **Mike's Pastry and Coffee Shop,** the specialties include homemade cannoli (filled with whipped cream or ricotta) and the best macaroons on earth. There are eclairs, turnovers, and butter cookies too. In the summer you can purchase a generous serving of Mike's homemade lemon Italian ice. Virgilio's is strictly take-out, while Mike's has a few tables.

Speaking of good things to eat, you can pick wild blueberries from the middle of July well into August at **Halibut Point State Park,** which must be one of the world's most perfect picnic spots. On the pleasant half-mile walk from the parking lot to the ocean you'll pass the rim of a defunct granite quarry, now filled with water (keep a firm hand on the youngest members of your group; the drop is precipitous and the water very deep). At the ocean the waves pound the shore creating great bursts of spray. Your kids will have a terrific time exploring the granite ledges and crevices that reach out to the ocean here at the northeast tip of Cape Ann. If you visit at low tide, you'll almost certainly find starfish, limpets, periwinkles, tiny crabs, and sea urchins in the tide pools that form in the rocks near the edge of the sea. Do be forewarned, however, that the rocks can be treacherously slippery. Swimming is absolutely not allowed, and with good reason — it's far too dangerous.

*Bring along a pair of binoculars so you can get a close-up view as the "gentle giants" make passes within yards of the boat and generally show off their stuff.*

If you would like to visit the crown jewel of the North Shore beaches, make a brief side trip to **Crane's Beach** in Ipswich. With more than five miles of white sand and dunes to wander, Crane's Beach has so much space that you can always find an uncrowded spot to claim as your own. Just be certain to arrive early enough in the day to get a parking space, particularly on the weekends.

On your way to the beach you'll drive down a country road that passes **Goodale Orchards,** where you can purchase fresh cider donuts in the eighteenth-century barn that serves as a store. Filled with fresh produce and flowers, all grown right here on the farm, the store also offers syrups and honey, cheese and preserves, and tons of old-fashioned candy. The bakers in the barn kitchen turn out scrumptious apple, pumpkin, and berry pies, which you can take home as the perfect dessert to end a day in the country. A glass wall separates the attached cider mill from the barn, making it easy to watch the entire cider making process, which relies on a century-old cider press. Cider is available in the store by the cup, half gallon, and gallon.

From mid-June through early July you can pick your own strawberries, and throughout July you can harvest raspberries. Blueberry pickers should plan to stop by mid-July through mid-August. Pumpkins line the stone walls and the driveway in the fall, when the orchards are open for pick-your-own apples. Specific picking dates depend upon the weather and the state of the crop, so you should definitely call ahead.

The farm also offers free, fifteen-minute, tractor-driven hayrides through the orchard for both kids and adults. Among the farm animals you might meet are pigs and a horse or two, goats, rabbits — even a sheep with a coat as thick as a rug who gets to roam at will, last we visited. Feel free to bring a picnic to eat at the table near the small pond, frequented by ducks and geese. As an extra touch, there's a swing set and a sand pile full of trucks to keep the younger members of your crew content.

For a pleasant evening's entertainment within a half hour's drive of Cape Ann, you can take in a show at the **North Shore Music Theatre** in Beverly. Here the fare tends toward revivals of hits like *Give My Regards to Broadway, 42nd Street*, and *1776*. Shows are produced in-the-round, which means you're never very far from the performers. Subject to availability, half-price children's rush tickets (for those twelve and under) are sold on the day of performance, except for Saturday nights. The theater also produces a ten-week series of Thursday morning performances that are perfect for the four- to eight-year-old crowd. The schedule usually includes a heavy dose of fairy tales and childhood favorites like *Cinderella* and *Peter Rabbit*.

Don't go home without spending an afternoon or an evening watching a performance by **Le Grand David and His Own Spectacular Magic Company**, also based in Beverly. From the moment the tuxedoed doorman ushers you into the lobby of the restored Cabot Street Cinema Theater, you know you're in for something special. You'll pass the

*A glass wall separates the attached cider mill from the barn, making it easy to watch the entire cider making process.*

clowns selling sweets at the candy counter as you move into the inner lobby, where antique and contemporary puppets often come to life in the hand-painted puppet theater even before the start of the main show. In the main theater take time to look at the posters and magic paraphernalia on display and to appreciate the pristine and elegant space.

Arrive early so you can find seats up front. Young children (those in the six to eight range; preschoolers don't really belong here) are happiest as close to the stage as possible so they can really follow the magicians' maneuvers. A seat at the end of a row is also highly desirable, since the troupe occasionally makes use of the aisles. Balcony seating is available too, which may appeal to children who have never had that opportunity before.

As the two-and-a-half-hour show unfolds, you'll meet Marco the Magi, the inspiration behind the company and Le Grand David's teacher. Marco, who grew up in Cuba and began practicing magic at age thirteen, spent five years assembling and training the company before its inaugural performance in 1975. They have been doing stage magic at the Cabot Street Theater year-round ever since, with occasional breaks for special appearances on television and at the White House. They've also recently restored a second theater in Beverly where they plan to offer more magic shows. When asked about his talents, Marco answers, "I have no supernatural powers. I want us all to have fun together, to share what is theater magic."

Fun is exactly what you'll have as Marco and his associates pluck silks from thin air, survive confinement in a box pierced with swords, levitate, summon doves and rabbits out of inanimate objects, and reel in goldfish from the audience. The show is fast-paced and exotic, layering one illusion on top of another in the midst of continuously changing props, costumes, and backdrops. The cast seems to grow and grow, weaving musical numbers and comedy into the magical tapestry of stage art that blossoms before you.

At intermission time there's more to do than stretch your legs. The clowns carry trays of refreshments down the aisles, or you can walk to the second floor café for frozen yogurt, pastries, and coffee. The old player piano performs cheerfully in the lobby as children ogle the keys that move without the help of fingers. When the show is all over, the cast gathers in the lobby to sign autographs and shake hands, a fitting finale to a dashing performance.

Le Grand David

*Don't go home without spending an afternoon or an evening watching a performance by Le Grand David and His Own Spectacular Magic Company.*

**CAPE ANN.** To reach Gloucester, take Route 128 north to its conclusion, the Gloucester rotary (Grant Circle). Take the first exit off the rotary onto Washington Street and continue into downtown Gloucester.

**BEVERLY.** Take Route 128 to exit 18. Follow signs to Beverly, traveling on Route 22.

**CAPE ANN CAMP SITE. Directions:** Follow Route 128 north to exit 13. Turn left on Concord Street and continue less than a mile to Atlantic Street. Turn right onto Atlantic Street, following signs to Wingaersheek Beach. Entrance to campground is on your left. **Season:** Memorial Day through Columbus Day. **Admission:** Charged. **Telephone:** (617) 283-8683.

**WINGAERSHEEK BEACH. Directions:** Follow Route 128 north to exit 13. Turn left on Concord Street. Continue less than a mile. Turn right on Atlantic Street and continue about 2 miles, following signs to beach. **Season:** Memorial Day through Labor Day. **Admission:** Parking fee charged. **Telephone:** (617) 283-1601 (Cape Ann Chamber of Commerce).

**GOOD HARBOR BEACH. Directions:** Follow Route 128 north to Grant Circle. Take second exit from circle onto Route 128 extension. Continue through another traffic circle. Turn left at second set of lights onto Route 127A and follow signs to beach. **Season:** Memorial Day through Labor Day. **Admission:** Parking fee charged. **Telephone:** (617) 283-1601 (Cape Ann Chamber of Commerce).

**STAGE FORT PARK. Directions:** Traveling north on Route 128, take exit 14. Turn right on Route 133, which becomes Essex Avenue, and continue into Gloucester. When you come to the end of the street, turn right and then immediately left into the park. **Season:** Memorial Day through Labor Day (lifeguards stationed); park accessible all year. **Admission:** Parking fee charged. **Telephone:** (617) 283-1601 (Cape Ann Chamber of Commerce).

**HAMMOND CASTLE MUSEUM. Directions:** Following Washington Street into downtown Gloucester, you'll come to the Joan of Arc statue. Turn right on Middle Street and then right on Stacy Boulevard. Continue on Stacy Boulevard, crossing drawbridge and then bearing left on Western Avenue. Turn left on Hesperus Avenue at sign for castle, which is located on Hesperus Avenue. **Season:** Year-round. **Admission:** Charged. **Telephone:** (617) 283-2080.

**DAUNTY FISHING FLEET. Directions:** Ticket office located at Rose's Wharf, 415 Main Street in downtown Gloucester. **Season:** Late June through Labor Day; weekends in spring and fall. **Admission:** Charged. **Telephone:** (617) 283-5110.

**CAPE ANN WHALE WATCH.** Information is the same as for Daunty Fishing Fleet.

*The eighteenth-century barn/store at Goodale Orchards offers fresh cider donuts, syrups, cheeses, and "tons of old-fashioned candy."*

Goodale Orchards

**VIRGILIO'S ITALIAN BAKERY. Directions:** Located at 29 Main Street in downtown Gloucester. **Season:** Year-round. **Admission:** Free. **Telephone:** (617) 283-5295.

**MIKE'S PASTRY AND COFFEE SHOP. Directions:** Located at 37 Main Street in downtown Gloucester. **Season:** Year-round. **Admission:** Free. **Telephone:** (617) 283-5333.

**HALIBUT POINT STATE PARK. Directions:** Follow Route 128 north to Grant Circle. Take third turn off circle and continue 6 miles on Route 127 to Gott Avenue. Turn left, following signs to park. **Season:** Year-round. **Admission:** Free. **Telephone:** (617) 369-3350.

**CRANE'S BEACH. Directions:** Located on Argilla Road in Ipswich, 2 miles beyond Goodale Orchards. **Season:** May through Labor Day; off-season rates after Labor Day through September. **Admission:** Parking fee charged. **Telephone:** (617) 356-4354.

**GOODALE ORCHARDS. Directions:** From Route 128, take exit 20N. Follow Route 1A through Hamilton. Turn right on Argilla Road at sign for Crane's Beach. Continue 2 miles to orchards, on the right. **Season:** Mid-June through December 24. **Admission:** Free. **Telephone:** (617) 356-5366.

**NORTH SHORE MUSIC THEATRE. Directions:** From Route 128, take exit 19 and follow signs to theater. **Season:** Mid-June through mid-September. **Admission:** Charged. **Telephone:** (617) 922-8500.

**LE GRAND DAVID AND HIS OWN SPECTACULAR MAGIC COMPANY. Directions:** From Route 128, take Route 22 exit. Follow Route 22 about 2 miles to the traffic light. Turn right (to avoid going the wrong way on a one-way street) and continue 1 block to Cabot Street. The theater is facing you, across the street and slightly to the left. **Season:** Year-round. **Admission:** Charged. **Telephone:** (617) 927-3677.

**For further information** or lodgings and restaurant suggestions, contact the Cape Ann Chamber of Commerce, 33 Commercial Street, Gloucester, MA 01930. Telephone: (617) 283-1601.

# Sturbridge

Your trip to Sturbridge will revolve around **Old Sturbridge Village,** an expansive indoor-outdoor living history museum that chronicles the life and work of an early-nineteenth-century rural New England community. As you pass a day in the village, you'll become familiar with the sights, sounds, smells — even the tastes — of an 1830s country

town. It's the kind of place that encourages children to indulge their fantasies, to pretend that they actually live in the village. In the course of their play, they absorb a hearty dose of early American heritage.

Old Sturbridge Village encompasses more than two hundred acres, including woodlands, fields, gardens, a working farm, and more than forty restored buildings, many of which have been transported to the site from towns throughout New England. Old Sturbridge is staffed by costumed interpreters who go about the chores that would have occupied real village residents 150 years ago.

The center of the village includes several residences and commercial ventures such as the bank, general store, and law office. A replica of a 150-year-old newspaper or handbill, freshly pulled from the press in the print shop, makes a great souvenir. You'll see lots of craftsmen at work, including the broom maker, tinsmith, blacksmith, and cooper. A sawmill, a grist mill, and a carding mill represent other important nineteenth-century industries. Your nose is certain to lure you into the bake shop where you can purchase still-warm, old-fashioned cookies like Quakers and Joe Froggers.

You'll do a lot of walking here — and kids will do a lot of running too. There's plenty of space to spread out and try your luck rolling that new wooden hoop you just purchased at the general store. That's why it's important not to rush your visit but to take your time enjoying the village and the opportunities it offers.

*Hitch a ride aboard the open-sided horse-drawn wagon that will carry you over a covered bridge and along the edge of the mill pond.*

Because Old Sturbridge is a rural community, much of what you see will depend upon the time of year you visit. The seasonal rhythm begins with the birth of young animals in the spring, when you might also see a team of oxen pulling a wooden brush harrow behind them to smooth the soil before seeds are planted. Visit in the fall, and you're likely to see the same team hauling an ox cart piled high with dried hay. In the farmhouse itself women go about their chores, preparing vegetables for storage, making cheese in the dairy, cooking applesauce over the hearth. Farming was the way of life for many families in country towns in the 1830s, and the Freeman Farm shows how people worked together within a household to raise crops and livestock, with the goal of both taking care of their own immediate needs and producing a surplus for trade. The farm is a bit of a distance from the center of the village, but you can hitch a ride aboard the open-sided horse-drawn wagon that will carry you over a covered

Colin Lee

bridge and along the edge of the mill pond en route.

Throughout the year the village presents many special activities associated with seasonal events. Autumn, for example, is characterized by apple pressing, election day hoopla, and traditional Thanksgiving preparations. Visit during the last week in November, and you'll see turkeys roasting in reflector ovens and costumed interpreters participating in early American dances. The residences in the village abound with good smells as the women prepare early American holiday dishes like Marlborough Pudding and mince pies. At the Center Meeting House you can attend a service that includes psalms, sermon, and prayers culled from nineteenth-century records. Kids will particularly enjoy the turkey shoot. Costumed interpreters use smoothbore muskets, rifles, and black powder to compete for a grand prize (usually a live turkey). In the early nineteenth century live birds were often used in these contests, but village contestants focus their aim at paper targets, which are also historically accurate.

The village sponsors special participatory activities in the Visitor Center on selected weekends throughout the year. During the three-day weekend following Thanksgiving, for example, you can try your hand at grinding corn, making cider, and crushing herbs and spices. During "Wool Days," held in the spring when the sheep are sheared, children can

*At Old Sturbridge Village they "make history" every day, in places like the print shop, the sawmill, and the cooper's shop.*

*The Sheraton Sturbridge Resort and Conference Center offers convenient dining and lodging for long-term visitors to the Sturbridge area.*

Sheraton Sturbridge Resort

make a print from an old woodcut of a sheep, card wool, and use needle and thread to sew together a booklet called *Amasa Walker's Coat.* The booklet contains an eighty-year-old, nineteenth-century gentleman's recollection of the new overcoat, or "surtout," made for him in 1811 when he was twelve years old. Children keep both the booklet and the wool as remembrances of their day at Old Sturbridge. Call to request a calendar if you wish to schedule your visit to coincide with the special activities, which also include dramatic presentations and guided tours.

You'll find plenty to eat and drink in the village, varying from full meals served upstairs at the Bullard Tavern to cafeteria-style fare at the Farmer's Nooning. If you spend a weekend in the Sturbridge area, you might want to attend one of the lavish Sunday brunches offered by two local hotels. At Crabapples, a restaurant in the **Publick House Orchard** complex (which also includes several lodging options, shops, and other places to eat), you can choose what you fancy from baskets filled with cinnamon-fried apples, pancakes, French toast, eggs, and omelets. Finish up with a do-it-yourself ice cream sundae and enjoy it all in charming Victorian ambiance. The complex also houses the Publick House Bake Shoppe, where you can purchase fresh sticky buns, corn sticks, blueberry muffins, turnovers, and cookies to take along or to eat on the spot. The ceiling of the bake shoppe is covered with live ivy, which, along with the generous display of large potted plants, makes it feel as though you're snacking in a garden.

The **Sheraton Sturbridge Resort and Conference Center** offers a bounteous Sunday brunch featuring a broad selection of breads, cheeses, meats, seafood, fruits, and made-to-order omelets. When you've finished, head out back for a round of miniature golf. The course is embellished with models of buildings from Old Sturbridge Village, each one accompanied by an explanatory plaque complete with a photograph of the original. Educational minigolf, you might say.

If your budget is slim, instead of a fancy brunch opt for the poor man's buffet. As a rule, kids like hot dogs and kids like ice cream. For pure indulgence, have lunch or supper at **Sundae Creations,** where you can "take a dog and stuff it" as well as make your own sundae. Choose a regular hot dog, a foot-long version, or Polish kielbasa. Then start decorating it with whatever you choose from the twenty-five trays of toppings. In addition to mustards and relishes, there are grated carrots, onions, chili, barbecue sauce, Italian marinated salad, and all sorts of other stuff. Chew down your dog in the cheerful dining area or at one of several picnic tables out front by the parking lot. Then it's time to put together dessert. Choose one, two, or three scoops of ice cream and get to work gussying it up with crumbled Oreos, flamingo crunch, chocolate chips, nuts, marshmallow, pineapple sauce . . . you name it.

Speaking of budgets, you might be relieved to hear that you don't have to check into one of the resort hotels to stay overnight in Sturbridge. Several commercial campgrounds in the Sturbridge area and **Wells State Park**, the only state camping area in south-central Massachusetts, provide an alternative. Encompassing fifteen hundred acres of forest, including its own small mountain and ninety-three-acre Walker Pond, Wells State Park is a delightful spot for getting in touch with nature. The streams and marshes are populated by turtles, frogs, and several kinds of fish. Muskrats, beaver, deer, raccoons, chipmunks, squirrels, and fox also make their home here, along with ruffed grouse, owls, and an occasional hawk.

The park has fifty-five camp sites, available strictly on a first-come–first-served basis. Hot showers are available. There are a swimming beach supervised by a lifeguard (open only to campers), a boat launch, and five miles of hiking trails. Fishing and canoeing are popular activities here. During the summer park rangers conduct interpretive programs relating to the local flora and fauna.

While you're visiting Sturbridge, make a side trip to tiny Brimfield, where you can pick your own apples at **Cheney Orchards.** A family operation that dates back to 1911, the farm is currently operated by the fourth generation of Cheneys. "Charger," the rocking horse outside the apple barn, is a good sign that children are welcome here. Many of the trees are the semidwarf type, which makes picking possible even for the youngest members of the family. Purchase a half-peck container and fill it up with Macs, Cortlands, and other lesser-known varieties, depending upon which part of the orchard is open. On weekends the Cheneys often provide rides into the orchard on old Model A and Model T fire engines (call ahead to make sure, if this is important to you). If you can't make it during picking season, you can still select your own apples. Just step into the chilly cold storage room in the orchard store and choose what you like from the huge wooden bins.

*On weekends the Cheneys often provide rides into the orchard on old Model A and Model T fire engines.*

The salesroom has shelves of jams and jellies, relishes, dried fruits and nuts, syrup, honey, sweet cider, cheese, and homemade frozen apple pies. There's also scrumptious fudge. Prunes, plums, and ten varieties of pears are sold along with a real treat — tree-ripened peaches. During December you can walk through the farm and select your own Christmas tree. The Cheneys provide saws, but you'll need your own rope for getting your tree home. Treat yourself to a cup of hot mulled cider in the showroom while you check out the wreaths and other seasonal decorations.

## ACCESS

**STURBRIDGE.** Follow I-90 (Massachusetts Turnpike) to exit 9 and follow signs to Sturbridge.

**OLD STURBRIDGE VILLAGE. Directions:** Follow I-90 (Massachusetts Turnpike) to exit 9. Take Route 20 west for about 1 mile to Old Sturbridge Road and entrance to the village. **Season:** Year-round. **Admission:** Charged. **Telephone:** (617) 347-3362.

**PUBLICK HOUSE ORCHARD. Directions:** Follow Route 20 west about ½ mile to Route 131. Turn left and continue a short distance to entrance, on your right. **Season:** Year-round. **Admission:** Free. **Telephone:** (617) 347-9555.

**SHERATON STURBRIDGE RESORT AND CONFERENCE CENTER. Directions:** Located at 366 Main Street (Route 20) in Sturbridge, about ½ mile west of I-90. **Season:** Year-round. **Admission:** Free. **Telephone:** (617) 347-7393.

**SUNDAE CREATIONS. Directions:** Located in the Country Village, 420 Main Street (Route 20). **Season:** Year-round; call for hours during the winter. **Admission:** Free. **Telephone:** (617) 347-5772.

**WELLS STATE PARK. Directions:** Take exit 9 from I-90 (Massachusetts Turnpike). Go east on Route 20 to Route 49 north. Follow Route 49 north 1 mile to park entrance on the left. **Season:** Camping from Memorial Day through Labor Day. **Admission:** Charged. **Telephone:** (617) 347-9257.

**CHENEY ORCHARDS. Directions:** From Sturbridge, follow Route 20 west 4 miles to Brimfield. Turn right at light in Brimfield Center and then bear right, following signs for about 5 miles to orchard. **Season:** Apple picking from September through Columbus Day, depending upon the weather; showroom closed in June and July. **Admission:** Free. **Telephone:** (617) 245-9223.

**For further information** or restaurant and lodgings suggestions, contact the Sturbridge Information Center, Route 20, Sturbridge, MA 01566. Telephone: (617) 347-7594.

Children's Museum

*Two "climbers" emerge from the "bumper tree," a unique feature of Holyoke's Children's Museum.*

# Holyoke

No matter what time of year, there's plenty to keep a family happily occupied in Holyoke. Sure, pleasant weather always enhances a trip, but it's good to know that when you absolutely must pry your kids away from the television before you and they go crazy, there are options, sleet and slush be damned.

Begin your day at 444 Dwight Street, home of the **Children's Museum,** a bright, cheerful place with plenty to do. The exhibit space is divided into more than a dozen areas, encouraging a variety of play styles. Create huge soap bubbles, make waves, and shoot high-powered water pistols at moving targets. Make patterns with the sand pendulum or by stretching threads across the geo boards. Pass through the bumper tree, a series of long, stiff, colored (purple, green, orange, yellow, and red) tubes suspended from wires. Push them aside as you scuttle through like an ant, like a kangaroo, with your eyes closed, backward, any way you can imagine. Step inside the infinity mirror area for an endless number of reflections of yourself. Capture your image in midair in the frozen shadow enclosure. Clap your hands in front of the echo tunnel. Try your luck at matching up road signs with messages; what sign means you're approaching a busy intersection? Or perhaps you'd like to "drive" a moving van?

Need a respite from the pandemonium? Take a

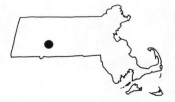

break in the puzzle hall or settle down in one of the four areas in the spacious two-story playhouse. One room is full of Legos, another contains foam blocks, while another is equipped with marbles and wooden blocks and chutes. The fourth is filled with dress-up clothes. Toddlers will feel safe in the Tot Lot, where they can test their balance and agility by navigating a carpeted ramp and stairs. They also can admire themselves in full-length mirrors, scribble at a chalkboard, or challenge themselves by climbing inclined nets. The area is fenced off from the rest of the museum so they can explore without fear of being trampled by energetic older kids.

All in all, there's loads to do. It's a great place to play with your kids as well as to observe them engrossed on their own. If you get hungry, you can have a bite in the self-service café in the foyer. Soup, sandwiches, and salad plates are available, along with oversized cookies, ice cream, and homemade muffins. You'll also want to visit the museum shop, where your youngsters can choose from a selection of imaginative toys, many of which continue the themes expressed in the museum exhibits. These toys encourage children to *do* something — whether it's growing a peanut plant, experimenting with optics, designing a puzzle, or pressing flowers.

Do you know where volleyball was invented? Right here in Holyoke. You'll learn this and much more at the **Volleyball Hall of Fame,** which occupies a small, handsome gallery upstairs in the same building as the Children's Museum. Back in 1895, William G. Morgan ran the physical education department at the Holyoke YMCA. He was looking for a game that was right for his older members and at first thought of tennis but decided it demanded too much equipment. Basketball was a success with younger members so he combined some of the elements of that game with the net from tennis and eventually came up with what we now know as volleyball. Through trial and error he found that the conventional basketball was too heavy and that the bare bladder of the basketball too light and small for his new game. He eventually asked the A.G. Spaulding & Bros. Company to come up with a satisfactory ball, which it did.

As Morgan explains in a radio interview that you can listen to at the Hall of Fame, "I might say right off that I at the time had no idea of any game similar to volleyball to aid me, so whatever was decided on was gotten by experience on the gymnasium floor." His remarks accompany a computer pro-

*Do you know where volleyball was invented? Right here in Holyoke.*

gram that traces the evolution of the game throughout the world.

Take a look at game artifacts like jerseys, old YMCA records, and volleyballs from important matches. Kids who play volleyball in school will be inspired by the color poster of the members of the 1984 United States Olympic Men's Volleyball Team, gold medalists one and all. By the way, did you know that volleyball is today the second most popular sport in the world?

**Annie's Attic,** also in the Children's Museum building, is a spacious, cheerful store chock-full of children's clothes at discount prices. You'll find well-known brands — Osh Kosh, Bugle Boys, Dr. Denton's, Billy the Kid, to name a few — marked about 30 percent below retail. Annie's carries children's clothes from infantwear up to size 14/girls and size 18/boys. There's a carpeted children's play area where youngsters can watch a "Sesame Street" video while you shop.

From 444 Dwight Street, it's just a short walk across **Holyoke Heritage State Park** to the Park Visitor Center, which chronicles the transformation of a tranquil Connecticut River farming community into an industrial boomtown. Holyoke was one of the earliest "planned" American cities. Nineteenth-century textile magnates from Boston, eager to increase productivity and profits, designed a city that included more than fifty cotton mills and more than four miles of canals to service them. Immigrants from many corners of the world flocked to Holyoke, lured by the availability of jobs, and soon industry diversified.

Through a series of exhibits and activities best suited to children ten years old and up, the park provides a lively sense of life during the height of the industrial era. Housed in a multilevel building reminiscent of a railroad roundhouse, the visitor center has a series of balconies that serve as exhibition spaces. The "paper loft," where rolls of paper are hung to dry the old-fashioned way, is reached by a towering black spiral stairway. In the "attic," tucked away in an upper balcony, you'll see all sorts of Victorian domestic memorabilia, including clothing, personal accessories, and old photographs.

Exhibits show how the Boston textile magnates mapped out Holyoke's streets and canals to serve housing and manufacturing requirements. The industrial fever took about fifty years to reach its peak, during which time the emphasis switched from the manufacture of textiles to fine writing paper. An

Holyoke Heritage State Park

*Multimedia displays at the visitor center of Holyoke Heritage State Park reveal the city's rich history. Holyoke City Hall towers in the background.*

extensive exhibit devoted to the technology of paper production includes authentic paper-making machinery. An interactive water power exhibit enables you to illustrate for yourself how the size of the pulleys and the length of the belts affects the amount of power produced.

The center has its own small theater where you can watch a twelve-minute film called *Holyoke and Its People,* which celebrates the city's ethnic diversity. The film reflects on the contributions of the Irish, European, Russian, and French-Canadian immigrants who built the dams, canals, and mills.

Outside the visitor center, five and a half acres of landscaped park overlook the canals and former mill buildings. There are picnic tables, and often you can catch outdoor concerts and ethnic festivals on the bricked plazas in the performance area. The park sponsors lots of special workshops and programs too, many of them specifically geared to children. Costumed guides might show how paper is made or teach the kids to create Victorian-era crafts. Call ahead to get a schedule of these programs.

Regularly scheduled weekend walking tours cover the Skinner Silk Mills, the Whiting Paper Company, workers' housing, and some of the city's fine examples of classic Victorian architecture. For a look at the alleys and canals that connect the mills, take a five-mile ride aboard the **Holyoke Heritage Park Railroad.** A tour guide will join you in the 1920s passenger car to answer your questions.

When you've finished exploring the park area, round out your trip to Holyoke with a visit to the home of one of the city's most successful industrialists. Built in the mid-1870s by silk manufacturer William Skinner, **Wistariahurst Museum** is an elegant Victorian mansion, enlarged by subsequent additions. Children will be intrigued by the leather-paneled room where the walls are covered with a combination of embossed leather and painted overlay showing exotic birds and plant life. The music room is fitted out with Tuscan columns and plasterwork that boasts musical instruments and cherubs. Kids often become bored in historic houses when the visit takes the form of an erudite guided tour. But at Wistariahurst you wander at your own pace, asking questions of the hostess as you wish. Take as little or as much time as you choose before heading out to the garden, where you will see authentic dinosaur tracks, and to the carriage house.

Arranged as a natural history museum, the carriage house is likely to be the high point of your visit

*For a look at the alleys and canals that connect the mills, take a five-mile ride aboard the Holyoke Heritage Park Railroad.*

to Wistariahurst for the youngest members of your entourage. There are mounted wildlife specimens native to the region, along with fossil prints and exhibits that focus on the geology of the area. Other displays cover the history of Holyoke and the Connecticut River. Dioramas draw you into the story of the city's growth, tracing the development of the lumber industry, fishing, transportation, and, finally, manufacturing. There's even a re-creation of the Skinner Mills. Several shelves in the carriage house contain Native American artifacts that touch on Eskimo, Plains Indian, and other Indian cultures.

After exploring the city's museums, stretch your legs with a hike in the country. **Mount Tom State Reservation,** just a ten-minute drive from downtown Holyoke, is a good place for a hike and a picnic (cooking fires are permitted in the existing fireplaces). Stop by the reservation headquarters (one and a half miles from the entrance) to pick up a map showing the twenty miles of trails. Near the headquarters building are a playground and a small nature museum with exhibits on geology and geography, along with collections of butterflies, insects, rocks, and birds. In the winter you can cross-country ski or ice-skate on Lake Bray. Do be aware, however, that there are no winter services. When your brood needs to warm up and get refueled, you'll have to pack up and head out.

*Mount Tom State Reservation, just a ten-minute drive from downtown Holyoke, is a good place for a hike and a picnic.*

## ACCESS

**HOLYOKE.** From I-90 (Massachusetts Turnpike), take exit 4 to I-91. Go north on I-91. Exits 16 and 17 lead into Holyoke.

**CHILDREN'S MUSEUM. Directions:** From I-90 (Massachusetts Turnpike), take exit 4 to I-91 north. Follow I-91 north to the second Holyoke exit. Take Route 202 north and follow signs to Holyoke Heritage State Park. Museum is located just across the plaza from park visitor center. **Season:** Year-round. **Admission:** Charged. **Telephone:** (413) 536-5437.

**VOLLEYBALL HALL OF FAME. Directions:** Located at 444 Dwight Street, in the same building as the Children's Museum. **Season:** Year-round. **Admission:** Free. **Telephone:** None.

**ANNIE'S ATTIC. Directions:** Located at 444 Dwight Street, in the same building as the Children's Museum. **Season:** Year-round. **Admission:** Free. **Telephone:** (413) 533-9672.

**HOLYOKE HERITAGE STATE PARK. Directions:** Follow directions to Children's Museum. **Season:** Year-round. **Admission:** Free. **Telephone:** (413) 534-1723.

**HOLYOKE HERITAGE PARK RAILROAD. Directions:**
Station located at Holyoke Heritage State Park. **Season:**
June through October; call for current information. **Admission:** Charged. **Telephone:** (413) 534-1723.

**WISTARIAHURST MUSEUM. Directions:** From I-90
(Massachusetts Turnpike), take exit 4 to I-91. Follow I-91
north to exit 16 (Route 202). Follow Route 202 (Cherry
Street) east; it will become Beech Street. Continue on
Beech Street 4 blocks to Cabot Street. Museum is located at
238 Cabot Street on your right, near the corner of Beech
and Cabot. **Season:** Year-round; closed the last 2 weeks in
August. **Admission:** Charged. **Telephone:** (413) 534-2216.

**MOUNT TOM STATE RESERVATION. Directions:**
From I-90 (Massachusetts Turnpike), take exit 4 to I-91.
Follow I-91 north to exit 17 west. Follow Route 141 west to
park entrance, about a 5-minute drive. **Season:** Year-
round; museum open Memorial Day through Labor Day.
**Admission:** Charged; free November through April. **Telephone:** (413) 527-4805.

**For further information** or restaurant and lodgings suggestions, contact the Greater Holyoke Chamber of Commerce, 69 Suffolk Street, Holyoke, MA 01040. Telephone:
(413) 534-3376.

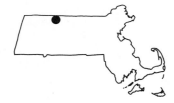

# Northfield

**B**elieve it or not, there are still ways a family can
get out and enjoy an activity-filled day in the
countryside without spending a fortune. Hiking,
camping, narrated boat trips, and plant tours are
among the options, as are canoeing and cross-country skiing, when you visit the Northfield area in
western Massachusetts.

At Northfield Mountain, Northeast Utilities
Service Company harnesses the Connecticut River
to produce enough electricity to light 190,000 miles
of residential streetlights. Since the Connecticut is a
natural resource owned by the public, Northeast
Utilities is required to provide the public with recreational and environmental programs in exchange for
its use. The public is reimbursed with a whole mountain to explore and enjoy. The scenery is spectacular,
and the fees — when there are any — are extremely
reasonable. You may well find that Northfield
Mountain is one of those places you return to frequently, always discovering something new.

The best way to become acquainted with the
mountain is to drop in at the **Northfield Mountain**

Northfield Recreational and Environmental Center

**Recreation and Environmental Center,** adjacent to the generating station. For just one dollar, you can buy a copy of the large-format, 160-page paperback book, *The Northfield Mountain Interpreter.* It is chock-full of photographs and information on the geology, flora and fauna, and social history of the Northfield landscape. The final chapter, "Take a Second Look and Think Twice," is a series of observation check-lists, which encourage you and your children to sharpen your senses as you take a close look at the natural world of Northfield Mountain. Did you know that if you get right down to the ground you can even hear the noisy movements of ants? Did you realize that sandy dune soil and the deep woods humus smell different? Can you find zigzag ridges of earth indicating where a mole has been digging a tunnel?

While you're at the center, pick up maps or tick-ets for the activities that interest you, then take time to check out the exhibit center, which focuses on "The Connecticut: A River at Work." Through a se-ries of interactive displays, your kids will learn about the significance of the river in the development of transportation and industry. Tiny models of a flat-boat, steamboat, and ferryboat light up in a river-scene diorama, as a taped narration explains the importance of the river in the movement of mer-chandise, people, and livestock. Water pours over a working model of a waterwheel, which illustrates how hydroelectric mechanical power works. There's also a display on ice harvesting and one on logging,

*Stories of Indians and pioneers enliven the narrated tour of the Connecticut River aboard the riverboat* Quinnetukut II.

where kids can use a peavey to heft a cumbersome log. A push button–operated wall exhibit shows how water levels rise and fall in Northfield Mountain's two reservoirs, according to electricity demand. Pick up an earphone and learn how a hydroelectric pump station works.

If you want to know more about hydropower, you can tour the underground powerhouse with its four reversible turbines, each one capable of generating 250,000 kilowatts. A bus will transport you to the entrance of a cavern. Here you'll get out and actually enter the mountain in order to reach the powerhouse, located half a mile into and seven hundred feet below the mountain's surface. The rock that you see alongside the modern generating equipment was deposited 400 million years ago.

Another bus takes visitors to the Upper Reservoir, where a guide explains the functions of the dams and dikes you see from the observation platform overlooking this three-hundred-acre manmade lake. The platform also offers a panoramic view of the Connecticut River Valley beyond. Each tour lasts about forty-five minutes.

Hiking is a favorite activity at Northfield Mountain, whether you want to trek up the mountain or simply take your children on a well-marked nature walk. Even very young kids can manage the Hidden Quarry Nature Trail, a mile-long series of loops with sixteen interpretive stops. You'll learn about geology and natural history as you pass by the dunes of Lake Hitchcock, the hidden quarry, a winter feeding station, and porcupine dens. You'll also learn about the interplay between power lines and wildlife.

If your hikers are experienced and have lots of stamina, you can choose instead to take a hike along the perimeter loop. Expect to spend about three hours completing the seven-mile route. Of course, lots of hiking options exist between these two extremes, as you'll discover when you examine your trail map. There's even a twenty-station physical fitness trail, where you can undertake a series of workouts designed to improve endurance and flexibility.

During summer and fall the center offers an unusual activity, riverboat rides. A twelve-mile, ninety-minute trip aboard the *Quinnetukut II* will make you feel as though you just stepped onto the set of *The African Queen*. Quinnetukut is the Indian name for the Connecticut River, and during the narrated cruise you'll hear about the Indians and about early pioneer settlements. You'll also learn how the river is used to fill modern industrial and recrea-

*The rock that you see alongside the modern generating equipment was deposited 400 million years ago.*

tional needs. A 44-foot passenger vessel, the *Quinnetukut II* has a covered (but open-sided) deck and seating for sixty.

With twenty-five miles of trails for ski touring and six miles of snowshoe trails, Northfield Mountain also attracts many winter visitors. Trails are divided into three levels — easiest, more difficult, and most difficult — with the less demanding ones at the lower elevations. Within the trail system the vertical drop is 805 feet. Try to plan your route so that you pass the Chocolate Pot, perched midmountain, where you can warm up with a cup of hot cocoa (or cool off with cold lemonade) and enjoy a high-energy snack before continuing on the trails.

Northfield Mountain is a great place to introduce your kids to cross-country skiing. Group and private lessons are available, and instruction is conducted in an area removed from the main trail system. Four hundred sets of rental skis are available, with a choice of wax or waxless surfaces. Snowshoes are rented as well. Other amenities include an outdoor barbecue where you can purchase hot dogs and hamburgers to enjoy at a picnic table out-of-doors or in the warmth of the center's lounge.

If you should visit the Northfield Mountain Recreation and Environmental Center in the fall, make a stop up the road at **Greenwood Farm,** a small, family-operated apple orchard. Here Neal and Louise Smith grow antique varieties of apples that they use to produce old-fashioned apple butter, apple jelly, and applesauce. A wedding gift of 25 young apple trees eight years ago has turned into an orchard of 625 trees. Still quite small, the orchard is intriguing because of the lesser-known varieties it contains. In addition to the familiar McIntosh, Delicious, and Cortland apples, the Smiths grow Ribston Pippin and Sops of Wine (both great for apple butter and applesauce), the latter being the oldest-known variety of apple in the world. For his hard cider (a much smoother product than typical New England hard cider), Smith grows true English cider apples with names like Kingston Black, Foxwelp, and Yarlington Mill.

Take a walk through the orchard; then drop in at the cider house to purchase apples and other made-on-the-premises products. A sampling table allows you to taste before making your purchases. Smith presses cider at least three times a week, almost always on Friday and Sunday afternoons. Call ahead if you want to be certain to see the process. All in clear view the apples are crushed into pumice in

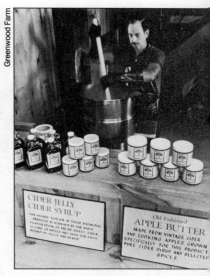

Greenwood Farm

*Apples grown and used in products made at Greenwood Farm include several lesser-known varieties: Ribston Pippin, Kingston Black, Foxwelp, and others.*

the grinder, then fed through a tube to the work station where Smith "builds the cheese" (wraps the pulp in netting) before feeding it through the 1930 vintage Palmer Press. During cider pressing the cider house is filled with the sweet scent of apples and the hum of machinery. Depending upon when you visit, you might also get to watch the production of jelly, syrup, apple sauce, and apple butter.

If you visit the area in the spring, you should stop in Turners Falls, where Northeast Utilities maintains the **Cabot Station Fishway.** Migrating fish manage to get past the falls by swimming over a series of rising pools, just as they navigated small natural rises in the river before the construction of dams. To get into the river above the dam, the fish have to enter the gate house fishway and travel through sixty-six pools, moving against the current. Eventually they are delivered above the dam.

At the fishway you can view the spawning migration of the American shad and the Atlantic salmon through large viewing windows. A guide explains to visitors that these two species are anadromous fish, which means they are born in fresh water, mature in the ocean, and then return to fresh water to spawn. On their spawning run, they overcome dams, falls, and fishways to travel to the habitat they require. Between May and June twenty-five to thirty thousand fish pass through the pools, which are also called fish ladders. The ladders are intended to help achieve a permanent restoration of the anadromous fish populations that flourished in the Connecticut River in preindustrial times.

In the summer the center operates **Barton Cove** in nearby Gill. Covered with hemlock and oak forest, this camping area is located on a rocky peninsula jutting out into the Connecticut River. With only twenty-two sites (and additional space set aside for group camping), Barton Cove doesn't get that crowded feeling. To further assure tranquility, campers are allowed to bring their cars into the campground only twice — to drop off their equipment and to reload when they're ready to leave. At all other times cars are restricted to designated parking areas removed from the tent sites. Each site is equipped with a fireplace and picnic table; drinking water, firewood, and sanitary facilities are available. Barton Cove has a maximum stay of seven consecutive days, unless there are unoccupied camp sites. Reservations are accepted. Daytrippers are welcome for picnicking and boating.

Swimming is not permitted at Barton Cove.

*Campers are allowed to bring their cars into the campground only twice — to drop off their equipment and to reload when they're ready to leave.*

Hiking, fishing (with Massachusetts license), and boating are the most popular activities. Bring your own boat or rent a canoe or small boat right here. Canoe instruction is available for beginners. In addition, if this is your family's maiden camping expedition, you may want to take advantage of the rent-a-tent program, cutting down on your initial equipment investment.

## ACCESS

**NORTHFIELD.** Follow I-91 to exit 28. Go east on Route 10 to Route 63. Turn left and go north about 1 mile to Northfield.

**NORTHFIELD MOUNTAIN RECREATION AND ENVIRONMENTAL CENTER. Directions:** Follow I-91 north to exit 28. Go east on Route 10 to Route 63. Turn right on Route 63, following signs to center, which is about a 10-minute drive from I-91. **Season:** Year-round Wednesday through Sunday; closed one week in the fall and one week in the spring. **Admission:** Free. **Telephone:** (413) 659-3713. **Note:** Cross-country skiing is available from mid-December through March, depending upon snow conditions; a trail-use fee is charged in addition to rental costs. Chocolate Pot and outdoor barbecue are available only on weekends. Plant tours are offered free of charge from May through October, but only children twelve years and older are permitted in the powerhouse. Call for tour availability.

*QUINNETUKUT II.* **Directions:** Cruises depart from the riverboat dock at the Riverview Picnic Area, on Route 63 across from the center. **Season:** June through mid-October. **Admission:** Charged; advance reservations recommended. **Telephone:** (413) 659-3714.

**GREENWOOD FARM. Directions:** Located on Route 63 in Northfield, just north of the center. **Season:** Mid-September through November. **Admission:** Free. **Telephone:** (413) 498-5995.

**CABOT STATION FISHWAY. Directions:** Follow I-91 to exit 27. Take Route 2 east to Turners Falls. Follow signs to fishway, which is located on First Street off Avenue A. **Season:** May and June. **Admission:** Free. **Telephone:** (413) 659-3714.

**BARTON COVE. Directions:** Take I-91 to exit 27. Go east 3 miles on Route 2 to campground entrance on the right. **Season:** Memorial Day through Labor Day; day use permitted through mid-October. **Admission:** Fees for services. **Telephone:** (413) 659-3714 (prior to camping season); (413) 863-9300 (during camping season).

**For further information,** contact Northfield Mountain Recreation and Environmental Center, R.R. 1, Box 377, Northfield, MA 01360. Telephone: (413) 659-3713.

# NEW HAMPSHIRE

Douglas Armsden/Strawbery Banke, Inc.

*Opportunities for discovery await youngsters behind every door at Portsmouth's historic Strawbery Banke, whose buildings date as far back as 1695.*

## Portsmouth

The jewel of New Hampshire's brief stretch of coastline, Portsmouth is a thriving seaside city that's fun to visit spring, summer, or fall. From boat rides and unusual museums to live entertainment and lovely parks, there's plenty here to keep you occupied for a weekend or longer.

A good way to introduce your family to Portsmouth is to spend a couple of hours at **Strawbery Banke,** a ten-acre living history museum that sheds light on four centuries of history and culture. The oldest building in the museum dates back to 1695, and the youngest was constructed in 1945. The neighborhood (and the museum) gets its name from the abundance of wild berries that once flourished right here, on the shores of the Piscataqua River.

There are seven furnished houses to visit, showing how people lived at different points in history. Other buildings contain formal exhibits, including displays of artifacts unearthed at Strawbery Banke. Kids become detectives when they check out the display illustrating "stratigraphy," the process geologists and archaeologists use to date the layers of dirt. Our kids were quick to point out that the layer with the plastic shovel embedded in it was probably lots more recent than the layer with the arrowheads. In fact, archaeology is very much an active part of Strawbery Banke, and you're likely to see researchers at work, sifting soil in search of evidence of the past.

Kids also enjoy standing amidst the heaps of bark shavings, watching the cooper fashion wooden barrels and casks. They can see boat builders produce graceful wooden dories in the boat shop and watch the resident weaver turn yarn to cloth on her loom.

For those who want to get actively involved with a craft, the museum offers a hands-on domestic arts program suitable for children six years and older. The purpose is to give visitors a feel for the activities of daily life in nineteenth-century Portsmouth by leading them through the steps required to complete a simple project. Two classes are offered each day, each one including a brief demonstration and a half-hour workshop session. You might learn to piece a quilt square, cut a silhouette, spin yarn, paint on velvet, or make a basket. Each class is limited to ten participants. No prior experience is required, and all materials are supplied. To be sure of a space, register at the Walsh House as soon as you arrive at the museum.

You'll probably want to make a souvenir stop at the Dunaway Store, a cheerful barn of a gift shop where you can buy just about anything with a strawberry motif. Strawberries decorate dish towels, cake plates, even the handles of knives and forks. You'll find them on mugs, jewelry, and postcards too. Kids enjoy choosing penny candy (mostly at three cents apiece) from the old glass and wood counter, and maybe stocking up on marbles, jacks, or round dice.

If the weather starts to look threatening, head for the **Children's Museum of Portsmouth,** which has more than a dozen hands-on exhibit areas de-

*Kids become detectives when they check out the display illustrating "stratigraphy," the process geologists and archaeologists use to date the layers of dirt.*

signed to incite the curiosity and imagination of children three to thirteen. Your child can put on puppet shows, make movies on phenakistascopes and zoetropes, contribute to a communal weaving, or go eyeball to eyeball with a terrarium-bound turtle or snake. Here a kid can become a telephone operator — flipping switches, connecting wires and dialing very long distance at an old AT&T switchboard. He or she can put on headphones, pick up a mike, and go to work as a deejay at station WFUN, or try a stint as a postmaster, a supermarket clerk, or a computer programmer. Matter of fact, a child who wants to be a lobster when she grows up can even try her hand at that here. Just buckle on a padded red costume, complete with claws that look like huge pot holders, and clamber around the corduroy-covered foam "rocks" in the seascape area.

One of the museum's most popular exhibits is the Yellow Submarine, a nearly life-size model of an early sub of the type used to do research, underwater photography, salvage, and rescue work. It's a multilevel play structure, with tunnels, ladders, and bunks, places to hide, portholes to peek out of, and even a firehouse-style pole to slide down. All of which reminds us that Portsmouth even has a real submarine that you can visit.

At the **Port of Portsmouth Maritime Museum** you can climb aboard an important piece of maritime history. The USS *Albacore* (named after the albacore, a small, streamlined tuna known for its speed) was designed and built in the early 1950s at the Portsmouth Naval Shipyard, just across the Piscataqua River in Kittery, Maine. A departure from the usual submarine design of the day, her unique shape was later adapted for the rest of the navy fleet. Today she is the only submarine on exhibit in permanent dry dock. Fully exposed, she looks like a huge beached whale.

Your visit begins with a ten-minute film, *The Final Voyage of the USS* Albacore, which describes the trials of shipping the sub upriver to her new home here at **Albacore Park.** An engineer who once worked on the sub explains that "she was rough riding on the surface but smooth as silk below." After the film a guide leads you through the sub. Mind your head and shins as you climb through the low doorways and over the raised metal thresholds.

Be forewarned! A sub is a close, claustrophobic place. You'll see the tiers of narrow metal shelves that served as bunks for the crew, twenty or more men packed like sardines into a narrow compart-

*A child who wants to be a lobster when she grows up can even try her hand at that here. Just buckle on a padded red costume, complete with claws.*

ment. Visit the engine room, check out the sonar signal ejectors, and peer through the periscope. Kids can take a seat in the control room and do a bit of steering while they ogle the dozens of dials and gauges that fill the control panel. You'll get a look too at the officers' quarters, the captain's stateroom, the pantry, the radio room, and the kitchen, as well as the broom closet–style bathroom facilities. Notice too the backgammon and checker boards inlaid in the tops of the dining tables. By the time you leave, your kids may realize that life aboard a sub is no picnic.

Speaking of which, you probably need some refueling. Try **Annabelle's Handmade Ice Cream,** tucked away in the bottom of a brick building that opens onto a quaint back street. There's something wholesome about this friendly spot, and you'll sense it as soon as you see the sign hanging out front — a linoleum block showing a chubby young miss feeding an ice cream cone to a happy cow. Ice cream cone mobiles twirl above the pine counter, and there are half a dozen wooden tables should you choose to eat in — not a bad idea since Annabelle's also serves fresh soups and sandwiches.

*A young lobsterman hauls 'em in at the Children's Museum of Portsmouth.*

The big attraction is, of course, the ice cream, which comes in winsome flavors like strawberries and cream, New Hampshire maple walnut, southern praline pecan, and Kahlua chocolate chip. Have a cone, or go all out and have a peach melba sundae with fresh peaches and whipped cream and homemade melba sauce. There are frappes and ice cream sodas too. You can even have a custom-made ice cream sandwich, a generous scoop of your favorite flavor firmly lodged between two homemade chocolate chip cookies. If you still haven't had your fill, purchase one of Annabelle's ice cream cashew caramel turtle pies to take home.

But you're not ready to head home because there's still lots to do. Head for **Prescott Park,** a lovely expanse of lawns, fountains, and gardens overlooking the harbor. Pay a brief visit to the tiny **Sheafe Warehouse Museum,** housed in the only remaining gundalow warehouse. Gundalows, or sailing barges, drew only about four feet of water when fully loaded. For two hundred years they plied the Piscataqua waterway off Portsmouth, carrying timber, military supplies, and farm produce. The museum contains photographs and memorabilia relating to the gundalows and to Portsmouth's early history. Take a good look at the model schooner carved by Captain Edward Adams, one of the last gunda-

*...ter a picnic,*
*...p a blanket, and*
*...down to the park as*
*...e sun begins to set.*

low captains, when he was a child. Adams and his son Cass were renowned wood carvers, and hundreds of the birds and boats they crafted are exhibited here.

Come evening take advantage of one of Portsmouth's best bargains and one of the pleasantest family entertainment offerings we've come across, the **Prescott Park Arts Festival.** For six weeks each summer the festival presents a lively schedule of theater, music, and dance. Put together a picnic (or plan to buy your supper from the pushcarts stationed near the edge of the park), pack up a blanket, and head down to the park as the sun begins to set. Hunker down on the lawn near the outdoor stage and listen to reggae, jazz, or folk music. See a musical, watch a mime, enjoy a fiddle contest, or admire the talents of the New Hampshire Ballet Theatre. If your kids get sleepy, they can conk out right under the stars.

A visit to Portsmouth would seem incomplete without a boat trip, and **Portsmouth Harbor**

Denise Fox

*The outdoor stage Prescott Park Arts festival is a true bargain in family evening entertainment.*

**Cruises** offers some good choices. Kids will favor the ninety-minute harbor cruise aboard the *Heritage*, an open-decked wooden vessel that can hold forty-nine passengers. Because of its build, the *Heritage* is able to navigate waterways too narrow for the larger sightseeing boats, which means you'll get a good look at the islands, channels, and coves that give the harbor so much of its character. You'll glide past tankers, lobster boats, tugboats, and even submarines, as your captain tells stories about kings, patriots, and privateers, all of whom are a part of the seaport's colorful history.

After you finish in Portsmouth itself, you ought to investigate a few points of interest south of town. At **Artisan Outlet Village** you can stock up on sneakers, overalls, and other youthful necessities at discount prices. This shopping mall comes disguised as a long gray barn. On the inside you'll be greeted by Muzak, carpeted floors, and a very unfactory feeling. The place is so clean and orderly that it's hard to believe you can purchase Osh Kosh and other trendy kidstuff for 20 to 50 percent below retail prices. You'll find lots of discounted imported toys and baby equipment too. We were enchanted by a collapsible mesh tent that keeps mosquitoes off an alfresco baby the way a cheesecloth cage keeps flies off a cake.

*With some diligent rack slapping, you can come up with super bargains priced up to 85 percent below retail.*

There are good buys for big folks here too — clothing, shoes, and accessories from the likes of Izod, Reebok, Christian Dior, and Perry Ellis. While everything is priced low, with some diligent rack slapping, you can come up with super bargains priced up to 85 percent below retail.

Continuing south for another few minutes, you arrive at **Water Country,** which bills itself as a family water park. At the huge pool you can ride the manmade waves. Hydroplane down the supersteep Dive Boggan or hold your breath as you navigate the twists and turns on the giant slides. Then again, you could take a plain old swim in the oversized swimming pool. Younger children can enjoy themselves in the play area or the shallow kiddie pool or team up with a parent for a ride in a bumper cycle boat. Once you've gotten thoroughly waterlogged, stretch out in the sun on a chaise longue. Water Country has a hefty admission fee, but one way to economize is to plan your visit for late afternoon on a sizzling hot day. The park is open until 8 P.M., and the rates drop at 4:30.

Continue south another ten minutes to Rye, to **Odiorne Point State Park,** perched right on the edge

*Strawbery Banke boat builder Doug Martin works on an Amesbury skiff.*

of New Hampshire's last remaining stretch of undeveloped coastline. Pannaway Plantation, the state's first permanent white settlement, was established here in 1623 by fishermen from England. Fort Dearborn, an army base, was built on the point to protect Portsmouth Harbor from possible attack during World War II.

Odiorne Point has inland trails to explore, as well as a rocky stretch of shoreline and both saltwater and freshwater marshes. The Visitor Center has a saltwater aquarium, a "touch table" covered with local flotsam and jetsam, and exhibits focusing on the natural and social history of the park. It serves too as headquarters for the park naturalists and volunteers who oversee an extensive series of summer programs. Picnic tables are out in the open and tucked away in the shade, many of them with ocean views. Grills are available if you want to have a cookout, and there is a small playground for young children. Put it all together, and you've got a lovely, peaceful place to while away an afternoon, with the bustle of Portsmouth only minutes away.

### ACCESS

**PORTSMOUTH.** From I-95, take exit 7 (Market Street) and follow signs to downtown area.

**STRAWBERY BANKE. Directions:** From I-95, take exit 7, Market Street. Follow signs toward downtown area. Bear left on Bow Street and follow brown signs to Strawbery Banke, which is located on Marcy Street, across from the waterfront. **Season:** May through October. **Admission:** Charged. **Telephone:** (603) 433-1100.

**CHILDREN'S MUSEUM OF PORTSMOUTH. Directions:** From I-95, take exit 7 and follow signs to downtown area. Follow signs to Strawbery Banke and continue past Strawbery Banke to the museum, which is located at 280

Marcy Street. **Season:** Year-round. **Admission:** Charged. **Telephone:** (603) 436-3853.

**PORT OF PORTSMOUTH MARITIME MUSEUM and ALBACORE PARK. Directions:** From I-95, take exit 7 and follow signs to Albacore Park, about ¼ mile. **Season:** Year-round. **Admission:** Charged. **Telephone:** (603) 436-1331.

**ANNABELLE'S HANDMADE ICE CREAM. Directions:** Located at 49 Ceres Street (near the junction of Market and Bow streets) in the downtown area. **Season:** Year-round. **Admission:** Free. **Telephone:** (603) 431-1988.

**PRESCOTT PARK. Directions:** Follow directions to Strawbery Banke. Prescott Park is located across from Strawbery Banke on Marcy Street. **Season:** Early July through mid-August (six weeks). **Admission:** Small donation requested. **Telephone:** (603) 436-2848.

**SHEAFE WAREHOUSE MUSEUM. Directions:** Located in Prescott Park. **Season:** Memorial Day to Labor Day. **Admission:** Free. **Telephone:** None.

**PORTSMOUTH HARBOR CRUISES. Directions:** Ticket booth located at 64 Ceres Street. The street begins near the junction of Market and Bow streets in downtown. **Season:** Mid-June through October. **Admission:** Charged. **Telephone:** (603) 436-8084.

**ARTISAN OUTLET VILLAGE. Directions:** From downtown Portsmouth, follow Route 1 south for about 1 mile. Turn right on Mirona Road (immediately after McDonald's) and follow signs. **Season:** Year-round. **Admission:** Free. **Telephone:** (603) 436-0022.

**WATER COUNTRY. Directions:** Located on Route 1, 3 miles south of downtown Portsmouth. **Season:** Memorial Day through Labor Day. **Admission:** Charged. **Telephone:** (603) 436-3556.

**ODIORNE POINT STATE PARK. Directions:** From downtown Portsmouth, follow Route 1A to Rye. Entrance to park will be on your left. **Season:** Year-round. Visitor center open late June through late August. **Admission:** Charged. **Telephone:** (603) 436-8043.

**For further information** or restaurant and lodgings suggestions, contact the Greater Portsmouth Chamber of Commerce, Box 239, 500 Market Street, Portsmouth, NH 03801. Telephone: (603) 436-1118.

# Weirs Beach

Weirs Beach is a place for having fun, for indulging in pleasures like do-it-yourself ice cream sundaes and giant water slides. Natural and man-made attractions combine to make Weirs Beach one of New England's oldest and favorite family resorts. Here you can swim in Lake Winnipesaukee, take a leisurely sightseeing cruise, and munch on cotton candy and fried dough. The pier, which stretches out over the lake, is lined with stands selling souvenirs, beach toys, and just about any kind of scrumptious junk food you can imagine. It also boasts tons of electronic games and amusements, as well as a lakeside miniature golf course. Often crowded, always festive, Weirs Beach is a great place to enjoy playing with your kids, big or small.

You'll know you've arrived when you spot the **Weirs Beach Water Slide,** a maze of tubes overlooking Lake Winnipesaukee. Just like ski trails, the slides are labeled according to the ability level required to navigate them. Beginners can hear the echo of their own screeches as they careen toward a splash finish on the seventy-foot-long Tunnel Twister. The Flash Flood (intermediate) propels riders with a foamy froth of white water. The Super Slide (advanced) is the longest water slide in the Northeast. Labeled "expert," the Sling Shot "features a thirty-two foot acceleration tube which launches you into the high-banked curves at an amazing velocity." This adventure is reserved for "the slider seeking the ultimate sliding experience." One of the best ways to determine your level is to do some observing before taking the plunge yourself.

Water-slide aficionados will want to make a brief side trip to **Alpine Ridge,** to experience the Cannonball Express, which simulates the effect of being shot out of a cannon and catapulted into a pool of water below. Prefer to have your fun on the dry side? Take a ride up the mountain on the aerial skylift and then descend via alpine slide.

You don't have to go to the ocean anymore to get a taste of the surf. A family attraction including two glitzy eighteen-hole miniature golf courses, a videoarcade, and a turtle car ride for small children, **Surf Coaster** features New England's first wave pool. The pool is nearly half an acre in size, and while the shallow end is massaged by waves gentle enough for a toddler, the deeper section entertains some serious artificial surf. We're talking waves substantial enough for a bit of body surfing, waves just perfect

*Just like ski trails, the water slides are labeled according to the ability level required to navigate them.*

*You won't often see the* Mount Washington *looking like this. The "Mount" provides three-hour, fifty-mile lake cruises for as many as twelve hundred passengers.*

for raft riding. Unlike at the ocean, surf's up all the time, and there aren't any undertows to worry about. Four water slides, varying in pitch and length, add variety to Surf Coaster's appeal.

In addition to unlimited use of the pool and the slides, the one-time admission fee entitles you to use the changing rooms and showers and to stretch out on the sun deck in a lounge chair. (There are additional fees for raft or locker rentals.) Small children will get a kick out of grappling with a series of climbing nets (they'll feel like Tarzan) and wiggling their way through the ball crawl (a cage of yellow and red lightweight balls) in the adjoining Kiddie Play Park.

For an exercise in juvenile hedonism, head for **Funspot.** Older kids will consider this video nirvana, as they choose from the more than three hundred electronic games that compete for their quarters. The bumper cars in the shapes of pigs, puppies, and bears are a big hit with the younger crowd. You'll find them up on the second floor, along with other rides just perfect for preschoolers. A shooting gallery, miniature golf, a driving range, and a snack bar round out the activities. You ought to know that Funspot is open twenty-four hours a day during the summer, should you be stricken by a 3 A.M. craving for Donkey Kong.

*Funspot is open twenty-four hours a day during the summer, should you be stricken by a 3 A.M. craving for Donkey Kong.*

Need a high-calorie, high-energy break? Go to the **Kellerhaus;** just be sure to go hungry. A multi-room gift shop that makes its own candy, Kellerhaus offers an ice cream buffet that is an experience in gluttony. Sundae dishes are offered in four sizes, and the purchase of the dish determines the size of your concoction, because you can have it filled with as many scoops of ice cream as it will hold. The buffet

*Watch that first step! The Winnipesaukee Railroad is a great way to introduce children to rail travel.*

contains tons of toppings — banana chips, peanuts, macaroon crunch, marshmallow, and real whipped cream for starters. Syrups come in flavors like blueberry, pineapple, chocolate, and butterscotch. Eat your creation at a table overlooking the lake.

For a thorough overview of New Hampshire's largest lake, you can't do better than to take a cruise aboard the **M/V *Mount Washington,*** a 230-foot excursion boat that holds twelve hundred passengers. A perennial lakes area attraction, the "Mount" carries on a tradition originated in 1872 by her predecessor, the side-wheel steamship *Mount Washington.* The cruise includes a commentary covering points of interest along the shore and tales of local history and legend. The Indians referred to the lake as "the beautiful water in a high place," and it's easy to see why as you loop in and out among the 274 islands that dot glacier-formed, spring-fed Winnipesaukee. The fifty-mile round trip cruise takes a little over three hours, so be sure to consider your child's temperament and patience quotient before signing on. It's fun to include a meal in your trip, perhaps the luncheon buffet. Or take an early morning cruise and opt for breakfast instead. Children enjoy acquainting themselves with the boat's every nook and cranny, including the ice cream parlor, where they can purchase a sustaining snack.

For a shorter lake cruise take a ride on the *Sophie C,* the mailboat that delivers packages and letters to people who live on the Winnipesaukee islands. It's fun to see folks come out to meet the mailboat and to listen to the captain's lively commentary as he combines the roles of mailman and tour boat operator. The *Doris E,* which is not a mailboat, offers similar cruises on a more frequent schedule, including a sunset trip. Each boat holds 150 passengers and sells light snacks. The trips last one and three-quarters hours. The *Mount Washington,* the *Sophie C,* and the *Doris E* are all operated by the **Winnipesaukee Flagship Company,** which can provide complete fare and schedule information (see ACCESS section at end of chapter). No matter which you choose, you'll get to savor the beauty of a sparkling lake gracefully framed by three mountain ranges: the Belknap Mountains, the Ossipee Mountains, and the Sandwich Range.

By the time you've spent a few hours enjoying Weirs Beach, you're sure to have noticed the train that periodically pulls up to the Victorian station overlooking the beach. **Winnipesaukee Railroad** offers scenic rides using early-period diesel locomotives. You can take your young ones aboard for a round trip to Meredith and back (under an hour), a good activity to keep in mind in case of rain. The train skims along the edge of the lake, affording great views of Meredith Bay and Paugus Bay. Longer trips are available too, but this one seems about right for kids — long enough to get a good taste but not quite long enough for the novelty to wear off.

For a change of pace and an opportunity to combine entertainment with education, make a half-hour side trip from Weirs Beach to visit **The Science Center of New Hampshire,** a complex of imaginative indoor and outdoor exhibits designed to introduce children to the science of plant and animal communities. The center encompasses a two-hundred-acre wildlife refuge, where bear, deer, bobcat, and other native animals live in spacious natural enclosures. As you explore the refuge, you'll learn about the leopard frogs, diving beetles, and muskrats that inhabit the shallow water and muddy bottom of the marsh community, the snapping turtles and diving loons of the lake community, and the nuthatches, great horned owls, mice, and shrews that share the forest community with the white-tailed deer.

*It's fun to see folks come out to meet the mailboat and to listen to the captain's lively commentary as he combines the roles of mailman and tour boat operator.*

As you follow the trails through the center, you'll encounter sixteen outdoor exhibits that use puzzles, games, and even live animals to teach about New Hampshire's natural communities. Several buildings along the trail contain interactive exhibits designed to help kids learn more about a particular type of animal. In the Bear Facts Exhibit, for example, kids can test their bear IQ at a question board with hidden answers. Do bears hug their victims to death? Lift the flap, and you'll discover that they don't. In truth, they attack with their teeth and claws. The Murphy Bird Exhibit challenges kids to match the physical characteristics of different birds (fat bill, long legs and toes) with their eating habits (cracks open seeds, eats flying insects). During the summer months staff members give fifteen-minute minitalks focusing on different aspects of plant and animal life, and you can watch "Up Close to Animals," a forty-five minute live animal presentation held twice each day in the attractive visitor center. Allow at least two hours for your visit and feel free to bring along a picnic.

## ACCESS

**WEIRS BEACH.** Follow I-93 to exit 20. Take Route 3 north to Weirs Beach, about ½-hour drive from the interstate.

Turn right at sign for Weirs Beach and continue ½ mile to docks. **Note:** Parking can be very difficult so try to arrive early in the day.

**WEIRS BEACH WATER SLIDE. Directions:** Located on Route 3 in Weirs Beach. **Season:** Memorial Day through Labor Day; weekends only until mid-June. **Admission:** Charged. **Telephone:** (603) 366-5161.

**ALPINE RIDGE. Directions:** Follow Route 3 (which becomes the same road as Route 11) north to Laconia. Turn right on Route 11A and continue to entrance. Located on Route 11A in Gilford. **Season:** Memorial Day through Labor Day. **Admission:** Free; fees for activities. **Telephone:** (603) 293-4304.

**SURF COASTER. Directions:** Take Route 3 north to Weirs Beach. Turn right at Dexter Shoe store onto Route 11B. Surf Coaster is on 11B. **Season:** Memorial Day through Labor Day; weekends only until mid-June. **Admission:** Charged. **Telephone:** (603) 366-4991.

**FUNSPOT. Directions:** Located on Route 3, about 1 mile north of Weirs Beach. **Season:** Year-round. **Admission:** Free. **Telephone:** (603) 366-4377.

**KELLERHAUS. Directions:** Located on Route 3 just north of Weirs Beach. **Season:** Year-round. **Admission:** Free. **Telephone:** (603) 366-4466.

**WINNIPESAUKEE FLAGSHIP COMPANY. Directions:** *The Mount Washington* departs from Weirs Beach, Center Harbor, Alton Bay, and Wolfboro. The *Sophie C* departs from Weirs Beach only. The *Doris E* departs from Weirs Beach and Meredith. **Season:** Late May through mid-October for the "Mount"; mid-June through early September for the other two boats. **Admission:** Charged. **Telephone:** (603) 366-5531.

**WINNIPESAUKEE RAILROAD. Directions:** Train stops at Weirs Beach. Ticket office and station overlook the dock. **Season:** Memorial Day through Columbus Day; weekends only, except daily from July through Labor Day. **Admission:** Charged. **Telephone:** (603) 528-2330.

**THE SCIENCE CENTER OF NEW HAMPSHIRE. Directions:** From I-93, take exit 24. Travel east for 4 miles on Route 25 to Holderness. Turn left on Route 113 and continue 1 block. Turn left at sign to center. **Season:** May through October. **Admission:** Charged. **Telephone:** (603) 968-7194.

**For further information** or restaurant and lodgings suggestions, contact the Weirs Beach Chamber of Commerce, Box 336B, Weirs Beach, NH 03246. Telephone: (603) 366-4770.

# Lincoln and North Woodstock

**A** generous slice of child heaven awaits in the White Mountains of New Hampshire. Base yourself in the vicinity of Lincoln and spend a weekend checking out one attraction after another. For a more economical approach, make a daytrip to the area. New Hampshire is not a very big state, and the interstate highways make the southern section of the White Mountains accessible in less time than you might expect. By the time they've gone spelunking or splashed down giant water slides, your kids will be so worn out they'll hardly notice the ride home.

**Hobo Railroad** is the newest of the White Mountain tourist attractions, premiering in 1987. The big draw here is Diamond Eddie's magnificent wonder wheel, a great big ferris wheel with enclosed red compartments named after individual White Mountains. You might ride in Loon, Whaleback, or Lafayette. Each compartment contains a pair of facing wooden benches and can easily accommodate a family of six. You're welcome to bring along snacks, not a bad idea since the ride lasts eight to ten minutes (you can't expect a kid to go forever without sustenance).

The other major activity is a ride aboard the Hobo Picnic Train. The fourteen-mile trip along the Pemigewasset River comes complete with stunning mountain views. You can ride coach or opt for first class (not too hobolike) and have a meal aboard. Your lunch will come attractively packed in a "bindle stick" — that's a bandana on a stick to all you would-

Alan Thomas/Hobo Railroad

*Can you imagine a "hobo" railroad that offers a first class section? This one does.*

be vagabonds. There are brass racks overhead and plush red seats. First-class accommodations include a table to unpack your sandwich, chips, cookie, and drink, so you can sit back and savor life on the rails.

Hobo Railroad is a good place to remember when you want to plan an evening activity with your kids. On some nights there are band concerts at the foot of the ferris wheel (dancing encouraged). The frame of the 108-foot-high wheel is studded with colored lights, which make it a cheerful sight when night falls. Little kids can play on the swings or get to work in the sandpile, which is equipped with a fleet of large and sturdy toy construction vehicles. Train rides are also offered each evening.

For a cool treat on a hot day, try **The Whale's Tale Waterpark and Fantasy Farm,** a flashy entertainment duo that has something for toddlers as well as teens. Admission entitles your kids to ride the merry-go-round, scrambler, and other rides as often as they wish. You'll have to pay extra if they want to try the speedboats (bring along dry sneakers and a change of clothes, just in case). Other attractions include a clown show, the "ball crawl" (imagine swimming in a sea of colored Ping-Pong balls, and you'll begin to get the idea), and a moonwalk to bounce on. The youngest in your group can feed the goats and other barnyard beasts in the special pen in the petting zoo.

The adjoining Whale's Tale is an aquatic amusement park. You can hop aboard an inflatable yellow float and ride the "Lazy River" through a "canyon" studded with boulders. Machine-made waves provide excitement in the giant wave pool. Fly down one of the giant water slides or coast down the slower flume slides. Nonswimmers can cool off at Whale Harbor, a water playground equipped with high-powered squirt guns.

The park provides changing rooms and life preservers; just be sure not to forget the bathing suits. A snack bar overlooks the "beach." Your ticket to the Whale's Tale includes admission to Fantasy Farm. A special reduced-price admission is offered after 5 P.M., but do be aware that Fantasy Farm closes at 6 P.M. The waterpark remains open for several hours after that.

Oldest of the area's amusement attractions is **Clark's Trading Post,** which features a family of trained native New Hampshire black bears that like to be rewarded for their antics with spoonfuls of ice cream. They perform, "unmuzzled and unleashed,"

The Whale's Tale Water Park and Fantasy Farm provide a two-for-one treat for lovers of rides and amusements.

in a circular cage with the audience sitting and standing all around on two levels. Watch Pearl and her pals drink out of a cup, roll a wooden spool, climb posts, swing on tires, and generally try to please the crowd, just as bears have done here for the past sixty years. Their show takes about half an hour and is presented several times a day.

You'll want to hop aboard the open-sided White Mountain Central Railroad, powered by a standard gauge, wood-burning, smoke-billowing steam locomotive. Take care, though. As you pass through the covered bridge near the start of your two-and-a-half-mile journey, you enter "Wolfman's territory"! What's that noise? What's that metallic blur racing through the trees? Help! It's Wolfman himself, waving a club, dressed caveman style in fake fur, driving a jalopy. He appears and disappears, harassing passengers. He even shoots off his rifle a few times to the delight of the youngsters aboard. The kids harass right back, heeding the conductor's advice: "The best way to have fun with Wolfman is to aggravate him."

*What's that noise? What's that metallic blur racing through the trees? Help! It's Wolfman himself.*

Give yourself a couple of hours to amble down "Main Street," where you can have your picture taken in Victorian regalia at the photo parlor, stuff yourself silly on a do-it-yourself ice cream sundae, ogle the antique fire engines in the reproduction Pemigewasset Hook and Ladder Fire House, and admire the collections of old-time advertising memorabilia and electrical and mechanical devices in the Americana Building. The Clark Museum has intriguing collections of early typewriters, swords, hotel china, and children's games like Round the World with Nellie Bly and Komical Konversation Kards.

While you're strolling on the brick street, you'll pass by a tall wooden fence. It appears a mite rundown, but that's nothing compared to the scene that awaits beyond the gate. At Tuttle's Haunted House, all the floors are slanted, and bottles and billiard balls roll mysteriously uphill. You'll be led through the house by a series of guides who deliver a packaged patter that runs along these lines: "When Dad Tuttle died, they didn't have to bury him. They just rolled him out here in his bed and let him soak into the ground." You get the idea.

Across the street at the Mysterious Mansion, a normal enough looking Victorian house, you are greeted by an ominous fellow in formal attire who admonishes those afflicted with claustrophobia, fear of the dark, or equilibrium problems to refrain from entering. You'll learn that the house is inhabited by a famous wizard and that it is located directly over . . . a gravity point. Forewarned, you enter and take a seat. A brass bar is pulled up in front of you, the wizard speaks and does a bit of magic, and before you know it the flames on the candles are burning upside down and the ceiling slides beneath your feet, as the piano flies overhead!

Just beyond the mansion, your kids are sure to catch sight of the small pond filled with "water bugs." These circular seacraft are actually aquatic bumper cars, the idea being to bash into one another, with the added excitement (and likelihood) of getting good and soaked in the process. Bring along an extra pair of sneakers. Small kids do best to ride with their parents, at least until they get the hang of the controls. Each "ride" is five minutes. There's an adjacent sandpile full of trucks for those too young to rough it in the boats.

In contrast to Hobo Railroad, Fantasy Farm, and Clark's Trading Post are two natural attractions, Lost River Reservation and Polar Caves. Kids love a physical challenge, and at the **Lost River Reservation** they'll have plenty of opportunity to get good and dirty as they slither and slide through dark, tight places, navigating caves and crevasses. You'll be given a map of the three-quarter-mile riverbed hike, with descriptions of points of interest along the way. The leaflet contains another sort of important information too; it tells you if you'll have to crawl or slither on your belly or just plain be small and agile to get through the rocky formations formed during the Ice Age. You don't have to go into the caves; you can stick to the boardwalks if you like, although your kids probably will never let you forget it.

*You don't have to go into the caves; you can stick to the boardwalks if you like, although your kids probably will never let you forget it.*

Loudspeakers placed along the walks deliver information on the geology, ecology, and social history of the Lost River. The river itself was discovered inadvertently in 1852 by a fellow named Lyman Jackman, who fell through a huge mass of debris only to find himself in what is now called Shadow Cave, through which the river still runs.

Huge granite walls rise on either side as you descend Kinsman Notch toward the riverbed. Twenty-five thousand years ago the notch was covered by a sheet of ice a mile thick. Today mosses and lichens, primitive nonflowering plants, cling to the rocks, and the exposed roots of tall trees force their way into the cracks, seeking nourishment. All in all, the scenery is spectacular.

Although less than a mile long, the trip through

Dick Hamilton/NH Office of Vacation Travel

*"You go ahead, son. I'll catch up." The scenery is worth the effort at Lost River Reservation.*

the riverbed will take about an hour, and it involves lots of stair and ladder climbing. Sneakers are helpful, particularly if you want to go into the dark, tight places. It's also a good idea to bring along a flashlight. Carrying a child in a backpack is no easy feat, and strollers are absolutely out of the question. If you choose to bring preschoolers, you're going to have to keep a hand on them every moment and you'll need to stay on the boardwalks and forgo the caves. Kids from age seven on up will have the best time here. It's eerie to enter a cave, feel the dampness, and listen to the river course past, unseen except for a glimmer of moving water illuminated by a few small candles.

You pay an admission fee to hike along the riverbed and explore the caves, but the other activities at Lost River are free. You can take a look around the Ecology Center, a small cabin containing preserved specimens including a bobcat, ruffed grouse, and gray fox. One display details the life cycle of a fern, and another explains how the pitcher plant eats insects. Peer into the magnified bug box and see if you can identify the grasshopper, bumblebee, sapsucker, and other residents of the notch. In the tiny Geology Center, you'll learn how swirling water creates friction on rocks, resulting after many centuries in the rounded basins popularly called potholes. There are also several hiking trails, and if you're hungry you can take time out to purchase lunch at the cafeteria in the lodge.

Take care not to bang your head or twist your ankle when you visit **Polar Caves,** where great chunks of granite deposited many thousands of years ago by glacial melting form a labyrinth of tunnels and passageways. Caution: stamina, dexterity,

Neal Hamburg

*Stamina, dexterity, and a willingness to get a bit grubby are required for a successful foray into Polar Caves.*

and a willingness to get a bit grubby are required for a successful foray. There are steep stairs and rocky paths to descend, and the footing is sometimes unsure. Kids need to be mature enough to understand that there's nothing amusing about running or showing off here. Not that the adventure won't be fun. Children seem to thrive on the creepy ambiance in dark places with names like Fat Man's Misery and the Cave of the Eternal Chill. And for you older folks, rest assured. Detours provide a way to avoid the more challenging caves, so you too will be able to get by. Polar Caves are best saved for children seven and up. If you have smaller children along, they might be happier spending the time feeding the resident goats, geese, and rabbits. Stop in at the Maple Sugar Museum for a taste of maple candy or lick on an ice cream at the Polar Bar. There are also a gift shop and a cafeteria. Allow about an hour for your visit.

## ACCESS

**LINCOLN AND NORTH WOODSTOCK.** Follow I-93 north to exit 32. Follow signs to Lincoln (Route 3) and North Woodstock (Route 112).

**HOBO RAILROAD. Directions:** Located on Route 3 in Lincoln just off I-93. **Season:** Memorial Day through mid-October. **Admission:** Charged. **Telephone:** (603) 745-2135.

**THE WHALE'S TALE WATERPARK AND FANTASY FARM. Directions:** Follow I-93 to exit 33. Follow Route 3 north about ½ mile. **Season:** Memorial Day through Labor Day; weekends only before June 25. **Admission:** Charged. **Telephone:** (603) 745-8810.

**CLARK'S TRADING POST. Directions:** From I-93, take exit 33 to Route 3. Located on Route 3 in Lincoln just off I-93. **Season:** Memorial Day through mid-October. **Admission:** Charged. **Telephone:** (603) 745-8913.

**LOST RIVER RESERVATION. Directions:** From I-93, take exit 32. Follow signs to Route 112, then west 6 miles to North Woodstock and the reservation. **Season:** Mid-May through late October. **Admission:** Charged. **Telephone:** (603) 745-8031.

**POLAR CAVES. Directions:** Follow I-93 north to exit 26. Take Route 25 west through Plymouth to Polar Caves. **Season:** Mid-May through mid-October. **Admission:** Charged. **Telephone:** (603) 536-1888.

**For further information** or restaurant and lodging suggestions, write White Mountains Attractions, North Woodstock, NH 03262. Or call the White Mountains Visitors Center at (603) 745-8720.

# The Kancamagus Highway

Following the path of the Swift River to Passaconaway Valley, climbing the flank of Mount Kancamagus, crossing a three-thousand-foot-high pass, and winding along the Pemigewasset River, the Kancamagus Highway is a thirty-four-mile stretch of incomparably pretty road. Children usually moan at the thought of taking a "scenic ride," but this one is different. There are plenty of opportunities to interact with, rather than simply look at, the scenery.

The Kancamagus traverses the White Mountain National Forest, connecting Conway to Lincoln. It offers a convenient woodland experience that's perfect for families. You'll never be far from civilization, but you'll certainly feel as though you've shed your everyday routines. Spend a day, a weekend, or a week introducing your kids to an unspoiled forest environment. Teach them to identify the flora and fauna and acquaint them with the satisfaction that comes from having climbed a demanding mountain trail. Introduce them to stream fishing or watch them shiver as they take a dip in a bubbling mountain river. Let yourselves lose track of time, just relaxing in the woods.

Although many trails originate at the highway, two deserve special mention. Plan to spend two to four hours on the **Boulder Loop Trail,** a nearly three-mile route through broad-leafed and evergreen forest, ascending to about one thousand feet above the Passaconaway Valley. A real "hike" as opposed to a less demanding "walk," the trail requires sturdy footgear.

Yellow trail blazes make the Boulder Loop Trail easy to follow. There are also eighteen numbered stops keyed to a leaflet describing the plant life and

Ross Connelly

*Every stop along the Kancamagus — campground, hiking trail, or fishing spot — marks the start of an adventure.*

geological features of the terrain. (Leaflets are available at the information centers, as noted in the ACCESS section.) More than fifty thousand years ago, the Wisconsin ice sheet gathered in Canada and then expanded southward until it blanketed every mountain and valley in New Hampshire. During the melting years, the ice accumulated frozen soil and broken chunks of rocks, which it dragged across the land much like a giant sheet of sandpaper. This process continued until the last of the ice disappeared, about ten thousand years ago. The scoured and scratched granite you see along the trail is the result of the glacial activity, which wore the soil away and exposed the bedrock.

The trail passes through deciduous forest before moving into evergreen territory, where spruce mix with broad-leaf trees. Continuing on, you'll come out in the open where you'll be rewarded with views of the Kancamagus Highway and the Swift River. Eventually you'll come to the "Ledges," a series of sheer stone faces (take care to keep children far from the cliff edges).

For a much less demanding hike, try the **Rail 'n River Nature Trail,** a three-quarter-mile loop beginning and ending at the Passaconaway Historic Site (George House). An interpretive leaflet is available. Fairly flat, the route is stroller and wheelchair accessible. Part of it follows an old railroad grade, a vestige of the logging railroads that crossed the valley from the late 1800s to the early 1900s, hauling logs from the mountains to sawmills in Conway and Bartlett. During your walk you'll see depressions left by railroad ties as well as evidence of a railroad crossing. With the help of the leaflet, you can teach your kids to identify trees including the tamarack, white pine, rock maple, black cherry, and red spruce.

The high point of the walk is the "fish pools." When the Swift River comes into view, lower your voices and tread quietly. You'll soon come upon some deep pools, a favorite habitat for brook trout. It is sometimes possible to see the fish, but they disappear at the slightest sign of movement so you'll have to sneak up.

The state of New Hampshire and the White Mountain National Forest cooperate in a fish-stocking program, and the anglers in your family may want to try their luck (those sixteen years or older must have a valid New Hampshire fishing license). Small flies and worms are considered the best lures, and early morning and early evening are the best times of day for trout fishing.

*When the Swift River comes into view, lower your voices and tread quietly. You'll soon come upon some deep pools, a favorite habitat for brook trout.*

There is something special about a waterfall, and two good ones can be found within easy hiking distance of the highway. It takes only about half an hour to make the round trip trek to **Sabbaday Falls,** a series of cascades that travel through a narrow flume. Descriptive signs on a viewing platform overlooking the flume point out rock formations. And you can sit on a flat rock at a pool near the bottom and cool off your toes (absolutely no swimming here). For a longer walk, continue up the trail beyond the viewing platform, wending your way along the rocky bed of the Sabbaday Brook.

Allow one to three hours for the one-and-a-half-mile round trip to **Champney Falls,** named for Benjamin Champney (1817–1907), an early White Mountain artist. If the weather has been particularly dry, you won't find much action at Champney, but from the bottom of the falls you can follow a path two hundred feet to the base of Pitcher Falls, which almost always has water going over it.

If you'd like to swim in a mountain stream beneath a waterfall, head for **Lower Falls,** where the Swift River drops over a fall about ten feet high, forming a large pool. Lots of broad flat rocks provide places to spread out on to dry in the sun after an invigorating dip. It's hard to think of a choicer place to spend a hot summer afternoon. Swimming is also

Ross Connelly

*Named for early White Mountain artist Benjamin Champney, Champney Falls is a picture-perfect trailside resting place.*

permitted in the swimming holes in the Swift River behind the **Jigger Johnson Campground,** but Lower Falls is the only spot with a lifeguard on duty.

Half a dozen campgrounds are strung out along the Kancamagus, each one consisting of family units with an individual parking spur, cleared area for a tent, open fireplace, and picnic table. Trailers are permitted, but no special facilities are provided for them. All of the campgrounds operate on a first-come–first-served basis with no reservations accepted. Seventy-five-site Jigger Johnson Campground is a favorite with families, partly because of the sandbars and swimming holes in the river out back. The campground also holds weekly evening campfire programs followed by a marshmallow roast. Subjects vary from tree identification to the history of the White Mountain National Forest to the life and times of the early area inhabitants. The programs are open to the public. Just bring along a blanket to sit on (or wrap up in).

*You might want to treat your kids to a ride aboard the Loon Mountain Gondola Skyride, the longest aerial lift in the state.*

Before leaving the Kancamagus you might want to treat your kids to a ride aboard the **Loon Mountain Gondola Skyride,** the longest aerial lift in the state. It takes just eleven minutes to reach the summit in one of the bright red enclosed four-passenger gondolas. You'll watch the mountains rise in front of you and the valley seem to drop below as you travel seven thousand feet to the summit. Up top, the views of the Presidential Range are outstanding, particularly if you climb the four-story summit observation tower. There are also a short, marked nature trail and a newly developed cave walk that provides insight into mountain geology. There's a cafeteria at the summit too.

## ACCESS

**KANCAMAGUS HIGHWAY.** The highway (Route 112) is accessible from I-93 in Lincoln or Route 16 in Conway. The highway is open year-round.

**INFORMATION CENTERS.** There are three information centers along the highway, all operated by the U.S. Forest Service. **Saco River Station** is at the east end of the highway, about 100 yards from Route 16. **Season:** Memorial Day through Labor Day. **Telephone:** 603-447-5448. **Passaconaway Historic Site (George House)** is located 12 miles west of Conway. **Season:** Mid-June through Labor Day; weekends from Memorial Day through mid-June and Labor Day through Columbus Day. **White Mountains Visitors Center** is located at the junction of I-93 and the Kancamagus Highway in Lincoln. **Season:** Year-round. **Telephone:** 603-745-8720.

**BOULDER LOOP TRAIL. Directions:** The trail originates opposite Blackberry Crossing Campground, 6 miles east of the Passaconaway Historic Site (George House) on north side of highway.

**RAIL 'N RIVER NATURE TRAIL. Directions:** Trail originates at the parking lot for the Passaconaway Historic Site (George House).

**SABBADAY FALLS. Directions:** Entrance to trail to falls is 3 miles west of the Passaconaway Historic Site (George House) on south side of highway.

**CHAMPNEY FALLS. Directions:** Entrance to trail to falls is 2 miles east of the Passaconaway Historic Site (George House) on south side of highway.

**LOWER FALLS. Directions:** Located across from Blackberry Crossing Campground, 6 miles east of Passaconaway Historic Site (George House) on north side of highway.

**JIGGER JOHNSON CAMPGROUND. Directions:** Located just east of the Passaconaway Historic Site (George House) on north side of highway. **Season:** Late May through late October. **Admission:** Camping fees charged. **Telephone:** None.

**LOON MOUNTAIN GONDOLA SKYRIDE. Directions:** Located at the western entrance to the Kancamagus Highway. **Season:** Memorial Day through mid-October; weekends only until mid-June. **Admission:** Charged. **Telephone:** (603) 745-8111.

**For additional information,** contact the Saco River Station, Kancamagus Highway, Conway, NH 03818. Telephone: (603) 447-5448), or the Forest Supervisor, White Mountain National Forest, Laconia, NH 03246.

# North Conway

O ften called the gateway to the White Mountains, North Conway is a prosperous resort town surrounded by spectacular scenery. Attractions in the immediate area can occupy many days, and you may well find it one of those places you return to year after year, using the village as a base from which to explore the many pleasures of the Mount Washington Valley.

A trip through the countryside by rail is a good way to introduce yourself to the area. Train travel is a novelty for lots of today's kids, an adventure rather than just a way of getting from one place to another. If your kids fall into this category, treat them to a ride

aboard the **Conway Scenic Railroad.** Purchase your tickets at the telegraph and ticket office in the century-old Victorian railroad station, where you'll also find displays of railroading artifacts like old conductors' gear, timetables, tickets, and lanterns. There's a gift shop too, where you can purchase your own striped engineer cap.

Board early so that you can claim a window seat in one of the open-air cinder collector club cars or comfortable enclosed coaches. When it's time to chug forth, the conductor calls out "All Aboard!" and gives a "highball," a hand signal that lets the engineer know everything's ready. The engineer answers with two toots of his whistle, and off you go. The train rumbles past geese, horses, and cows, past cornfields and people swimming or canoeing, as it travels along tracks constructed by the Portsmouth, Great Falls, and Conway Railway in 1872. The trip is occasionally interrupted by the trainman's commentary, which focuses on the history of the railroad and intriguing features of the passing panorama, like a tunnel that provides cows with safe passage under the tracks. There's a short layover in Conway, just time enough to pick up a soda and popcorn for the return trip. The whole journey takes about one hour.

If you find yourself with a little spare time before or after the train trip, your kids might like to stop by the attractive park next to the station. There's lots of play equipment, including a slide, swings, seesaws, and some interesting climbing apparatus. Grown-ups can take a break at the picnic tables while kids let off steam.

Another way to get a view of the valley is to travel up a mountain and look down. One of the first ski lifts in the country, the **Mount Cranmore Skimobile,** provides a fun ride to the top of its namesake, in warm weather as well as cold. If you're used to ascending mountains on lifts that hang from overhead cables, you'll find a ride on the skimobile a fascinating change. The one-passenger red-and-green metal cars (you can fit a small child on your lap) squeak and rattle as they struggle upward along an elevated wooden trestle. The top of the mountain offers walking trails and fabulous views of Mount Washington, Mount Chocorua, Mount Whittier, Mount Kearsarge, Mount Jackson, and Mount Resolution. There are blueberries and raspberries to pick in season too, so be sure to bring along a container if you want to help harvest the crop. For a more serious hunger, treat yourself to lunch at the Summit House restaurant.

*If you're used to ascending mountains on lifts that hang from overhead cables, you'll find a ride on the skimobile a fascinating change.*

*Hear that lonesome whistle blow aboard the Conway Scenic Railroad.*

Come winter, return to Mount Cranmore for some pleasant family skiing. A triple chair lift serves the summit, and a double chair caters to those using the South Slope Beginner's Area. The twenty-nine trails and five open slopes feature 100 percent snow-making coverage from base to summit. Mount Cranmore has been dramatically updated in recent years, with the addition of a new day lodge and an expanded base lodge. There are also a ski shop and equipment rental facility, an all-day nursery, and a ski school.

Still another way to get in touch with the North Conway area's natural setting is to spend some time on the gentle, clear, clean Saco River. The White Mountains are the perfect place to introduce your children to the joys of canoeing, and the folks at **Saco Bound** will outfit you with all the equipment and trip planning advice you need. They offer a straight rental service, pick-up service, and guided day trips, and they'll help you get started even if you've never canoed before.

Spend a half day or full day paddling along the river, stopping for a swim or a picnic as the mood strikes. Or plan a more ambitious canoe camping trip. The most popular stretch of the Saco is the forty-five-mile section extending from just below Center Conway to Hiram, Maine (you'll paddle across the New Hampshire–Maine border in the first hour of your trip). The banks are studded with white pine and silver maple, framed by the mountains beyond, and you'll seldom be more than a few minutes from a beach. In summer the water is very shallow, making it perfect for beginning paddlers. A one-day trip (allow at least six hours, including lunch and swim breaks) will take you to a pick-up point near the Canal Bridge in Maine, a distance of about eleven miles.

During the summer weekends, Saco Bound has to turn away dozens of canoe rental requests, so advance reservations several weeks ahead are a must. The demand is considerably less midweek, when the river is also less congested.

It would be a shame to visit North Conway without hiking a mountain trail or taking a dip in a pristine lake. At **Echo Lake State Park,** just a ten-minute drive from the center of town, you can do both. A mile-long trail circles the lake, affording an easy, level walk. If your group has lots of stamina, opt instead for a three-and-a-half-mile hike up the White Horse Ledge Trail, which will take you to the top of the soaring stone face that overlooks the lake. Start out in the morning and bring along a picnic lunch. By the time you've completed the round trip (about three and a half hours), you'll be ready to cool off with a plunge in the lake. The swimming area is carefully marked, including a shallow section for nonswimmers. Picnic tables and fireplaces are set among the pine trees, and rowboats are available for rent.

Back in North Conway you'll want to check out the dozens of attractive specialty shops. Baseball card collectors will have a field day at the **North Conway Baseball Card Shop,** where they can choose between old cards and new according to their interest and budget. There are cards here for the serious collector and for the beginner, current cards and packs of unopened cards from past years, old team sets and complete mint sets. There are cards for fifty dollars and cards for a nickel, as well as hard plastic cases and soft plastic pocket sheets for storing and displaying them. If you have cards you'd like to convert to cash, bring them along for an estimate. You might end up selling instead of buying.

The shop is also well stocked with associated memorabilia like autographed photos of famous ball players, old programs, and sports magazines. Team logos emblazon the racks of jerseys and jackets as well as novelty items like mugs and bumper stickers. And, of course, baseballs are available. All in all, this pleasant, spacious shop is a good spot to keep in mind, especially for rainy weather.

*There are cards here for the serious collector and for the beginner, current cards and packs of unopened cards from past years, old team sets and complete mint sets.*

Just yards from the card shop you can indulge your offspring with a visit to the **Fun Factory,** where they can hang out in the extensive arcade (more than fifty of the latest pinball and video games) or speed down the giant double water slide. The challenging miniature golf course, built on a hillside with plenty of opportunity to end up in a water trap, makes great family evening entertainment. When you've finished your session on the links, reward yourselves with an ice cream from the snack bar.

For good, unpretentious food in a pleasant atmosphere where kids feel welcome, you can't do much better than the **Big Pickle,** just steps from the center of the village. The spacious knotty pine and brick dining room has a generous counter along with lots of round and rectangular tables. In addition to all the usual breakfast items, you can choose an omelet (six varieties), blueberry or cheese blintzes, or the house specialty, an Egg McBagel (one egg, bacon, and cheddar cheese on a bagel). Lunch leans toward sandwiches, ranging from old reliables like grilled cheese and the trusty BLT to more exotic numbers like grilled swordfish on an onion roll. There are hot and cold subs, hamburgers, and salads too, and seven types of beer.

The Big Pickle serves only breakfast and lunch, so you'll need another solution for dinner. **Anthony's Pizza & Subs** is a delicious and economical choice. It's housed (along with an ice cream shop and a delicatessen) in an old gas station. At the end of a busy day, taking the kids to a restaurant for a lengthy dinner might well be courting disaster; instead get one of these delicious crusty pies to take back to your room or to eat on a red slatted bench on the sidewalk out front. In warm weather it's fun to watch the parade of people along Main Street. You can also order a hot or cold sub, along with terrific made-on-the-spot calzone.

Just a short trip up the road from North Conway you can get an entertainment-filled crash course in New Hampshire history. At **Heritage–New Hampshire** you'll "board" the good ship *Reliance* for a voyage that carries you across the ocean from England to Mason's Grant in the New World. Sea gulls squawk, sails billow, lightning flashes, and the ocean foams and heaves (this last, on a movie screen). After sixty days and nights "on the dreadful and doleful sea," you come in sight of "the white hills of New Hampshire." The year is 1634.

Disembarking from the ship, you begin your

*You can get an entertainment-filled crash course in New Hampshire history at Heritage–New Hampshire.*

walk through a series of scenes depicting different periods and events in the state's history. Real trout swim in the pool at the base of Amoskeag Falls, which the Indians called "the fish place" long before the birth of Christ. As you walk farther, winter descends and you become sensitive to cold and scarcity. You enter a tiny cabin where a mother croons the sad strains of "Barbara Allen" as she cuddles her child in the loft. You'll pass by a barn where a farmer planes boards, content in the warmth and companionship provided by his horse, pigs, and oxen.

Time marches on. You find yourself in Portsmouth Square. More than a century has passed since your arrival in the New World. A sign outside the Blue Bib tavern notes a charge of four pence a night for a place to sleep, with the notation that no more than five will have to sleep in one bed. As a woman dumps her waste water from her second-story home, she calls out in frustration, "All this talk about revolution! Get it over and be done with it." Soldiers march on the outskirts of town. And then suddenly you find yourself attending one of the first speeches George Washington made as president. After the mechanized mannequin delivers its lines, the "sky" brightens with fireworks.

*Real trout swim in the pool at the base of Amoskeag Falls, which the Indians called "the fish place" long before the birth of Christ.*

As you continue your journey, you make the acquaintance of Daniel Webster, who remarks, "The gift of gab has stood me well. One of my first clients was charged with murder, and I defended him well. Fortunately, he was hanged." Then move on to the Industrial Revolution and a visit to the Amoskeag Mills, where fifty miles of cloth were produced in a single hour in the 1850s. Kids who complain about their allowances may be sobered to learn that back then a child under ten earned seventy-five cents a week, working twelve hours a day for six days.

Before you know it, the Civil War arrives. Content to be back on his farm, a survivor quietly reminisces about the horrors of the conflict, observing that "more men died of disease than in battle." As the century comes to a close, conclude your trip on a cheerful note with a simulated train ride through Crawford Notch and a visit to Echo Lake.

Heritage–New Hampshire is full of the kind of special effects kids love. And since you move through the scenes at your own pace, there's plenty of time for children to let their imaginations dwell on what it would have been like to be a child way back when. Allow about an hour for your visit. And be sure to keep Heritage-New Hampshire in mind in case of rain.

*The* Story Land Queen *swan boat and the* Pirate Boat *are two of the rides at Story Land.*

Young children will enjoy **Story Land,** right next door, where familiar childhood tales come to life. Costumed characters greet visitors, and thirteen rides carry out the storybook theme. Take a trip in Cinderella's pumpkin coach or climb aboard the Huff, Puff and Whistle Railroad. Drive your own Model T, glide across the pond in a little swan boat, or ride in a pirate ship. There's a child-size roller coaster too. Preschoolers will be thrilled to make the acquaintance of the three little pigs and Little Bo Peep complete with sheep. Cheerful and well-maintained, Story Land is ideal for children seven and under.

Teenagers might enjoy a stop at **The Grand Manor Antique and Classic Car Museum,** just a couple of miles down the road. The museum's collection of restored classic and antique cars pays homage to America's love affair with the automobile. A 1932 Buick Victoria Convertible and a 1956 Mercedes Benz, 300 SL, Gull Wing Sports Car are typical of the cars displayed, which range in vintage from 1915 to 1957.

For a special outing, treat your older children to an evening at the theater. **The Mount Washington Valley Theatre Company** performs musicals at the Eastern Slope Playhouse in the center of North Conway throughout the summer. A recent season featured *Damn Yankees, Man of La Mancha,* and two other shows.

Or attend a performance sponsored by the **Arts Jubilee,** the ongoing performing arts festival that provides the Mount Washington Valley with weekly entertainment in the summer and monthly events the rest of the year. Events are held at several different locations in the North Conway/Glen area. The fare runs the gamut from barber shop quartets to a traditional symphony orchestra, from jazz to folk to ballet.

## ACCESS

**NORTH CONWAY.** Follow I-93 to Lincoln. Turn right onto the Kancamagus Highway (Route 112). Travel east 35 miles to the end of the highway. Turn left onto Route 16 and continue north about 6 miles into North Conway.

**CONWAY SCENIC RAILROAD. Directions:** Train station is located on Main Street (Route 16) in the center of North Conway. **Season:** Mid-June through late October; weekends in May and Thanksgiving weekend. **Admission:** Charged. **Telephone:** (603) 356-5251.

**MOUNT CRANMORE SKIMOBILE. Directions:** Traveling north on Route 16 into North Conway, turn right onto Kearsarge Street at the traffic light in the center of town. Follow signs. **Season:** Scenic rides daily from early July through mid-October. Skiing from December through March, depending upon the weather. **Admission:** Charged. **Telephone:** (603) 356-5544.

**SACO BOUND. Directions:** Located on Main Street in North Conway, across from the Eastern Slope Inn. **Season:** Year-round. **Admission:** Free. **Telephone:** (603) 447-2177.

**ECHO LAKE STATE PARK. Directions:** Follow Route 16 north through North Conway to the junction with Route 302. Turn left on Route 302 and follow signs. **Season:** June through Labor Day. **Admission:** Charged. **Telephone:** (603) 356-2672.

**NORTH CONWAY BASEBALL CARD SHOP. Directions:** Located on Route 16 just south of the center of North Conway, on the right-hand side if you are traveling north. **Season:** Year-round. **Admission:** Free. **Telephone:** (603) 356-3349.

*This 1934 Ford, displayed at The Grand Manor Antique and Classic Car Museum, appeared in the final scene of the 1967 movie,* Bonnie and Clyde.

**FUN FACTORY. Directions:** Located on Route 16 in North Conway on the same side of the street as the North Conway Baseball Card Shop. **Season:** May through October; water slide operates from Memorial Day through Labor Day. **Admission:** Free; fees for activities. **Telephone:** (603) 356-6541.

**BIG PICKLE. Directions:** Traveling north on Route 16 (Main Street) through the center of North Conway, turn right on Seavey Street. Restaurant is located on the right about ¼ mile from Main Street. **Season:** Year-round. **Admission:** Free. **Telephone:** (603) 356-3954.

**ANTHONY'S PIZZA & SUBS. Directions:** Located at the corner of Main Street and Kearsarge Street in North Conway. **Season:** Year-round. **Admission:** Free. **Telephone:** (603) 356-3954.

**HERITAGE–NEW HAMPSHIRE. Directions:** Located on Route 16, 5 miles north of North Conway in Glen. **Season:** Memorial Day through mid-October. **Admission:** Charged. **Telephone:** (603) 383-9776.

**STORY LAND. Directions:** Located on Route 16, 5 miles north of North Conway in Glen, adjacent to Heritage–New Hampshire. **Season:** Mid-June to Labor Day; weekends through Columbus Day. **Admission:** Charged. **Telephone:** (603) 383-4293.

**THE GRAND MANOR ANTIQUE AND CLASSIC CAR MUSEUM. Directions:** Located 3 miles north of North Conway on Route 16 in Glen. **Season:** Daily June through Labor Day; weekends year-round except March and April. **Admission:** Charged. **Telephone:** (603) 356-9366.

**THE MOUNT WASHINGTON VALLEY THEATRE COMPANY. Directions:** Performances are held at the Eastern Slope Playhouse on Route 16 (Main Street) in North Conway. **Season:** July through Labor Day. **Admission:** Charged. **Telephone:** (603) 356-5776.

**ARTS JUBILEE. Directions:** Summer performances and summer box office located at the Grand Manor 3 miles north of North Conway on Route 16 in Glen. Fall and winter events are held at the Mount Cranmore Racquet Club. **Season:** Year-round. **Admission:** Charged, to most events. **Telephone:** (603) 356-9393.

**For further information** or restaurant and lodgings suggestions, contact the Mount Washington Valley Chamber of Commerce, P.O. Box 385, North Conway, NH 03860. Telephone: (603) 356-3171.

# Lake Sunapee Region

**A** quiet, off-the-beaten-track section of the Granite State, the Lake Sunapee region lies high in the mountains of western New Hampshire. A rural area that has escaped the glitzy "improvements" that characterize so many vacation destinations, Lake Sunapee serves as an excellent base for introducing your kids to activities that range from cross-country skiing to mining minerals, from picking apples to canoeing. You could spend a day here, checking out a reconstructed fort, taking a lake cruise, hiking a mountain trail, or you could settle in for a weekend of skiing or swimming and sunning, depending on the season. All of the attractions mentioned in the chapter are located less than an hour from Sunapee Harbor.

Sunapee Harbor has a low-key, lazy feel to it. Little kids dig in the sand or throw crumbs to the ducks near the edge of the lake while their older siblings toss a Frisbee on the broad lawn that stretches back toward the road. During the summer weekly outdoor band concerts are held here. It's fun to bring along a picnic and spend an inexpensive evening listening to the music by the lake while the kids play nearby.

If you'd like to get out on the water, you can rent a motorboat, sailboat, paddleboat, or canoe at **Osborne's Marine,** right on the harbor. Ski boats and water skiing equipment are available too. It's wise to call ahead to inquire about boat availability if you plan to visit on a weekend. Like to do some fishing? Osborne's is also a good place to pick up any tackle or bait you need.

Prefer to get out on the water while leaving the driving to someone else? Take a ninety-minute trip aboard the **M/V** *Mount Sunapee II.* Captain Dave goes out of his way to make sure that each child who cruises with him gets a chance to steer the ship. The whole family will enjoy listening to his lively anecdotes about the history and lore of the lake. Sit back in a comfortable chair on the upper deck and soak in the sun or hunker down in the enclosed lower area if the weather is cool, as you glide by lighthouses and elegant summer homes with Mount Kearsarge, Mount Sunapee, and Mount Ascutney looming majestically in the background.

**Mount Sunapee State Park** has a lovely beach just perfect for children. Spread your blanket on the grass or on the sand. The barn-red concession sells sandwiches and other snacks, and there are swings

*Captain Dave goes out of his way to make sure that each child who cruises with him gets a chance to steer the ship.*

and slides for kids to work out on when they're waterlogged. Older children enjoy swimming out to the raft. There is nothing honky-tonk about the beach. As you look around the lake you won't see any neon signs, just a few simple summer camps nestled between the trees.

During the summer you can take a ride to the top of Mount Sunapee aboard one of the park ski lifts and hike the trails from the summit, including one that leads to Lake Solitude. The half-hour walk is mostly through the woods, although the trail does come out in the open at the White Ledges, offering fine views of the lake. Do be aware that swimming is not permitted in Lake Solitude. Bring along provisions if you want to picnic on the mountain or stop in at the summit cafeteria, which operates weekends during the summer months.

In the winter treat your family to some downhill skiing at the Mount Sunapee Ski Area (within the state park), which has twenty-five trails on thirteen slopes, with snowmaking capability from top to bottom. The trails are accessible by seven lifts, including two triple chairs. One section of the mountain, called the Province Area, is set aside just for beginners. It has four easy slopes and is serviced by its own pony lift and chair lift. The ski school offers private and group lessons. The Children's Nursery in the base lodge accepts children from one to six years of age, which means you can ski unencumbered with an

*Serene Marine. Motorboats, sailboats, paddleboats, and canoes all can be rented at Osborne's Marine, Sunapee Harbor.*

Gladys Mujica

older child while a younger one takes a break. Other facilities include a retail shop, a rental and repair shop, three cafeterias, and one pub.

Families that favor cross-country skiing should make tracks for the **Norsk Touring Center** in nearby New London. The seventeen trails are classified easiest, more difficult, and most difficult. They vary in length from one to more than six miles. The Norsk Touring Center adjoins the Lake Sunapee Country Club, which offers restaurant and lodgings facilities, and a ski shop with rental equipment for children and adults. You can even rent a pulka (child-carrying sled) for hauling along a small nonskier. Just starting out? Sign up for a group or private lesson, and you'll be on your way before you know it.

If you visit the Sunapee area in the fall, put apple picking at the top of your list. Two-hundred-year-old **Gould Hill Orchards** is a family business, and the atmosphere is warm and friendly. The farm grows thirty-nine varieties of apples and also produces its own sweet cider and maple syrup. The Orchard Store is located in a white barn (be sure to notice the horse weathervane up top) attached to the main house. Here you can purchase peaches, pumpkins, and homemade jams and jellies. Check inside the tin pie safe for scrumptious apple crumb, peach, and strawberry-apple pies made in local kitchens. And, of course, there are the apples — chunky wooden boxes of them informatively labeled according to character and use.

At Gould Hill Orchards visitors are encouraged to get out on the land and enjoy the spectacular scenery. Pick your own apples against a mountain backdrop that encompasses views of Kearsarge, Crotched, Gunstock, Monadnock, and even Mount Washington, crowned with flaming autumnal foliage. This is a particularly good orchard for children because the short, semidwarf trees make the fruit easy to reach (no climbing, please). Containers are furnished, and you'll be charged by the pound, so pick as few or as many apples as you like. Feel free to bring along a picnic to enjoy in the orchard.

While the fall foliage is spectacular, it's also delightful to take a spring walk through the hilltop orchard when the trees are in full blossom. In the winter months it's fine to stop by with a pair of cross-country skis for exploring the acreage. (There aren't any tended trails; it's strictly do-it-yourself.) During the holiday season the store is well stocked with locally crafted ornaments, balsam wreaths and roping, and gift boxes of apples.

*You can even rent a pulka (child-carrying sled) for hauling along a small nonskier.*

*The fun continues year-round in the Lake Sunapee region, thanks to the Norsk Touring Center.*

For quite a different kind of harvesting, visit **Ruggles Mine** in Grafton, where you can collect minerals to your heart's content. Just getting to the mine is a bit of an adventure. Make sure your car is feeling its oats before setting out for the top of Isinglass Mountain, because the last 1.3 miles of the trip are a challenge as you negotiate the steep dirt road leading to the summit and the mine entrance. As you drive out of the woods and into the parking lot, a panorama of mountains and valley unfolds, featuring views of Cardigan, Kearsarge, and Ragged, to name just a few of the peaks.

Pay your admission fee in the small shop, where you can buy or rent hammers, mineral picks, chisels, and a canvas collecting sack for squirreling away your hoard. To save a bit of money, bring your own equipment. Kids love having their own hammers to work with, so you might want to bring a few along, plus individual collecting bags. Most of the mine is an open pit, but there are some tunnels to explore so a flashlight can come in handy too (the store also stocks these).

As you enter the mine (actually the hollowed-out center of a mountain), make sure you take a minute to read and discuss the posted safety rules: "Do not run, do not climb wall, do not throw anything, do not go beyond barriers." Standing in the center of the open pit, you'll feel as though you've stepped into an old western movie set. It's hard not

*Standing in the center of the open pit, you'll feel as though you've stepped into an old western movie set.*

to keep an eye alert for hostile cowboys or Indians lurking stealthily on the ridge far above.

Now it's time to get down to business collecting minerals. One hundred fifty types have been found in the cave. You'll almost certainly find mica, feldspar, quartz, and garnet. Less usual finds include tourmaline, aquamarine, and golden beryl with smoky quartz center. Most of your activity will involve striking away at the stone surfaces, extracting minerals. You're permitted to chip pieces off the walls and to remove large chunks of rock from the mine. Be sure to wear sneakers or sturdy hiking shoes since the going is tough underfoot, and you'll appreciate the extra traction. Many of the surfaces are damp, and some of the cave floors are covered with water. Kids should wear long pants to avoid skinned knees.

In the snack bar section of the shop, which is likely to be cozily warmed by a wood stove if the weather is cool or dank, you can purchase pizza, hot dogs, candy, and drinks. The shop stocks minerals harvested in the mine so that you can purchase samples of treasures you weren't able to find. At the small museum you can view mining equipment such as Grafton's first-ever road grader (later used in the mine); a rotating, dumping ore cart on rails; a water pump used to keep the mine dry; and an exhibit of specimens discovered here.

For a taste of frontier life during the French and Indian War era, make a side trip to the **Fort at No. 4,** a re-created prerevolutionary settlement complete with a palisade, province houses, and lookout tower. A historical reproduction of the original fortified village of Charlestown, New Hampshire, the village poses serenely on twenty acres of meadow bordered

*Give your kids their own hammers and chisels and set them loose on a prospecting expedition in Ruggles Mine.*

Ruggles Mine

by the Connecticut River. First settled by families from Massachusetts, No. 4 was the northwesternmost English-speaking village in the New World in the 1740s. Here a handful of farmers and militiamen took part in skirmishes with the French and their Indian allies as they struggled to preserve this distant outpost of English influence. A ten-minute slide show introduces the fort and its history. The tiny settlement was the victim of land title disputes, isolation (its nearest neighbor was thirty miles distant and travel was difficult), a short growing season, and political instability. Twelve families lived in the community in 1743.

*A sign in the stairwell warns, "Caution: take care to descend ladders backward. Captain's orders."*

The most dramatic feature of the settlement is the ten-foot-high stockade fence, the pickets set far enough apart to allow musket fire issued from within the fort to find its mark. The fence wraps around three sides of the settlement, and the fourth is protected by the Great Chamber Building, complete with a watch tower you can climb into. (A sign in the stairwell warns, "Caution: take care to descend ladders backward. Captain's orders.")

Within the stockade you'll find replicas of the cabins and lean-tos built by the original settlers. They are furnished to represent eighteenth-century domestic life. Crafts such as cooking, candle dipping, weaving, woodworking, and the molding of musket balls are often demonstrated in the buildings by costumed guides. Sliced apples dry over the smoldering hearth in the Captain Steven Phineas House, and peacock-blue candles hang by their wicks from wooden drying racks in the Dr. Hastings House, where a turkey feather fan is used both to fan the fire and to clear away the cobwebs. You might find a weaver at work on a rag rug at a huge wooden loom in the Lieutenant Willard House, where wool is being carded and spun into yarn. Elsewhere you'll see a huge wooden dugout that sank in Lake Sunapee in 1800 while carrying clay to New London to make bricks, a display of metal tomahawks, early metal ice skates, and an eel spear.

In addition to the fourteen structures within the stockade, there are several others right outside to visit: a working blacksmith shop, a pit saw, corn barn, and horse barn. The museum shop contains lots of inexpensive period toys like quill pens, metal dice, tin whistles, and reproduction colonial and revolutionary currency. There are also kits for making your own berry basket, birch-bark dugout, and cornhusk doll.

# ACCESS

**LAKE SUNAPEE REGION.** The area is accessible via I-89 in New Hampshire or from I-91, exit 8 in Vermont.

**OSBORNE'S MARINE. Directions:** Follow I-89 to exit 12A. Take Route 11 south to Sunapee Harbor. Marina is located adjacent to the dock at the harbor. **Season:** April through mid-November. **Admission:** Rental fees. **Telephone:** (603) 763-2611.

**M/V *MOUNT SUNAPEE II.* Directions:** Boat departs from Sunapee Harbor. **Season:** Mid-June through mid-October; weekends only from mid-May through mid-June and Labor Day through mid-October. **Admission:** Charged. **Telephone:** (603) 763-4030.

**MOUNT SUNAPEE STATE PARK. Directions:** From I-89, take exit 12A. Follow Route 11 south to Route 103B. Follow Route 103B south to state park entrance. **Season:** Summit rides from late June through Labor Day and weekends during foliage season. Skiing from December through April, depending on weather. Beach open from mid-June through Labor Day. **Admission:** Fees charged for summit ride, skiing, and beach. **Telephone:** (603) 763-2356.

**NORSK TOURING CENTER. Directions:** Follow I-89 to exit 11. Take Route 11 east to New London. Turn right on Country Club Road (sign at intersection reads Seaman's Road on the left, Country Club Road on the right) and follow signs to Norsk, about a 10-minute drive from I-89. **Season:** December through April, depending upon weather. **Admission:** Charged. **Telephone:** (603) 526-4685.

**GOULD HILL ORCHARDS. Directions:** From I-89, take exit 5. Take Route 202/9 to Hopkinton Village. Turn left onto Route 103. Turn right on Gould Hill Road, following signs to orchard. Total distance is 3½ miles from I-89. **Season:** August through May. **Admission:** Free. **Telephone:** (603) 746-3811.

**RUGGLES MINE. Directions:** Follow I-89 to exit 11. Take Route 11 in the direction of Andover. In Andover take Route 4 in the direction of Grafton. At the Grafton Village Green, bear left at sign for mine. Continue to follow orange arrows. **Season:** Mid-June through mid-October; weekends only from mid-May through mid-June. **Admission:** Charged. **Telephone:** (603) 763-2495.

**FORT AT NO. 4. Directions:** Located on Route 11, ½ mile east of exit 7 off I-91. Also accessible from exit 12, I-89. Follow Route 11 to Charlestown and fort entrance. **Season:** End of May through mid-October. **Admission:** Charged. **Telephone:** (603) 826-5700.

**For further information** or restaurant and lodgings suggestions, contact the Lake Sunapee Business Association, P.O. Box 400, Sunapee, NH 03782. Telephone: 1-800-258-3530; in New Hampshire (603) 763-2495.

*A working blacksmith shop stands just outside the Fort at No. 4 stockade.*

# RHODE ISLAND

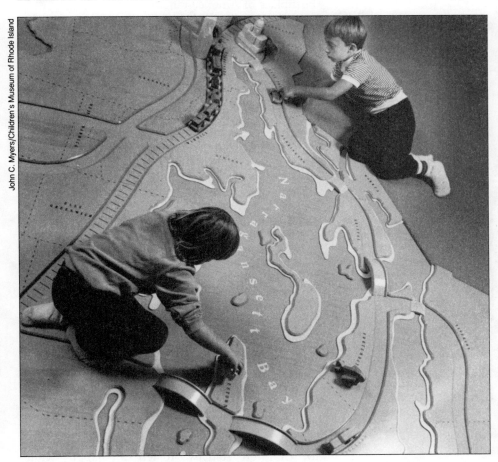

*At the Children's Museum of Rhode Island, kids get an overview of the Ocean State unlike any other.*

## The Pawtucket–Providence Area

**S**prinkled throughout the distinctively urban Pawtucket–Providence section of Rhode Island, you'll find a combination of attractions that's hard to beat. Begin with a lively children's museum and a rambling park complete with zoo, planetarium, and nine lakes; add a professional baseball club; tack on a spiffy amusement park; and suddenly you've got a quartet of attractions that appeals to a broad band of ages and interests. If your brood includes a mature, mechanically inclined kid or two, you may want to add to your list a nearby historic site billed as the birthplace of American industry.

The emphasis is on active participation at the **Children's Museum of Rhode Island.** Housed in the romantic Pitcher Goff mansion — a mid-nineteenth-century Victorian with leaded-glass windows, a wraparound sun porch, and a fanciful stairwell complete with illuminated newel post — the museum is a cozy, friendly place to explore. There aren't any "Don't Touch" signs, which means you can relax while your children explore.

Exhibits change frequently, but your kids can always cook up an imaginary storm in Grandma's Kitchen, hauling out pots and pans and more unusual equipment like an old-fashioned hand-cranked ice cream maker. Another room is outfitted with a climbing structure complete with lots of places to hide. The cushioned upper deck is cleverly draped with netting to keep enthusiastic small fry from inadvertently flopping overboard. Down below are tunnels to crawl through and curtains to draw when the need for privacy strikes. There is also a generous supply of foam cushions, just right for stacking, building walls, making furniture, or whatever else a clever kid conjures up.

From tangrams to mazes to jigsaws, there's plenty to consider in the puzzle room. You're also likely to see exhibits devoted to nature (with plenty of specimens to touch and smell), make-believe (dress-up clothes and a play firehouse), puppetry, and music. Encourage your kids to explore the exhibits but be patient when they just want to sit down and spend half an hour playing with a construction toy. Children from two to ten can happily while away an hour or two here.

For an inexpensive, variety-filled excursion, **Roger Williams Park** is hard to beat. Designed in 1878 by H. W. S. Cleveland, the Victorian-era park encompasses 430 acres of landscaped terrain, ponds, lakes, drives, and walkways. Your children will probably want to begin at the zoo, which is one of the oldest in the country, containing both domestic and exotic animals. The Farmyard, a complex of rough-hewn barns with shingled roofs, is the home of familiar animals like goats, domestic cattle, and the Rhode Island Red (better known as "Little Rhody"), the famous chicken from the smallest state. Do warn your kids to keep their hands away from the animals, however. A sign by the donkey (who happens to emit an almost melancholy howl unlike anything

*A child can always find a special lap to cuddle up in at the Children's Museum of Rhode Island.*

we've ever heard from a donkey) reads, "Stay back. I can bite." The sign by the pigs is more definite: "Caution! We bite!"

Young equestrians should be sure to see the pair of endearing miniature horses. These compact animals were used to pull ore carts in the English coal mines and were first brought to this country in the late 1800s to work in the mines in West Virginia and Ohio. Today the horses, which measure thirty-four inches or less from the ground to the lowest hair of their mane, are used primarily as pets.

You'll want to visit the Nature Center, where children learn about concepts such as adaptation as they walk past a series of environments that vary from tropical rain forest to desert. Thanks to windows that begin low down on the walls, all the environments are easily visible even to toddlers. At the center's see-through beehive you can watch the worker bees leave the hive and return with pollen and nectar to make into honey. After learning all about the ways in which plants and animals evolve in order to meet the demands of their environment, kids are asked this question: "Humans have a special adaptation which helps them to survive in almost any environment. What is it? Hint: You're using it when you think about this."

As you walk through the zoo, you'll see llamas and wolves, zebras, a camel, monkeys, deer, elk, sea lions, and polar bears. Many of the large animals are housed in spacious outdoor enclosed areas rather than in cages. Be sure to take a look at the unusual ring-tailed lemurs. Found in the wild only on the African island of Madagascar, they live in troops of twelve to twenty. Primitive relatives of the monkey, they leap from trees and hang by their long, striped tails. With red eyes, white faces, and a dark mask around the eyes, the gray-brown creatures are fascinating to watch.

There are exotic birds too, including the ostrich, flamingo, golden eagle, penguin, and wild turkey. You'll encounter common waterfowl as you traverse the network of wooden paths and bridges in the exhibit area devoted to the ecology of wetlands. A visit to the zoo involves a lot of walking, so be sure to bring along a stroller or backpack for the short-legged members of your party.

When you need a break, stop at the café just beyond the zoo entrance; near here you can buy hot dogs, hamburgers, pizza, ice cream, and the like. Eat at a booth inside or outdoors at a round green picnic table.

*Young equestrians should be sure to see the pair of endearing miniature horses.*

The zoo is only the beginning. Drive around the park, and you'll discover all sorts of other features: pony rides, a carousel, even a paddleboat to rent if you want to use your own energy to navigate the ponds. There are about ten connecting waterways. Another way to see them, and to get an introduction to the history of the park at the same time, is to take a twenty-minute narrated trip aboard a small motor launch, which passes under stone bridges as it makes its way from one body of water to another.

The park also contains the Museum of Natural History, with exhibits that include American Indian, Eskimo, and Pacific artifacts, along with displays on earth sciences and regional wildlife. In the Narragansett Bay Room, where exhibits center on local customs and innovations, we learned how the barrier beach–coastal pond complex along the southern Rhode Island coastline was formed. We also learned about Prudence Island Farm, where oysters have been grown in a man-made pond since 1977. The oysters grow by attaching themselves to strings of scallop shells that are hung from a floating grid, and the pond can support about a million of them. At a third exhibit, this one devoted to interpreting the growth of industry in Providence, we discovered that the city was the acknowledged costume jewelry capital of the world in the late nineteenth century. Exhibits rotate frequently, but these are typical of those you will see. The museum also has a planetarium with shows Saturday and Sunday afternoons.

If your kids have never seen oranges growing on trees, take them to the Greenhouses and Gardens, where (depending upon the time of year) they'll see oranges, limes, grapefruit, kumquats, and figs. The greenhouses have broad walkways and are accented with statuary and benches. They're filled with lush and exotic foliage. See if your kids can find the vibrant orange and periwinkle-blue bird of paradise, the prayer plant, the cornstalk plant, a cactus ten feet high. Outside are a well-tended rose garden and a graceful Japanese garden.

Throughout Roger Williams Park you'll find good spots for settling down with a picnic, feeding crumbs to the ducks and geese that frequent the ponds, or perhaps tossing a Frisbee.

For less than the price of a movie, your family can enjoy a good baseball game, courtesy of the **Pawtucket Red Sox,** an affiliate of the Boston Red Sox. The purpose of minor league baseball is to develop new talent so that when the Boston Red Sox run into a problem — perhaps an injured pitcher —

*Young hopefuls get right out there on the field for some hands-on instruction from PawSox players, some of whom may well turn out to be the major league stars of tomorrow.*

they can call on their support club at Pawtucket to fill the void. Fans come to Pawtucket because they want to scout out future Red Sox stars. In recent years they certainly haven't been disappointed. Mike Greenwell and Ellis Burks are just a couple of the players who have moved on to the big time after preparing in Pawtucket. Games are played at small and cozy **McCoy Stadium,** which received a massive face-lift in 1987 and early 1988.

Free youth clinics are scheduled throughout the summer, and you may want to call ahead for specifics. They provide an opportunity for young hopefuls to get right out there on the field for some hands-on instruction from PawSox players, some of whom may well turn out to be the major league stars of tomorrow.

Many amusement parks are sad and seedy, neglected places that look as though they've landed on hard times. Nothing could be further from the truth at **Rocky Point Park,** a cheerful, well-maintained spot with a lively family atmosphere. Part of the reason Rocky Point appears so natty is that each winter the rides are dismantled, adjusted, reassembled, and treated to fresh paint and upholstery. When the park reopens in the spring, it is fresh and sparkling, just like the shimmering waters of neighboring Narragansett Bay. Perched at the edge of the famous bay, Rocky Point regularly enjoys a soft sea breeze, most welcome on a hot summer afternoon.

There's plenty to do here, for toddlers to teens — parents too. The preschool set will enjoy a spin on the miniature helicopters, motorcycles, Red Baron airplanes, and trucks, as well as the full-size merry-go-round. Older kids get a kick out of the sixteen-hundred-foot flume ride (be prepared to get splashed!), New England's only Loop-Corkscrew-Coaster, and the Sky Diver. There are bumper cars and other rides as well. Everyone will enjoy a spin on the Rocky Point Express Train or an aerial journey on the cable cars. Other entertainment includes live rock music performed on an outdoor stage and a skee ball arcade where you can win prizes.

Rocky Point is also a good place to indulge in a classic shore dinner, Rhode Island style. It boasts "the world's largest shore dinner hall," a cavernous modern dining room that overlooks the bay and can seat *four thousand* people. The complete dinner includes olives, relishes, cucumbers and Bermuda onions, brown and white bread, Narragansett baked clams, Rocky Point clam fritters, baked fish, Creole sauce, watermelon — and a boiled lobster or half a

*Among its many options, Roger Williams Park offers good old-fashioned pony rides.*

broiled chicken. Of course, French fries and corn on the cob are also part of the package, in case you're still hungry. The dinner can be ordered at a lower price without the lobster or chicken. For those with a more modest budget or less ambitious appetite, there's another good choice: the all-you-can-eat chowder, clam cakes, and watermelon special. All meals are available in reduced portions (at reduced prices) for kids. With an attractive setting, lots to do, and plenty to eat, Rocky Point Park is a pleasant way to pass the better part of a day.

At the **Slater Mill Historic Site,** you can visit the first factory in America to successfully produce yarn using water-powered carding and spinning frames. During the ninety-minute guided tour (best saved for children twelve and older), which covers the Old Slater Mill and two neighboring buildings, you'll learn about the technical accomplishments that made this possible and about the social changes that accompanied American manufacturing's transition from handcraft to machine production.

It's hard to understand how a machine works just by staring at it, but that's no problem here. The site calls itself "the museum where the machines work," and your guide will demonstrate the operation of many of the machines on exhibit. The sounds and motion of the machinery in action make it easy to imagine what it was like to toil, day after day, in an early factory. For another perspective on the life of a factory worker, you'll visit the Sylvanus Brown House, which is furnished in accordance with possessions listed in an inventory left behind by a nineteenth-century Pawtucket mechanic who died in 1824. The third building on the tour is the Oziel Wilkinson Stone Mill, which has been reconstructed to represent a nineteenth-century machine building shop complete with both woodworking and metalworking equipment.

## ACCESS

**PAWTUCKET.** Go north on I-95 to exit 28 or south on I-95 to exit 29.

**CHILDREN'S MUSEUM OF RHODE ISLAND. Directions:** Take I-95 north to exit 28 (School Street). Cross School Street and go straight up Vernon Street. Turn left on Summit Street and left again on Walcott Street. The museum is the first building on the right, within 5 minutes' drive of I-95. Traveling south on I-95, take exit 29 (Downtown Pawtucket). Stay to the right on Broadway for ¼ mile. Pass the Exchange Street traffic light and then turn left into the Pawtucket Congregational Church/Children's

*A guide demonstrates one of the many working machines at Slater Mill Historic Site.*

Laura Raposa

Museum parking lot. **Season:** Year-round. **Admission:** Charged. **Telephone:** (401) 726-2590.

**ROGER WILLIAMS PARK. Directions:** Take I-95 south to exit 17. Turn left and follow Elmwood Avenue about ½ mile to the park entrance, on your right. **Season:** Year-round. **Admission:** Free to park grounds and museum; admission charged to zoo, planetarium, and for rides. **Telephone:** (401) 421-3300.

**PAWTUCKET RED SOX (McCOY STADIUM). Directions:** Take I-95 south to exit 2A (Newport Avenue, Pawtucket). Follow Newport Avenue 2½ miles. At the light, turn right on Columbus Avenue. McCoy Stadium is approximately 1 mile along Columbus Avenue, on the right. From the south, take I-95 north to exit 28 (School Street). At the bottom of the exit ramp, go right. About 100 feet after the second set of lights, go left on Pond Street. Follow Pond Street ½ mile to stadium. **Season:** April through August. **Admission:** Charged. **Telephone:** (401) 724-7303.

**ROCKY POINT PARK. Directions:** Traveling north or south on I-95, take exit 10 (Route 117) at Apponaug. Follow Route 117 east about 4 miles. Turn right onto Warwick Neck Avenue and left onto Rocky Point Avenue, following signs to park. **Season:** Memorial Day through Labor Day. **Admission:** Charged. **Telephone:** (401) 737-8000.

**SLATER MILL HISTORIC SITE. Directions:** Take I-95 north to exit 28 (School Street). Turn left from the exit ramp, continue straight, then cross Main Street Bridge. Turn right on Roosevelt Avenue and follow to mill site. Traveling south on I-95, take exit 29 (Downtown Pawtucket). Turn right on Fountain Street and right again on Exchange Street. Turn left on Roosevelt Avenue and continue to the mill. **Season:** March through December. **Admission:** Charged. **Telephone:** (401) 725-8638.

**For further information** or restaurant and lodgings suggestions, contact the Greater Providence Convention and Visitors Bureau, 30 Exchange Terrace, Providence, RI 02903. Telephone: (401) 274-1636.

# Newport

An elegant island community with a glamorous past, Newport has been called both "the millionaire's playground" and "the yachting capital of the world." Its traditions of wealth and social prestige are very much in evidence. Newport provides a window into a fascinating, glittery world, quite alien to most of us, and most appealing to children eight years of age and older.

The quickest, pleasantest way to get your bearings is to get out on the water in an hour-long narrated cruise aboard the *Viking Queen.* Sit on one of the wooden benches on the open upper deck or find a cozy spot in the enclosed area below if the weather is raw. Ogle the forest of masts that decorate the edge of the harbor as you head out into the bay to get a waterside view of Newport. You'll cruise beneath Newport Bridge and get a good close-up of "Clingstone," an eighteen-room house built on an island so tiny that it's really nothing more than a clump of rocks. You'll enjoy fine views of the elegant yachts rocking gently at anchor in Brenton Cove, and you may well get a glimpse of modern racing sailboats with their colorful jibs puffed out. The captain's stories about the history and people who make Newport famous are often spiced with mention of past and current real estate prices.

You'll also be able to see several of the famous Newport mansions or "summer cottages," including **Hammersmith Farm,** one of the best to visit with children. In fact, you can combine your cruise with a visit to the farm. Depart by boat from the Goat Island dock on the waterfront in downtown Newport. Cruise through the harbor and bay to the private dock at Hammersmith. Disembark and take a guided tour. Then return to the dock where the boat will pick you up for the return trip to Goat Island.

*Sights such as this are common off Newport, home of The Museum of Yachting.*

Kids like arriving this way, which is (more or less) the way celebrities arrived when Jacqueline Bouvier married John F. Kennedy in 1953. Twelve hundred guests toasted the couple beneath pink-and-white-striped tents on the grounds of Hammersmith Farm, where Jacqueline spent summers as a girl. The only working farm left in Newport, Hammersmith, built in 1887, is the most informal and rustic of the famous "summer cottages." The twenty-eight room, shingled home sits on fifty rolling acres with landscaping that varies from expansive flower gardens to pastures where cows still graze. The broad lawn and meadows stretch down to Narragansett Bay, site of the dock once used to berth the presidential yacht.

Your guided tour of the house begins in the handsome foyer (check out the wonderful mushroom lamp), where you'll receive a short lecture on the history of the house. The house's appearance today results from a massive redecoration effort in 1959, and the luxurious bouquets of fresh flowers found throughout the rooms come from the Hammersmith gardens.

In the dining room, your kids will be pleased to note that the separate table for children is set in an alcove framed with three floor-to-ceiling glass panels overlooking the grounds and the bay. The center panel could be electronically lowered, disappearing into the basement and allowing young diners free access to the great outdoors.

Children also are intrigued to discover that the house has thirteen fireplaces and seventeen bathrooms, and that it was managed by a staff of sixteen servants. They enjoy peeking into bedrooms where famous people like President and Mrs. Kennedy, the Kennedy children, and Indian Prime Ministers Jawaharlal Nehru and Indira Gandhi once slept. You'll see the room that President Kennedy used as an office when in residence at Hammersmith, sometimes called his "Summer White House." From the bedroom windows you'll catch a glimpse of the "castle," a rambling yellow farmhouse lived in today by Mrs. Hugh Auchincloss, whose family has owned Hammersmith for four generations, and where Jacqueline Kennedy Onassis stays when she visits Newport. It's fun to imagine the affluent young summer residents playing backgammon, thumping away at the piano, and generally entertaining themselves in the "Deck Room," where teak beams stripe the ceiling and a stuffed pelican hangs overhead.

*The only working farm left in Newport, Hammersmith, built in 1887, is the most informal and rustic of the famous "summer cottages."*

The house tour takes about forty-five minutes, but you'll want to give your kids plenty of time to run around the grounds. Children tend to fall in love with the miniature horses that congregate just yards away from the gift shop, a children's playhouse in its former life. They also like to explore the nooks and knolls, which include lots of intriguing statuary and gardens, stone arches, and even an alley of silver lindens. As one young man observed, "This place is wicked awesome for hide 'n seek!"

Since mansions are a main reason for visiting Newport, you may well want to visit more than one, but give the kids a lunch break in between and they'll enjoy it more. If you're looking for a quaint or trendy place to eat, you won't have much trouble because Newport is filled with such spots. Finding an inexpensive, simple restaurant is more difficult. For families, the **Newport Creamery** chain, with its extensive sandwich menu and its own ice cream, offers the best bargain.

Want to splurge on a late afternoon snack? **La Patisserie,** a second-story tearoom, is the place to go. With its seven wooden tables, brass fixtures, and lace curtains, it will make you feel as though you've suddenly been transported to a European pastry shop. Children can step right up to the large glass case to select their treats, but it won't be easy. How do you decide between a slice of chocolate toffee torte or chocolate mousse cake? A napoleon or a cream horn? There are also homemade cookies, tiny jewel-like fruit tarts, and individual iced cakes with scrumptious fillings. Add a bottle of fruit juice (or a steaming cup of cappuccino or café au lait), and you're in business. La Patisserie also offers fresh cheese Danish, fruit muffins, scones, croissants, or French bread. Better order up a few to stave off hunger on the trip home at the end of the day.

Once fed, return to sightseeing. Let's face it. Most kids find old house tours boring. They can't get excited about a Duncan Phyfe table or a Chippendale sofa, and one portrait tends to look a lot like another. It's different at **The Astors' Beechwood.** No ordinary mansion tour, this, but an ongoing theatrical presentation where you're part of the action. Explain to your children beforehand that the costumed staff members are assuming nineteenth-century roles and that they won't acknowledge the present. The more you're willing to enter into the game, the better time you'll have at Beechwood, where visitors are cast as Mrs. Astor's guests.

The year is 1891, and the occasion is the tenth anniversary ball (the Astors purchased the cottage in 1881). Throughout your stay the costumed people you meet will familiarize you with the house and help you to get ready for the big event. Instead of

The Astors' Beechwood

*The "staff" at The Astors' Beechwood encourages visitors to get into the act.*

tour guides and ticket takers, you'll make the acquaintance of people like Winifred Crump, who has worked her way up from twentieth to fourth housemaid in just twelve years. Winnie currently spends most of her time cleaning the three-hundred-plus mirrors in the cottage. Or you might be introduced to Trevor Ashley Doddington III, yachtsman, polo player, and philanthropist, who has a reputation for being flirtatious.

Beechwood re-creates Newport's Gilded Age, the late 1800s, when Caroline Schermerhorn Astor presided as the queen of Newport aristocracy. Not only did she have the biggest ballroom in town, but she had it designed with wavelike windows that capture the reflection of the ocean beyond. The idea was to make guests feel as though they were dancing on water, a servant explains, adding, "Me personally, I think it was the wine with the seven-course dinner what made them feel that way."

As the servants show you through the cottage, they discuss their mistress. You'll learn that Mrs. Astor was a devoted mother — "why she spent a full half hour a day with her children!" — and that she constantly bickered with her next-door neighbors, the Vanderbilts — "they only spent ten minutes a day with their children." You'll discover that twenty-four varieties of roses grow in the garden and that Mrs. Astor arranged to have the red and white roses bred to create the pink that is known as the Astor Rose. You'll also discover that in ten years, Mr. Astor has spent only two weeks at Beechwood. He much prefers to gad about on his yacht.

As you head for the grand staircase, the servant points out that of course those under the age of eighteen may not use it. (Tell him your kids are nineteen, just short for their age, and you'll be able to slip them by.) Upstairs you'll tour the bedrooms, and a ladies' maid will help you store your gowns ("you brought forty or fifty of them with you for the season, didn't you ma'am?"). In Mr. Astor's room you'll see a painting of his yacht — "all women aboard, and not a lady among them," observes the maid, shaking her head in disapproval.

At this point you'll be given over to the care of one Angus MacTavish, a gardener, who treats you to a glimpse of the servants' quarters. ("The girls aren't allowed to have gentlemen callers," he explains, "but they are allowed to have relatives, and it's amazing what a lot of brothers, uncles, and cousins they turn up.") He'll then take you to the kitchen for a sample of Mrs. Astor's famous strawberry tea, before usher-

*The more you're willing to enter into the game, the better time you'll have at Beechwood, where visitors are cast as Mrs. Astor's guests.*

ing you out into the garden and back into the twentieth century.

Before leaving, cross the spacious back lawn leading toward the ocean. Go through the gate, and you'll find yourself on Cliff Walk, the famous footpath that cleaves to the very edge of the Atlantic. As the name indicates, the path is high and the drop on the ocean side treacherous, so do be sure to keep a hand on small children; toddlers are best off in backpacks. If you turn right, you'll walk past Marble House (rumor has it that suffragettes hung out and smoked cigars in the Chinese teahouse in its garden). Turn to the left, and you'll pass Rosecliff (modeled after the Grand Trianon at Versailles) and The Breakers (inspired by an Italian Renaissance palace). With the ocean on one side, the mansions on the other, Cliff Walk is mighty impressive.

For a picnic spot with a water view, try **Fort Adams State Park,** named for one of the largest seacoast fortifications in the country. The existing fort was built in 1824. It was designed to accommodate twenty-four hundred men and 468 cannon during time of war, but at no time in its history was it fully armed or garrisoned. You can't tour the fort, but you can walk around the outside.

The park has picnic tables, fireplaces, two fishing piers, a small beach, and several playing fields. At **The Museum of Yachting,** located on the park grounds, photographs, models, and nautical artifacts document "The Golden Age of Yachting — 1885–1914," when Newport earned its reputation as a playground for the rich. The park is also the home of the **Fort Adams Sailing Association,** Rhode Island's only public sailing facility. Sailboats varying in length from six to twenty-four feet are available for rent (at very reasonable fees) by the hour or by the half day. Call ahead for additional information.

Newport pays homage to tennis as well as yachting. If there are any serious players in your brood, you should make a stop at **The International Tennis Hall of Fame,** which is housed in the former Newport Casino, an elegant Victorian complex with lots of latticework. American lawn tennis got its start right here at the Casino, where the first National Championships were held from 1881 until 1915, when the tournament moved to Forest Hills, New York. One room is devoted to court tennis, another to the Davis Cup. There are also displays of tennis art, tennis memorabilia, and tennis trophies, along with exhibits that focus on the manufacture of tennis equipment and tennis fashions. The casino has a

Michael Baz/International Tennis Hall of Fame

*American lawn tennis got its start right here, where the International Tennis Hall of Fame is now located.*

450-seat theater where tennis films are shown. It also boasts a dozen grass courts, the only such courts in the country open to the public. But that's not all. There's also a restored court tennis court, like the ones royalty enjoyed in thirteenth-century Europe.

Before leaving the Newport area, consider a side trip to Portsmouth, where you can visit the **Green Animals Topiary Gardens.** It takes only about twenty minutes to drive to the gardens from downtown Newport, but if you'd like to turn the trip into an adventure, consider traveling by train aboard the **Old Colony and Newport Railway,** with its 1930s vintage equipment. The trip takes about forty minutes each way, with a fifty-minute layover at the gardens.

Topiary, which has been practiced for centuries, is the art of manicuring living plants into geometric figures and animal shapes. The gardens here contain more than eighty examples of topiary including sixteen animals and birds. See if your kids can find the giraffe, the ostrich, the mountain goats, the elephant. Finding them is particularly fun because the gardens are crisscrossed by a maze of pathways that incorporate other features such as rose arbors, a very proper pet cemetery, and espaliered trees. A small museum houses a good collection of antique toys and children's furniture.

Preservation Society of Newport County

*Is it a plant or an animal? Kids can decide for themselves at Portsmouth's Green Animals Topiary Gardens.*

## ACCESS

**NEWPORT.** From the north, follow I-95 south to Providence. Take I-195 east to Route 114. Follow Route 114 south into Newport. From the south, follow either I-95 or Route 1 to Route 138. Take Route 138 east to Route 114 south into Newport.

**VIKING BOAT CRUISES. Directions:** Follow Route 114 (which becomes Broadway) south to Summer Street. Turn right on Summer Street, which becomes Vanzandt Avenue. Turn left on Second Street. Go 10 blocks and turn right on Marsh Street. Marsh Street becomes a causeway leading to Goat Island. After crossing causeway, bear left to parking area and ticket office. **Season:** Mid-May through mid-October. **Admission:** Charged. **Telephone:** (401) 847-6921.

**HAMMERSMITH FARM. Directions:** From Route 114 in Newport, follow signs for Ocean Drive and Fort Adams State Park. Hammersmith is adjacent to Fort Adams. **Season:** April through October; weekends in March and November. **Admission:** Charged. **Telephone:** (401) 846-0420.

**NEWPORT CREAMERY. Directions:** Located at 208 West Main Street, 181 Bellevue Avenue, and 49 Long Wharf Mall in Newport. **Season:** Year-round. **Admission:**

Free. **Telephone:** In order that branches are listed above (401) 846-2767; (401) 846-6332; (401) 849-8469.

**LA PATISSERIE. Directions:** Follow Route 114 (Broadway) into Newport. Turn right on Washington Square (where Broadway comes to an end), then left on Thames Street. Located on the second floor at 136 Thames Street in downtown Newport. **Season:** Year-round. **Admission:** Free. **Telephone:** (401) 847-0194.

**THE ASTORS' BEECHWOOD. Directions:** From Thames Street, turn left on Touro Street. Continue several blocks and turn right on Bellevue Avenue. Located on Bellevue Avenue in Newport. **Season:** June through October. **Admission:** Charged. **Telephone:** (401) 846-3772.

**FORT ADAMS STATE PARK. Directions:** From Route 114, follow signs for Ocean Drive and Fort Adams. **Season:** Year-round. **Admission:** Parking fee charged during the summer. **Telephone:** (401) 847-2400.

**THE MUSEUM OF YACHTING. Directions:** Located in Fort Adams State Park. **Season:** Memorial Day through Columbus Day. **Admission:** Charged. **Telephone:** (401) 847-1018.

**FORT ADAMS SAILING ASSOCIATION. Directions:** Located in Fort Adams State Park. **Season:** Mid-June through September. **Admission:** Boat rental fees. **Telephone:** (401) 849-8385.

**THE INTERNATIONAL TENNIS HALL OF FAME. Directions:** Located in the Newport Casino at 194 Bellevue Avenue. **Season:** Year-round. **Admission:** Charged. **Telephone:** (401) 849-3990.

**GREEN ANIMALS TOPIARY GARDENS. Directions:** From downtown Newport, take Route 114 north about 10 miles to Portsmouth. Turn onto Cory's Lane and follow signs to garden. **Season:** May through September; weekends in October. **Admission:** Charged. **Telephone:** (401) 847-1000.

**OLD COLONY AND NEWPORT RAILWAY. Directions:** Follow Route 114 (Broadway) into Newport. Where road forks, bear right on West Broadway. Continue several blocks and then turn right on Marlborough Street. Marlborough becomes West Marlborough, which ends at intersection with America's Cup Avenue. Turn left on America's Cup Avenue and continue to terminal, located across from the Newport Fire Department Headquarters. **Season:** July through Labor Day. **Admission:** Charged. **Telephone:** (401) 624-6951.

**For further information** or restaurant and lodgings suggestions, contact the Rhode Island Tourism Division, 7 Jackson Walkway, Providence, RI 02903. Telephone: (401) 277-2601.

# VERMONT

Paul O. Boisvert/New England Culinary Institute

*Depend on Vermont — and the student chefs at Montpelier's New England Culinary Institute — to serve up something extra special for the entire family.*

## Arlington and Manchester

Luxuriate in the splendor of some of the Green Mountain State's handsomest mountains and what some call its loveliest river as you explore Arlington and Manchester in southwestern Vermont. Here you can introduce your children to the pleasure and tranquility of a wilderness canoe trip even if you have never lifted a paddle before. Hike in the mountains, catch trout in a stream so clear you can see the fish glide by, or cross-country ski along trails that used to belong to Abraham Lincoln's descendants.

Off on a side road in Arlington, Jim and JoAnn Walker operate **Battenkill Canoe, Ltd.** Their purpose is to introduce visitors to the beauty and soothing qualities of Vermont's rivers and to provide fun and adventure at a set-it-yourself pace. Canoes can be rented for a minimum of one and a half hours, but Battenkill Canoe recommends you allow yourselves at least three hours to experience the river. Children must be six years of age or older. Other than that, there are few rules.

*At Battenkill Canoe the emphasis is on "unhurried floating."*

At Battenkill Canoe the emphasis is on "unhurried floating." Staff members take the time to talk over your trip with you. If you're a novice, they give you paddling pointers. Lessons are available too, but you don't need formal instruction to spend a pleasant day on the Battenkill. Some families prefer to set out and learn as they go while others like to take a family lesson first.

The Battenkill, or " 'Kill," is a Class 1 river, which means it has no white water and no standing waves. It does have a good current and a mile of what is labeled "quick water." A twisty, narrow river, the 'Kill passes through heavily wooded areas as well as past open fields. At Arlington proper you'll come to a red covered bridge where you may want to take time out for a swim. The river varies in depth from several inches to twenty feet, and right below the bridge is a favorite place for taking a dip. Gravel bars have developed in the river too, some adjoining the riverbanks and others forming islands in the middle of the water. Some of them are so established that they are covered with grass and wildflowers. They also make great places for taking a break and doing some sunning or swimming.

The 'Kill is famous for its trout fishing, and if you call in advance, Battenkill Canoe will arrange a guided float fishing trip. An expert angler will take you to the choicest spots and introduce you to techniques of canoe scouting, such as how to paddle without scaring the fish. The wildlife you'll encounter along the river isn't limited to fish, however. The great blue heron, osprey, and kingfisher often make appearances, as do many other kinds of birds.

Each rental includes a premium Blue Hole canoe, life vests, cushions for children to sit on, paddles, and a waterproof dry bag for the protection of your camera, wallet, or other objects that shouldn't get wet. Two adults and two children can be accommodated in one canoe. Rental fees also include shuttle service, which means a staff member will meet you at a prearranged spot along the river to transport you back to the starting point and your car. All in all, Battenkill Canoe makes a river trip convenient and simple. Just be sure to pack a picnic suited to the appetite you're likely to work up afloat.

For a truly memorable experience, combine canoeing with camping. Set out for a couple of days on the river, pulling up at **Camping on the Battenkill** to spend the night. There are 102 sites here, mostly wooded with some in an open meadow. Tent campers are separated from recreational vehicles. Amenities include flush toilets, hot showers, and a playground. Fishing and swimming in the river are the most popular activities. The campground has been in business for more than twenty-five years and attracts lots of repeat customers, so reservations are essential, and they must be secured by a deposit. Single night stays are possible during the week but not on weekends.

While you're in Arlington, it's fun to shop or browse at **Candle Mill Village,** a complex of eight craft and specialty shops housed in three old buildings: an eighteenth-century grist mill, a hay barn, and a colonial house where Tories conducted secret gatherings during the revolutionary war. The buildings are perched on the banks of a mountain stream complete with its own small waterfall and rock ledges that are fun to clamber over. Picnicking is encouraged, and wading is quite all right too.

The village takes its name from the Candle Mill, which stocks about fifty thousand candles. There are candles in the shapes of animals, plants, and cupcakes, candles that float, and candles that drip in a rainbow of colors. You can even dip your own. Just purchase some plain candles and carry them over to the pots of colored melted wax. Following a series of quick dips, your candle will be different from anyone else's. (Be sure to supervise your kids carefully with the hot wax.)

Another store that particularly appeals to kids is the Rosebud Toy Company, where you are greeted by a sign that proclaims "Unattended children will be towed away." Along with a tempting selection of sophisticated imported and educational toys, there are lots of inexpensive items to choose from. You'll find bins and boxes filled with spinning tops, squirt guns in animal shapes, long flexible pencils, friction toys, wind-up dinosaurs, and miniature paint sets. Kids are free to play with the wooden train, but otherwise they'll need to exercise some restraint. As a sign posted by a life-size stuffed bear and her cubs clearly states, "If you touch my children, I will bite

*Rosebud Toy Company's "bearatorium" contains well over two hundred "species" of the popular shaggy beast.*

Rosebud Toy Co.

you. If you touch me, the proprietor will bite you." Populated by an eclectic selection of beasts, the "bearatorium" contains well over two hundred species, ranging from Napoleon Bearnaparte, who sports gold epaulets, to Ms. Bearman of the Board, nattily turned out in a pin-striped suit and a great role model for ambitious young women.

From Arlington it's just a fifteen-minute ride to Manchester, where you can visit **Hildene,** a twenty-four-room Georgian revival mansion built by Robert Todd Lincoln, son of President Abraham Lincoln. A brief slide show chronicles Robert's major achievements, including his tenure as secretary of war under President Garfield and as minister to Great Britain under President Harrison. In Robert's study your kids will see one of Honest Abe's famous stovepipe hats. In addition to hearing bits of gossip about the house's residents, they'll appreciate some of the architectural features like the pulley-operated dumbwaiter used to haul wine, luggage, furniture, and firewood from one floor to another.

"Hildene" means "hill and valley," and the setting for this 412-acre estate is as much a draw as the house. There are gardens to explore and footpaths to hike, varying from the Meadow Trail, an easy twenty-minute stroll, to the Cliff Trail, a more demanding mile-and-a-half walk that will take an hour or more depending upon the age and endurance of your offspring. In winter these trails and many others are groomed for cross-country skiing. Rental equipment is available, and hot drinks are dispensed in the warming hut.

No matter what time of year you visit, a stop at **Mother Myrick's Confectionery and Ice Cream Parlor** is essential. Splurge on scrumptious cakes and pastries. Wallow in the pure indulgence of Moonlight in Vermont (two scoops of vanilla crowned with Vermont maple syrup, whipped cream, and chopped walnuts) or drown your sorrows in a Mud Season Special (chocolate and coffee ice cream with butterscotch fudge and malt on top). All the traditional sundaes are served up too. The atmosphere is festive and upbeat, everything you could want in an ice cream parlor even if Mother Myrick's didn't have another drawing card, which it does — the candy room. Here you can watch the candy cooks stir fudge, dip buttercrunch in chocolate, and mold batches of sinfully sweet stuff on marble slabs. The aroma is so rich you'll feel as though you could put on pounds just by inhaling. You can buy the candy by weight or opt for one of

*Wallow in the pure indulgence of Moonlight in Vermont or drown your sorrows in a Mud Season Special.*

Peter Cooper/Hildene

*Beautiful Hildene encompasses 412 acres of gardens and footpaths. Cross-country skiing takes place here in winter.*

the dozens of nifty novelty containers filled with sweets of every imaginable persuasion.

Each of the three tracks at the **Bromley Alpine Slide and Scenic Chairlift** is more than two-thirds of a mile long. Control your own speed on the slide, traveling as fast or slow as you like down the mountain on a small sled. Or try a chair lift ride to the summit of Bromley Mountain, where you'll savor a spectacular panorama that encompasses parts of five states. You can descend from the 3,260-foot summit via chair lift, or you can hike down, taking time to enjoy the scenery and perhaps a picnic along the way.

If you pass through Bennington on your way to or from the Arlington/Manchester area, consider a refueling stop at **Mother Hubbard's** in downtown, the perfect spot for a late breakfast, lunch, or mid-afternoon calorie-laden snack. For lunch choose from soups, quiches, and cold and hot sandwiches (yes, you can get a hot dog). Mother Hubbard's also serves up tempting Danish pastries, fresh-baked cookies, and super-chunky ice cream. Nearby, **Geannelis'** has earned a reputation for serving good solid Vermont breakfasts (from blueberry muffins to homemade sausage) in an unpretentious, down-home setting.

Located in a sprawling red barn just south of Bennington, **Southern Vermont Orchards** sells apples, cider, and all sorts of other country food products. Inside the barn visitors can watch cider making (in season). A separate area in the barn houses a baking operation, which can be viewed through large windows. A cider donut accompanied by a cup of cider (cold or hot mulled) from the help-yourself counter makes a great snack. Just west of town visit **Fairdale Farms** to find out what happens to milk from the time it arrives by truck (from Vermont,

Mother Myrick's

*The aroma is so rich you'll feel as though you could put on pounds just by inhaling at Mother Myrick's.*

Massachusetts, and New York) to the time it's ready for the supermarket. You'll see where milk is pasteurized and homogenized. You might also see thousands of tiny half pints traveling along conveyor belts on their way to becoming part of someone's school lunch.

If time allows you to dawdle a while in Bennington, the town offers two attractions with kid-appeal. The **Bennington Battle Monument,** Vermont's tallest structure, honors the untrained Yankee soldiers who held their own against some of Europe's best-trained, best-equipped troops in the 1777 revolutionary war Battle of Bennington. The three-hundred-foot monolith, built in the late 1800s, offers spectacular views of the valleys and hills of Vermont, Massachusetts, and New York.

Not far away is the 1865 **Park-McCullough House,** a thirty-five-room mansion graced with eighteen fireplaces and ornately decorated in true Victorian fashion. The furnishings are those that actually belonged to three generations of the family that lived here. During the forty-five-minute guided tour be sure to notice the wonderful tricycle in the children's room, built in the form of a sulky and racehorse. Before the tour you might want to enjoy a leisurely round of croquet on the front lawn, or check out the carriage barn with its fine collection of carriages and sleighs as well as a children's playhouse, a replica of the main house.

## ACCESS

**ARLINGTON/MANCHESTER.** Follow Route 7 north, then Historic Route 7A north to Arlington. Continue north on Route 7A for 12 miles to Manchester.

**BATTENKILL CANOE, LTD. Directions:** Located ½ mile west of Historic Route 7A on Route 313 in Arlington. **Season:** May through October. **Admission:** Rental and instruction fees. **Telephone:** (802) 375-9559.

**CAMPING ON THE BATTENKILL. Directions:** Located on Historic Route 7A in Arlington. **Season:** Mid-April through October. **Admission:** Charged. **Telephone:** (802) 375-6663.

**CANDLE MILL VILLAGE. Directions:** Follow Historic Route 7A north to East Arlington Road. Turn right. At fork, bear right on Old Mill Road. Candle Mill Village will be on your right. **Season:** Year-round. **Admission:** Free. **Telephone:** The Candle Mill (802) 375-6068; Rosebud Toy Company (802) 375-2839.

**HILDENE. Directions:** Located on Historic Route 7A in Manchester Village, 2 miles south of the junction of Routes

7A and 30. **Season:** Mid-May through October; reopens for cross-country skiing in the winter. **Admission:** Charged. **Telephone:** (802) 362-1788.

**MOTHER MYRICK'S CONFECTIONERY AND ICE CREAM PARLOR. Directions:** Located on Route 7A in Manchester Center. **Season:** Year-round. **Admission:** Free. **Telephone:** (802) 362-1560.

**BROMLEY ALPINE SLIDE AND SCENIC CHAIRLIFT. Directions:** Follow Route 7A north to Route 11. Turn right. Located 6 miles east of Manchester on Route 11 in Peru. **Season:** Alpine slide from Memorial Day through Columbus Day. **Admission:** Charged. **Telephone:** (802) 824-5522.

**BENNINGTON.** Follow I-91 to exit 2. Follow Route 9 west to Bennington.

**MOTHER HUBBARD'S. Directions:** Located at 431 Main Street (Route 9) in downtown Bennington. **Season:** Year-round. **Admission:** Free. **Telephone:** (802) 447-0740

**GEANNELIS'. Directions:** Located at 520 Main Street (Route 9) in downtown Bennington. **Season:** Year-round. **Admission:** Free. **Telephone:** (802) 442-9778

**SOUTHERN VERMONT ORCHARDS. Directions:** Located 1½ miles south of Bennington on Route 7. **Season:** Mid-August through December. **Admission:** Free. **Telephone:** (802) 447-0714.

**FAIRDALE FARMS. Directions:** Located on Route 9, about 2 miles west of the intersection of routes 7 and 9 in downtown Bennington. **Season:** Mid-May through Labor Day; weekends until Columbus Day. **Admission:** Free. **Telephone:** (802) 442-6391.

**BENNINGTON BATTLE MONUMENT. Directions:** Follow Route 9 west past the Bennington Museum. Where Route 9 bears sharply left, about ⅛ mile past museum, bear right onto access road to the monument. **Season:** April through October. **Admission:** Charged. **Telephone:** (802) 447-0550.

**PARK-McCULLOUGH HOUSE. Directions:** Follow Route 9 west to Route 7 north to Route 7A (Northside Drive). Turn left on Route 7A, then right on Park Street, then left on West Street. Follow signs. **Season:** Late May through October. **Admission:** Charged. **Telephone:** (802) 442-5441.

**For further information** or restaurant and lodgings suggestions, contact the Manchester-and-the-Mountains Chamber of Commerce, P.O. Box 928, Manchester Center, VT 05255. Telephone: (802) 362-2100.

# Montpelier

**A** visit to Montpelier, Vermont's state capital, is a living history lesson. The attractive, gold-domed state house is friendly and accessible, a place where it's easy to see that government involves real people. Today's State House is Vermont's third. The first State House, a ten-sided wooden structure warmed by a two-story stove, was built in the early 1800s and torn down in 1836 because of overcrowding and deterioration. It was replaced by a second State House, set on a rise and modeled after a Greek temple.

A fire in 1857 destroyed just about everything except the granite columns on the portico. (During construction it had taken a team of four horses eighteen hours to transport a load of granite to Montpelier from the Barre quarries, about ten miles distant.) The columns were incorporated into the present building.

Vermont's is one of thirteen state capitols crowned with a genuine gold dome. Right up on top of the dome stands a white pine statue of Ceres, the Roman goddess of agriculture. And there's a lightning rod on top of her!

The **Vermont State House Tour** takes about twenty minutes. When you enter, take a good close look at the black-and-white checkered floor made from Vermont marble. With a bit of sleuthing, kids will find fossil imprints in some of the squares. The building has other idiosyncrasies too, like the cast iron stairs and balustrades, designed out of fear of another fire.

Upstairs your guide will show you the ceremonial office restored to its 1857 look. As you admire the restored Civil War flags, you'll learn that Vermont sent more men to fight and die in the Civil War than any other state. The tour also takes you into the D-shaped Representatives Hall, with its elaborate molded plaster ceiling, where Vermont's 150 state representatives plunk down in the same seats originally installed in the building in 1859. The thirty thronelike red chairs that fan out from either side of the speaker's desk are used by the state senators when the two houses of the legislature meet in joint session. In the green-carpeted Senate Chamber you'll see the tub chairs and black walnut desks used by state senators here since 1859.

The Legislature is usually in session from January through April, and you are welcome to take a seat in the gallery at the back of either room to watch

*Ceres, goddess of agriculture, stands atop Vermont's gold-domed state capitol.*

the proceedings (formal tours are not conducted at this time of year). If you do, you may be surprised to see some very young faces at work. Each winter eighteen eighth-grade students from throughout the state are chosen to spend eight weeks at the State House working as pages.

Just two doors away in the Pavilion Building you can visit the **Vermont Museum,** where the emphasis is on state history, including the early Indian occupation and the effect of the development of railroad and industry. The intriguing artifacts include the stuffed "King of the American Forest," the last panther shot in Vermont, back in 1881, and a plaster cast of a paw print left behind by a panther sighted in Randolph in 1941 and never apprehended.

The museum is not a stuffy place. As the brochure explains, "While boisterous behavior is not condoned, we do not expect visitors to move through the museum on tiptoe or limit their conversations to whispers." There are things to touch, and there's a "What is it?" case filled with old-time treasures to identify. See if you can find the sleeve holders (used to keep sleeves from drooping in the soup) and the snowball knocker (for getting snow out of a horse's hooves). In the Victoriana case you may find more intriguing items such as jewelry made from hair and a glass vial for collecting tears.

*See if you can find the sleeve holders (used to keep sleeves from drooping in the soup) and the snowball knocker (for getting snow out of a horse's hooves).*

If you'd like to have an elegant dinner but your kids don't trust any food with a sauce and your wallet throbs at the thought of ordering them pricey dishes they'll just ignore, try the **Elm Street Café,** a few minutes' walk from the museum and the State House. The café is the hands-on laboratory site for first-year students at the New England Culinary Institute, which trains future professional chefs. The prices are moderate for the types of dishes served, and the staff is always cheerful about fixing up a bit of plain pasta or chicken to placate a finicky young eater while parents savor more intriguing fare. There are even booster seats for little kids.

Sample items from the dinner menu include baked Vermont goat cheese in phyllo pastry and New England seafood stew. Lunch features imaginative soups like chilled cucumber beet borscht, and there's always a pasta special — cheese tortellini Alfredo with prosciutto and fresh basil, the day we stopped by.

If you're the sort of family that loves to eat a big breakfast out, start your day at the café. Conservative kids can feast on French toast, eggs, and pancakes, while more adventurous adults might choose buckwheat crêpes filled with fresh fruit and sour cream or shirred eggs with salmon and chives. Side orders include scones, croissants, and muffins made at the school's La Brioche bake shop just up the street, where you'll also find wonderful cookies, tortes, and pastries to eat there or take out. The bakery shares space with **Tubbs Restaurant,** where second-year students prepare mostly French cuisine. This is a more elegant establishment than the café, but the staff is very friendly and welcomes children. The menu tends to be pricey at dinner, but lunch is imaginative yet reasonable.

Now take a side trip just outside of town to **Morse Farm,** where sugaring is more than a seasonal event. If you visit in March or April, you'll see the sugar house in full swing, sticky and steamy, as the sap is transformed into syrup. At other times of the year, "Old Harry," who has lived on the farm all his life, will show you around the shack and tell you all about the equipment and how it functions. He'll also show you some slides that give a feeling for what it's like out tapping trees in the sugarbush. We noticed that in one picture the worker was wearing snowshoes. We wondered if that meant the slide was taken way back when, but Harry assured us that it was just last winter. Technology has affected much about the way the farm does its business — but not everything. Today twenty-five miles of blue plastic tubing are used to route the sap from the three thousand trees to the sugar house. In the past sap collected from individual trees was hauled down by a team of animals. Yet snowshoes are still the best way for workers to get to the trees to tend the tubing and see

*Snowshoes are still the best way for workers to get to the trees to tend the tubing and see to other chores when the snow is deep, as it often is in this part of Vermont.*

*It's unanimous! The cookies at the New England Culinary Institute are as good as you'll find anywhere.*

to other chores when the snow is deep, as it often is in this part of Vermont.

After spending about twenty minutes in the sugar house, you can choose Morse-grown produce to take home — pumpkins in the fall, strawberries in the early summer, and sweet corn in the late summer and early fall. The large gift shop offers country-style souvenirs and Vermont-made syrups, jellies, and condiments. Feel free to bring along a picnic to enjoy on the open deck overlooking a field of cows or in the enclosed porch where there are picnic tables. Actually you can put together a pretty respectable lunch right on the spot since the shop sells fresh-baked bread, Vermont cheeses, a bit of produce, and the like. The day we visited, we were able to buy some strawberries, a bag of fresh baking powder biscuits, and a container of fresh cream from the dairy case, to assemble some pretty respectable, although somewhat messy, strawberry shortcake.

Within half an hour's drive of Montpelier, you can learn how three other very different Vermont industries operate. Begin with a visit to the **Rock of Ages Quarry** in Barre. Actually there are several operating quarries here, producing the granite for monuments, sidings, floors, and other building parts. Stop at the Tourist Center for a look at the exhibits and to purchase tickets for a twenty-five-minute ride aboard the Rock of Ages Railroad. Kids feel as if they're right in the midst of the action as the diesel locomotive hauls the open railway car to the work area and the guide explains the skills and responsibilities associated with the different tasks undertaken by the quarriers you see at work.

You can also take a guided walking tour, or you can opt for a self-guided visit to the observation platform where you'll look out over a 350-foot hole that has been worked for well over a century. You'll get a sense of the rigors of quarrying as you gaze at the huge piles of "grout," granite not worthy of use in finished products because of its imperfections.

Gazing skyward you'll notice a maze of cables that support and operate the huge derricks, each of which can heft a forty-ton-plus load of granite. The same derricks ferry quarriers down to their work stations, but you'll also notice dozens of ladders. That's because many men prefer to rely on their own power to get in and out of the quarry. They wear safety helmets for protection against falling objects, goggles to protect their eyes, and earplugs to ward off the hearing loss that can be a hazard of working in such a noisy place. Because of the noise, the men communicate via a complex system of hand signals. Watch carefully to see if you can detect any "silent conversations." Before leaving this area, kids can climb aboard stationary "Hercules," an old locomotive that served the Barre and Chelsea Railroad and then the Rock of Ages Quarry before her retirement in 1958.

You can also visit the Craftsman Center to see how the mined granite is transformed into finished products. An elevated observation deck provides good viewing of the center below (which is bigger than two football fields), where cranes, forklifts, and conveyor belts are all part of the scene. Polishing, shaping, and hand-carving operations can also be observed.

Quite another type of product is produced at the **Ben & Jerry's Ice Cream Factory** in Waterbury. Ben & Jerry's product has become a part of Vermont folklore; and while the company has fanciful ice cream parlors in other parts of the state, this is the one and only factory. This is where *all* their ice cream is produced (rumor has it that expansion is on the

*Ben Cohen and Jerry Greenfield — the Ben and Jerry — are floating along on the success of their Vermont-made premium ice cream.*

Ben & Jerry's

horizon). It took five thousand cows to produce the milk needed to make the 2.5 million gallons of Ben & Jerry's ice cream churned out in 1986.

Your tour begins with a light-hearted slide show that underscores the fact that Ben and Jerry are just regular guys, that they are not your typical executive types. They got their start in the business by taking a five-dollar correspondence course in ice cream making back in 1977. Both got "A" in the course. You'll also discover that due to their unorthodox means of raising the capital necessary to build the factory, one out of every one hundred families in Vermont owns a share of the business.

The glassed-in mezzanine in the factory looks down on a sea of machinery including homogenizer, pasteurizer, flavor vat, and freezers. Your guide explains the nine steps involved in producing Ben & Jerry's ice cream: blending, pasteurizing, homogenizing, flavoring, freezing, adding chunks, packaging, bundling, hardening. The factory makes ice cream sixteen hours a day six days a week. Everyone gets a free sample at the end of the tour, but it will only whet your appetite for a more substantial treat.

That's no problem because there's a large ice cream stand right on the premises. Make your choice from "Today's Euphoric Flavors," like Cherry Garcia, Heath Bar Crunch, White Russian, New York Chocolate Fudge, and Fresh Georgia Peach. Eat your ice cream in a standard sugar cone or cart it off in a vanilla or chocolate homemade waffle cone. Opt for a fresh fruit sundae or try a chocolate chip cookie sandwich on a stick. If your group is large and ravenous, considering taking time out to devour a "Vermonster": 20 scoops of ice cream, 10 scoops chopped walnuts, 7 scoops fresh strawberries, 5 scoops whipped cream, 4 scoops bananas, 4 scoops hot fudge, 3 scoops chocolate chip cookies, 2 scoops each Heath Bars, M&M's, Reese's Pieces, chocolate jimmies, and one giant homemade brownie.

At the picnic tables and lawn swings out front you can eat your ice cream overlooking a panorama of cows and mountains. One night each week in the summer, Ben & Jerry's shows outdoor movies. Bring your own chairs or blankets and hunker down to eat your sweet stuff while you watch a free full-length feature film beneath a starry Vermont sky. Shows begin at dusk. (Call for the day of the week.)

The factory also includes a large gift shop where the emphasis is on the humble cow. You'll find some mighty endearing stuffed bovines here, along with cows on mugs, T-shirts, table mats, toy trucks, jewel-

*It took five thousand cows to produce the milk needed to make the 2.5 million gallons of Ben & Jerry's ice cream churned out in 1986.*

ry, stationery, stickers, pot holders, purses, and just about anything else you might imagine.

Just two miles from the ice cream factory drop in at **Cold Hollow Cider Mill** to learn how apple cider is made. Depending upon when you visit, you might also see the production of cider jelly. Cider is made fresh daily except during July and August when the apple supply runs low and a movie about cider making is shown instead. Free samples — fresh and chilly in the summer, hot and spicy in the winter — are part of the fun.

Cold Hollow Cider Mill incorporates a large gift shop filled with Vermont food specialties including, naturally, pure maple syrup. Papier-mâché figures illustrate the evolution of maple syrup production from the time of the American Indians up to today. A movie about maple syrup making, *The Flavor of Vermont,* is shown year-round on request.

The gift shop includes a bakery where you can feast on fresh apple cider donuts, muffins, and chunky homemade cookies. Or buy fresh bread, cobbler, or strudel to take home.

*Free samples — fresh and chilly in the summer, hot and spicy in the winter — are part of the fun.*

## ACCESS

**MONTPELIER.** Follow I-89 to exit 8, which places you on Memorial Drive. Take first left on Bailey Avenue, then first right on State Street.

**VERMONT STATE HOUSE TOUR. Directions:** Located in the capitol, on State Street. **Season:** July through October, Monday through Friday. **Admission:** Free. **Telephone:** (802) 828-2228.

**VERMONT MUSEUM. Directions:** Located in the Pavilion Building at 109 State Street adjacent to the capitol. **Season:** Year-round. **Admission:** Donation requested. **Telephone:** (802) 828-2291.

**ELM STREET CAFÉ. Directions:** Traveling on State Street with the state capitol on your left, continue to first major intersection (court house on the left-hand corner) and turn left on Elm Street. Located at 38 Elm Street. **Season:** Year-round; closed the last 2 weeks of May and November. **Admission:** Free. **Telephone:** (802) 223-3188.

**TUBBS RESTAURANT. Directions:** Located at 24 Elm Street, Jailhouse Common. **Season:** Year-round; closed the last 2 weeks of May and November. **Admission:** Free. **Telephone:** (802) 229-9202.

**MORSE FARM. Directions:** From Main Street in Montpelier, follow signs to farm, which is on County Road. (Main Street becomes County Road.) **Season:** Year-round. **Admission:** Free. **Telephone:** (802) 223-2740.

**ROCK OF AGES QUARRY. Directions:** Take exit 6 off I-89 and continue 4 miles to Route 14. Cross Route 14 and continue about 3 miles, following signs to quarry. **Season:** May through October; train operates June through September. **Admission:** Free; charge for train ride. **Telephone:** (802) 476-3115.

**BEN & JERRY'S ICE CREAM FACTORY. Directions:** Follow I-89 to exit 10. Follow Route 100 north about 1 mile. Entrance on the left. **Season:** Year-round. **Admission:** Charged. **Telephone:** (802) 244-5641.

**COLD HOLLOW CIDER MILL. Directions:** Follow I-89 to exit 10. Follow Route 100 north 2½ miles to Waterbury Center. Mill is on the right. **Season:** Year-round. **Admission:** Free. **Telephone:** (802) 244-8771.

**For further information** or lodgings and restaurant suggestions, contact the Central Vermont Chamber of Commerce, Granger Road, Berlin, VT 05602. Telephone: (802) 229-4619.

# St. Johnsbury

The only town with this name anywhere in the world, St. Johnsbury is recognized as the cultural, retail, and industrial core of the Northeast Kingdom, that corner of Vermont that snuggles between the upper Connecticut River and the Canadian border. Notable events in the town's history include the 1831 invention of the platform scale by Thaddeus Fairbanks and the innovation of flavoring tobacco with maple sugar attributed to one George C. Cary. Today the name Fairbanks is nearly synonymous with scales, and maple products are distributed all around the world from St. Johnsbury. While you are in the area, you'll have the opportunity to tour a maple factory, as well as a factory involved in the production of a second traditional Vermont food specialty, cheese.

A visit to St. Johnsbury is a bit like embarking on a time travel adventure. Instead of rushing kids into the twenty-first century and the space age, this trip takes them back about a century. Main Street is lined with nineteenth-century structures that range from churches to ornate brick commercial buildings to Victorian mansions. It feels old-fashioned just walking the streets here. The surrounding countryside is filled with lakes and mountains and tucked-away rural towns that offer country fairs and craft shows, church suppers and band concerts. You can spend a day savoring the pleasures of St. Johnsbury on its own, or you can spend a weekend, using the town as your base while you set about exploring the neighboring communities as well.

Begin by paying a visit to the **Fairbanks Museum and Planetarium,** founded in 1889 by Franklin Fairbanks (of the same family that operated the Fairbanks Scale Company). An ornately carved, red sandstone Romanesque structure complete with tower, the museum celebrates natural history and culture. A naturalist and scientist, Fairbanks contributed his own extensive wildlife collection and garnered contributions of cultural artifacts from his well-traveled family and friends.

The main gallery is 130 feet long with a barrel-vaulted ceiling of golden-quartered oak. Somber yet cozy, with its stained-glass windows and rows of heavy oak and cherry display cases housing dozens of stuffed specimens, the gallery is the kind of room that makes you feel like whispering. Looking up, you'll see two long balconies lined with more exhibits, chronicling cultures visited by nineteenth-century St. Johnsbury travelers. You'll feel as though you're visiting a very special attic, one that contains a city's collective treasures.

The first exhibit your kids will notice as you enter is the huge stuffed bears. Two of them, the immense brown Kodiak bear with its frightening claws and the polar bear with its toothy grin, tower on their hind legs. Kids like to stand right up close to have their picture taken, and the museum staff doesn't mind a bit. Right across from the bears is a working Regina music box. Insert a nickel and listen as the broad copper disc comes to life, playing tunes from the Victorian era. The exhibit just behind the music box focuses on the history of St. Johnsbury, with special attention paid to locally manufactured products including orange-crush (a soft drink), maple-flavored "imperial kisses," crackers, horehound candy, pottery, and basket bottom chairs.

Wandering through the great hall, children will discover a giant clam from the East Indies, a nine-banded armadillo, a wild boar with splendid tusks, a South African rock python, and even a common kiwi, which has the largest eggs proportionate to its body weight of any bird in existence today. The opossums are displayed around a reconstructed hill, which shows the entrance to their underground nest. Meanwhile, above the ground, a mother struts by, her offspring neatly planted on her back, their tails firmly wrapped around hers for anchorage.

*Keep an eye out for the bug pictures by entomologist/engineer John Hampson, who turned his creative talents into artwork in the form of insect mosaics.*

Sean Kardon

*St. Johnsbury's Fairbanks Museum is where the buffalo roam in Vermont's Northeast Kingdom.*

Climb the narrow winding stairs to the upper galleries for a look at paper made from the bark of a mulberry tree (Japan), an embroidered child's hood with a tiger on top to scare off evil spirits and bells attached to scare off tigers (China), and a crystal collection. A sign next to an African fetish explains, "Strange, often revolting, the fetish was produced by the medicine-man to give protection against evil. If a fetish proved powerless, it was destroyed or given to the children as a toy." Other curiosities include photomicrographs of snow crystals. Taken by W. A. Bentley of Jericho, Vermont, in the late 1800s, these photographs of snowflakes show that no two flakes are alike. Keep an eye out too for the bug pictures by entomologist/engineer John Hampson (1836–1923), who turned his creative talents into artwork in the form of insect mosaics.

The cellar of the museum houses a collection of Fairbanks scales used to measure everything from grain to gunpowder, babies to yarns to candies. Weigh yourself on an old-time Fairbanks-Morse springless or an up-to-date Fairbanks digital model. Then move on to the Northern New England Weather Center, which prepares regional interpretive weather broadcasts. A wind direction and speed recorder spits out a graph registering variations in these weather components while a teletype machine records additional data. Today's weather maps are posted, alongside a chart decoding the weather symbols used on them so that you can make your own interpretation. Elsewhere in the cellar, you can test yourself for color blindness, experiment with a probability board, and use collision balls to demonstrate Newton's third law of motion: momentum lost equals momentum gained.

Try to plan your visit to coincide with a planetarium show. The fifty-seat facility is the only public planetarium in northern New England. Shows are geared toward helping you learn your way around the universe. You might find out what makes the northern lights light up or when to look for shooting stars.

The museum store is a pleasant place for a child to shop. There are lots of inexpensive items to consider, relating to the themes of the collections. Choose from field guides, prisms, inflatable celestial globes, science experiment kits, and dinosaur models for starters.

If you cross the street from the museum and walk toward the center of town, you'll soon come to the **St. Johnsbury Athenaeum,** built to serve as a public library and presented to the town by Horace Fairbanks in 1871. The elegant Victorian building has cathedral ceilings, soaring windows, spiral staircases, and fancy balconies. In the spacious children's room on the second floor, visiting kids are welcome to join in a summer bedtime story hour or flop down in a beanbag chair to take a break with a book. Kids who are used to sleek contemporary town libraries will find this one intriguing.

An art gallery, added to the athenaeum in 1873, has been left just as it was in the nineteenth century. An arched skylight provides natural light for the paintings in their heavy gold frames, mostly American works purchased directly from the artists, with a heavy preference for the Hudson River School. An enormous landscape, *The Domes of the Yosemite,* hangs opposite the entrance to the gallery.

Leaving the athenaeum, you'll face Eastern Avenue, home of the box office for **Catamount Arts,** which sponsors performing arts events in St. Johnsbury and the neighboring area. The bill of fare has included appearances by Rosenshontz, Circus Smirkus (a home-grown Vermont circus), and Peter, Paul, and Mary. Also a Super Heroes Film Festival, and a series of children's plays including *Charlotte's Web,* performed with "life-sized barn-yard animal puppets, actors, and a fantastic illuminated web," courtesy of the award-winning Louisville Children's Theater. Call or write ahead for a schedule.

You're probably hungry by now, so make tracks for the **Miss Vermont Diner,** an unpretentious,

*Kids who are used to sleek contemporary town libraries will find this one intriguing.*

cheerful place not far from the center of town where even the smallest fry feel welcome (high chairs are available). The spacious dining room, one huge wall of which is decorated with a mural showing a snow-covered Vermont landscape, has a small counter and lots of tables and chairs. Choose from burgers and sandwiches, salads and soups, and hearty fare like breaded chicken or grilled pork chops. The pies, in flavors like strawberry, blueberry, and banana cream, are outstanding.

A visit to St. Johnsbury wouldn't be complete without a stop at the **Maple Grove Maple Museum and Factory.** Ten-minute guided tours of the world's largest maple factory are given several times each hour. When you enter the brick plant, you'll be given a sample bag containing two types of candy. Heaps of candy boxes and rolls of labels surround you as your guide explains how the shrink wrap machine seals a plastic covering over the finished candies. The air is heavy with the scent of maple sugar as you watch a row of workers inspect and pack the candy by hand, pass an immense copper mixing bowl sticky with cream fondant, and view the rubber molds where the candy is shaped, cooled, and hardened. One room is full of empty rubber molds hanging over racks to dry. In another, women in plastic gloves spread the pieces of unmolded candy out on huge metal cookie sheets to dry. After that each piece receives a protective coat of sugar to keep it fresh.

*The air is heavy with the scent of maple sugar as you watch a row of workers inspect and pack the candy by hand.*

When you've completed your tour, stroll through the tiny maple museum where an evaporator may be steaming away, reducing sap to syrup. Here you'll also see old sugaring equipment like wooden ox yokes and spiles (the spigots used to tap trees for their sap). Then you'll enter the gift shop, which has a comfortable theater where you can watch a fifteen-minute color movie that takes you right out into the sugarbush to learn how the sap is extracted from the maple tree and transported to the sugar house.

The gift shop is the place to stock up on pure Vermont maple syrup, maple butter, and maple cream, and, of course, candy, which comes flavored in cranberry and blueberry as well as peppermint and maple.

If factory visits are popular with your family, take a brief side trip to **The Cabot Creamery** in Cabot. Located way out in the countryside, the creamery has a sparkling new visitor center complete with attractive tasting room and theater. You'll receive a warm welcome and a bright red-and-white

Cabot Creamery button to wear before being ushered in to watch a fourteen-minute videotape that begins by introducing the cow: "This is the housing for a hydrochemical conversion unit."

The film goes on to explain that the town of Cabot was settled in 1783 by Benjamin Webster, an uncle of the famous Daniel Webster. During the War of 1812 the town supported a dozen distilleries, selling lots of whiskey to the Canadians. In the early 1900s, the Cabot Creamery was just one of the 180 creameries in Vermont, which also had 66 cheese factories. The Cabot Creamery began a new life as a cooperative venture in 1919, a tradition that it still continues. Cheese making began in 1930.

Five hundred farmers, representing thirty thousand cows, belong to the coop today. Two hundred people work at the factory, turning the milk into cheese products. Each morning twenty trucks visit the member farms, collecting four thousand to six thousand gallons of fresh milk for delivery to the factory, where twelve million pounds of cheese are produced each year.

After the film, a guide leads you on a ten-minute tour of the factory, where workers in white go about manufacturing and packaging the cheese. Large viewing windows make it easy to see the processes involved, although the actual activity under way depends upon the time of day you visit and the products in process. You'll probably see "cheddaring," wherein huge slabs of cheddar are hand flipped in a continuous pattern for a full hour, permitting the acid level to develop evenly throughout the cheese, which looks like big blocks of pale yellow foam rubber. You might also see the cheese cut to size by a guillotine or fed into plastic bags. In the quality control lab technicians test the milk used to make the cheese for butterfat and take protein and bacteria counts. At the end of the tour you'll find out how the blast cooler is used to quickly reduce the temperature of the finished cheddar in order to prevent bacteria growth.

Back in the tasting room you can sample Cabot products, as well as special crackers and condiments. This is the place to purchase Cabot cheeses, butter, and yogurt, along with other Vermont specialty foods and novelty items, not to mention Ben & Jerry's ice cream cones.

If you like getting out into the small towns, you might think about an autumn visit. Renowned for the beauty of its fall foliage, the Northeast Kingdom welcomes a big influx of visitors each September

*Each morning twenty trucks visit the member farms, collecting four thousand to six thousand gallons of fresh milk for delivery to the factory, where twelve million pounds of cheese are produced each year.*

*You can watch cheese being made and then taste the end result at the Cabot Creamery.*

and October. Hike in the mountains, buy Halloween pumpkins and fresh apples and cider and be sure to attend a traditional New England church supper. Because numbers are limited, many require advance ticket purchase and assign seating times. Each town seems to have its own specialty. One church might hold an annual chicken pie supper while another favors ham and beans and still another offers up Vermont turkey. Live music and other entertainment are often part of the fun. To get a calendar of foliage season events in the area, write to the St. Johnsbury Chamber of Commerce (see ACCESS section).

Another annual fall activity is the series of excursions offered by **St. J. & L.C. Railroad, Inc.** You'll ride in one of four cars (two 1930s vintage P-70s and two retired Amtrak cars), pulled by an RS-3 locomotive. With frequent hairpin turns, the train zigs and zags from St. Johnsbury to Greensboro Bend, a fifty-seven-mile round trip. The trip takes three hours, allowing stops for photographing and just plain enjoying the scenery. You'll pass through Badger Gap and cross Pumpkin Hill Trestle. The conductors have a tendency to break into song, and another trainman will provide a bit of history about the railroad and this part of Vermont. In Greensboro the engine uncouples from one end, passes the cars, and couples up to the other end for the return trip. There are morning and afternoon excursions, and advance reservations are a must.

## ACCESS

**ST. JOHNSBURY.** Take I-91, exit 20. Follow Route 5 north into the center of town.

**FAIRBANKS MUSEUM AND PLANETARIUM. Directions:** Take Route 5 to South Main Street, which becomes Main Street. Museum is on the left. **Season:** Year-round.

**Admission:** Charged. **Telephone:** (802) 748-2372. **Note:** Separate charge for planetarium shows, which are held daily in July and August and weekends only during the rest of the year.

**ST. JOHNSBURY ATHENAEUM. Directions:** Take Route 5 to South Main Street, which becomes Main Street. Located on the right side of Main Street in the center of town. **Season:** Year-round. **Admission:** Free. **Telephone:** (802) 748-8291.

**CATAMOUNT ARTS. Directions:** Box office located at 60 Eastern Avenue in St. Johnsbury. Eastern Avenue intersects Main Street in front of the St. Johnsbury Athenaeum. **Season:** Year-round. **Admission:** Charged. **Telephone:** (802) 748-2600.

**MISS VERMONT DINER. Directions:** Located on Route 5 about 2 miles north of St. Johnsbury. **Season:** Year-round. **Admission:** Free. **Telephone:** (802) 748-9751.

**MAPLE GROVE MAPLE MUSEUM AND FACTORY. Directions:** Follow Route 5 north to Route 2. Follow Route 2 east 1 mile to museum and factory. **Season:** Museum and shop open Memorial Day through late October; factory tours weekdays year-round. **Admission:** Small charge for factory tour. **Telephone:** (802) 748-5141.

**THE CABOT CREAMERY. Directions:** Follow Route 5 north to Route 2 west, then Route 2 west to Marshfield. Follow signs to creamery. **Season:** Year-round. **Admission:** Donation requested. **Telephone:** (802) 563-2231.

**ST. J. & L.C. RAILROAD, INC. Directions:** From north or south, follow I-91 to exit 21. Drive into St. Johnsbury. Go through traffic light. Take next right turn and follow signs. **Season:** Mid-September through mid-October, weekends only. **Admission:** Charged. **Telephone:** (802) 748-3685.

**For further information** or restaurant and lodgings suggestions, contact St. Johnsbury Chamber of Commerce, 30 Western Avenue, St. Johnsbury, VT 05819. Telephone: (802) 748-3678.

# Index

Michael Lafferty

# About the Author

Harriet Webster is the author of *Trips for Those Over 50, Coastal Daytrips in New England, Favorite Weekends in New England,* and *Favorite Short Trips in New York State.* She wrote *Winter Book,* and *Going Places,* two nonfiction children's books. She's also the author of *Family Secrets: How Telling and Not Telling Affect Our Children.*

Her articles have been published in *McCall's, Mademoiselle, Family Circle, Parents, Working Mother, Better Homes and Gardens, Seventeen, Women's World, Bride's,* and *Yankee.* Her travel stories have appeared in *Americana, The Boston Globe, The Christian Science Monitor, Newsday,* and *Boston* magazine. She lives in Gloucester, Massachusetts.